Values
That Shape the World
Ancient Precepts, Modern Concepts

Faye Lincoln

Erick

Live by values
that shape the future.

Faye Lincoln
8-22-2021

Values
That Shape the World

Ancient Precepts
Modern Concepts

Faye Lincoln

dp Dialog
Press
Washington, DC

The print editions of this book are printed on acid-free paper.

Printed in the United States of America.

ISBNs:
978-0-914153-68-9; 978-0-914153-69-6 (PB)
978-0-914153-71-9, 978-0-914153-72-6, 978-0-914153-74-0 (HB)
978-0-914153-75-7, 978-0-914153-80-1 (Ebook/EPUB)

Cover and art design by Myles Hoenes; typesetting and eBook preparation by E. M. Jones; index compiled by Virginia Nolan. Cover image adapted from a photo of Mt. Sinai by Mohammed Moussa.

Modern book text is produced using a variety of collaborative software tools, including automated spellcheckers and text revision tools. It is possible for such software to create typographical errors or other textual changes beyond the control of the author, editors, or publisher. Please report errors to errata@dialogpress.com; changes, corrections, and additions can be found at ValuesThatShapeTheWorld.com.

Links, titles, and statistics were accurate as of press time; neither the author nor the publisher is responsible for pages or other resources that have expired or moved since the manuscript was prepared.

This book is dedicated to the loving memory of my parents, who, by some miracle, survived the Holocaust.

Table of Contents

Part II Edifices

Foreword:
How Values Build Bridges

Every civilization develops its own values; every generation has its own values. Are values relative or absolute?

As a young man, I used to hear many times from those of previous generations lamenting that the newest generation had lost its values, had compromised the cherished and sacred values of previous generations. I never understood their lament. Now that I have reached the "age of wisdom," I see a new generation which has developed its own set of values that, in my eyes, appear to have grossly abandoned the values of previous generations. I have come to realize how true and correct were the laments of the previous generations that the new generation abandoned the established values that helped create their world, embracing shallow new values. But these values will create what?

Are values absolute? Intergenerational? God-given? Or are they relative, generation-dependent, and human-made?

As a man of faith, I believe that there are core values that are Divine in origin, intergenerational, and absolute. Every generation is able to develop its own values. Those should certainly not abrogate the Divine values—but build upon them. New values should address new discoveries and new technology and apply them to modern life.

Values are not to divide or differentiate us. Values are to bring us closer to each other, to embrace each other and to respect each other; to build bridges between generations, nations, people, and civilizations.

Divine Values that are absolute include the belief in one God—omnipotent, omniscient, and transcendent; the sanctity of life; the right to privacy and property; seeking the truth; and pursuing justice and mercy upon all creatures. These are values that cannot and should not be replaced or changed; the existence of humanity depends on them. These values are those upon which we can build bridges among all of humanity. For these are the values that were given to all of humanity; based on them, humanity was able to survive and continues to survive. Without them, humanity is doomed to implode, self-destruct, and disappear. We have seen many civilizations abandon these values, partially or entirely, and those societies have eventually disappeared.

Having lived in the Liberal West, I have seen with my own eyes the deconstruction of Divine Values and their abandonment. This has led to moral relativism, ethical and moral decadence, and the absolute depravity of the civility of the masses. Lacking awe of the Almighty God, the degrading of human life, disrespecting privacy and property, spreading of falsehoods and fake news, the imposition of injustice to all, and cruelty to people and animals alike will lead to the implosion and self-destruction of the Liberal West

Now, however, I have the honor and pleasure to serve as the Senior Rabbi in the United Arab Emirates and the Association of Gulf Jewish Communities. The values that I was born into and raised with have come back to life for me. These "values of old" that I so cherish and live by have been resurrected for me. In a country based on the awe of God, with tolerance, one that embraces peaceful coexistence and harmonious living—these are not just concepts, but a way of life here.

Generational Values based on Divine Values extending throughout our modern and advanced world will help ensure that humanity is eternal. It is only through keeping those cherished and proven values near and dear that we can assure generations to follow a better and brighter future.

Rabbi Dr. Elie Abadie
Senior Rabbi, Jewish Council of the Emirates
Chief Rabbi, Association of Gulf Jewish Communities
Chairman, Council of Sephardic Sages
June 15, 2021

Acknowledgements

For all authors, writing a book is a long and challenging journey. Ideas must grow into written words which give rise to a manuscript. The research is painstaking, but the pivotal discoveries yield their own rewards. This part is personal. Then the teamwork begins, a second journey, to bring one person's product to the world. Here is where I, like all other authors, acknowledge the list of individuals who made this volume a global reality.

My husband Bill receives the first thanks. He supported me through this process from its inception. I would run ideas by him, and he would point to issues that should be emphasized. Often, I wrote late into the night. He would wake up, come into my office, and inform me that he could "hear words flying all around" as ideas were being written.

Sadly, Bill passed away six months before I finished the final manuscript. He suffered from microvascular strokes, accompanied by advanced dementia from his illness. In the end, he could not remember much or recognize many people. But he always remembered the day I completed the first draft of this book. Bill was my greatest supporter, and this book honors our twenty years of marriage.

Next, I thank Carl Tippets for making this book possible. Carl and I have worked together on many projects over the years. He set me on the path to research the cultural impact of the Holocaust, biblical history, and the geopolitics of the Middle East. Ultimately, it was Carl who encouraged me to write this book and he has been a key member of my editorial team throughout the process.

I am indebted to my good friends Edwin and Carol Black. Edwin's books were the best I ever read. I decided one day to travel from Utah to Seattle to meet him during a lecture, and then invited him and Carol to dinner in Washington, DC, while on business. During our first visit, we viewed texts and videos of the Arab Spring in Cairo as it was happening, sent by people on the ground. There have been many dinners since then, both in Washington, DC, and Salt Lake City. With his contacts in publishing, he rendered strategic guidance on the process of leaping from manuscript to global bookshelf.

My journey to the global editorial stage was handled deftly by Dialog Press, and their assistance made the final crucial leg of the process one of the most enjoyable of experiences. I am grateful for the Dialog team including but not limited to Eve Jones in New York City, Nick Charles in London, Carol Black, Virginia Nolan, also in NYC, Christine Randolph in Fort Wayne, Myles Hoenes in Detroit for his most excellent cover, and for the day-to-day support provided by the entire team.

Further thanks are due to Rabbi Ilana Schwartzman for the research she helped me with over the years. As I wrote this book, I discovered rather quickly that I needed a Rabbi who could direct me in my examination. I cherish those discussions which always pointed me in the right direction and provided necessary course corrections.

I am indebted as well to Rabbi Joel Schwartzman for his enthusiasm, lively discussions, and willingness to act as my rabbinical reviewer during the writing process. Through his expertise, we verified historical facts, clarified text, and strengthened the storyline into the focused effort it has become.

Yaakov Kuc started out as our family's personal tour guide in Israel, but his fascinating historical expertise and knowledge of the country ensured that we would be friends for life.

My greatest acknowledgement goes to my personal editor and one of my closest friends, Wayne Johnson. Two things are important when writing a non-fiction work. The first is to create the appropriate underlying structure that ties everything together and makes a book read seamlessly. The second is to create an emotional connection with the reader. Neither of these is easy to accomplish. Wayne is a master at this, an outstanding professor of literature, and an expert in the world of books and film script writing. Our working relationship was instantaneous, and our journey together based on a higher purpose while full of laughter.

Faye Lincoln
Salt Lake City
June 11, 2021

Introduction:
Values That Shaped My World

My parents were Holocaust survivors. As a young couple, they were delivered in a railroad freight car to the Auschwitz concentration camp during WWII, survived the horrors of the Holocaust, and emigrated to America after the war. Decades later, a colleague of mine wondered what it was like growing up as a child of parents who survived such an experience. That question eventually provided me the opportunity to journey down a fascinating path of discovery.

It isn't often you get a chance to think back over your life and reflect on what made you who you are. I can honestly say that it was not only my parents, but the entire culture of post-Holocaust survival that contributed to my growth. The question motivated me to think through the values that emerged from this environment and influenced my life.

My parents came from Poland. My mother grew up in a small town called Tomaszów, located near Łódź. Her family owned a successful textile factory which employed many people. They were Orthodox Jews, strong in their faith, whose love of business was passed down to us through a few surviving family members. My mother's three brothers, her parents, and her grandparents all perished in the war.

When it came to living in America, my mother always had street smarts, which she certainly received from her father. My mother stood only 4'9" tall, but she had a fierce sense of independence and an outsized willingness to take a stand for what was right. During her internment in Auschwitz, a German soldier brought her to a mass Jewish grave and demanded at gunpoint that she begin throwing more dead bodies of fellow Jews into the pit. She defiantly responded to him, "Over my dead body! You will have to kill me first." It is a miracle that she survived her ordeal. She was a practical and gutsy individual who knew that life could be hard. She had spirit with stubbornness; she was funny and could laugh her heart out. Even in her old age, she was feisty, loved people, and told commanding stories that captured everyone's heart.

My father and his family came from Warsaw, which for over eighty years was in the Pale of Settlement, that portion of eastern Russia separated from the rest of Russia where Jews were legally permitted to live. The family story is that my paternal grandfather, Abraham, had been a scholar and a rabbi, so the family was deeply involved in *Torah* and Talmudic study and had an incredible love of learning, also passed down through the generations.

Abraham was the oldest son in his family. The second oldest brother, my great-uncle Solomon, emigrated to America before World War II. My father was lucky to have survived, as most of his family perished after Poland was conquered by Germany. After the war, my great-uncle helped my parents come to America.

A kind and gentle soul, my father was a hard worker, disciplined, and honest. He would always steer me in the right direction, allowing my own character and independence to shine through. His love was always steadfast and kind, never domineering or overbearing, allowing me to be whatever I wanted to be.

I am the product of these two families, comprised of a rich heritage of people, most of whom I never had the opportunity to meet except through memories recounted by my parents and remaining relatives. Out of six million Jews who died during the Holocaust, the statistical chance that any one of them could have survived the evils of those years was a miracle in and of itself. My parents lost a baby boy at two years of age in Poland because of the Germans and later lost a girl, who died at the age of seven in America.

Holocaust survivors and their children realize what it means to endure the harshest conditions of imprisonment, hard labor, torture, and starvation. Life as we know it was utterly devalued. The personal values that the survivors brought to bear enabled them to live through this experience and to successfully restart their lives in another country. My parents were fortunate to have survived the concentration camps for over a year. Their values, based on their Jewish culture, came through loud and clear.

Today, many people deny that the Holocaust occurred. They deny that six million Jews, along with many Poles and others, were mercilessly exterminated by the Germans, or they attempt to downplay the enormity by insisting that fewer than six million Jews were killed. The number was six million. But whether it was five million, four million, or 1.5 million (the number of Christian Armenians killed by the Ottoman Turks during World War I), it should not make a difference. We all should be morally outraged at the cultural degeneration that would lead a country to willfully exterminate an entire population of people. That so many Jews lost their lives less than one generation ago epitomizes what little regard Hitler's Reich had for the sanctity of what they considered to be the "wrong" kind of human life.

Prompted by my colleague's curiosity about my having grown up in a Holocaust survivor family, I asked myself, where did such evil come from? What was its purpose? What can we learn from it? And so began a ten-year journey during which I attempted to grasp the rationale of how such evil came to exist in this world. Researching the Holocaust, I began by focusing specifically on the question of how a culture could have descended to the level that such a horrific event could take place. What kind of society, I asked myself, willingly grants permission for so many people to vengefully hate, to utterly devalue life, or to blatantly remain passive while exterminating six million Jews? It is humankind's responsibility to decide whether we stand for goodness or for evil and to know the difference.

This book is not about the darkness of the Holocaust; it is about the values that emerged from such a tragic event. It is about the strength of the living light that comes from each of us, a light that shapes this world for the better. Out of evil and destruction came an enduring tenacity and resilience in a people who have touched so many.

Determined to come to America, my parents arrived with no money but with a tremendous will to live. It was a strange land where they knew no one other than my father's uncle, who financed their travel. They brought with them the courage to try to outlive the horrors they had survived and start all over again. How many people are given the chance to rebuild their lives?

The values my parents lived by as I was growing up near Detroit in a post-Holocaust culture are what I remember most. As they started over, my parents worked hard and saved their money. My father was a tailor and my mother a seamstress, skills which helped them survive in the concentration camps without having to endure the harsher labor others were subjected to, which certainly would have killed them. They sewed uniforms in the camps. When they arrived in America, sewing was their livelihood. Always honest, with the utmost integrity, they did not make much money, but they enjoyed success in a new land with family and friends. I carry that honesty and integrity with me every day of my life.

Even with little money, my parents found ways to live well, and I was rarely wanting for anything. They sent me to a good college, the University of Michigan, to become educated and allow me to become the best person I could be. Without today's computers, video games, high-definition televisions, or the latest digital technologies, my friends and I would visit each other's homes. We were never bored.

My parents sent me to music camp, let me ski, play tennis, and encouraged me to travel. All around, I had a wonderful childhood. I recall one of my friends taking dance lessons and teaching several of us what she learned because our parents could not afford to send us for lessons. We practiced in our backyards and then put on neighborhood charity shows for several years to raise money for the local Leukemia Society. I wonder if today's video games teach children how to be creative, have fun, and help others?

Truth and honesty, as well as the difference between right and wrong, were taught by my parents and my culture. The ethics of Judaism were embedded in our culture and shaped our decisions every day. We memorialized the history of the Holocaust to remind us of the danger that this might happen again—to any people. Decisions in our daily lives were made based on our sense of fairness, equality, ethics, and moral wisdom. These values were a given.

Right or wrong, I believed that we, as Jewish people, must live up to a standard that was somehow higher. We had to be just a little smarter, work a little harder, give a little more, and develop a sense of what needed to be done in this world to make it a better place. I never felt different from those who were not Jewish, but instead felt the need to live up to my parents' expectations. As Holocaust survivors, my parents could lead a better life in America, but their child's quality of life had to exceed that of their generation. This expectation was embedded in my culture.

Growing up in our Jewish culture, the most important goal was to become well-educated. This was the highest expectation that Jewish parents had of their children, for boys and girls equally. I learned to love reading at a very early age. As a young child, I remember huddling on my front porch on rainy days under a tent of umbrellas, losing myself in books. Given the high standards of our schools, I was always diligent in doing my homework. We were all expected to do well in public education, whether we were from Jewish or non-Jewish families.

When I say that education was important, I really mean something more than just doing well in classes. It was the atmosphere of being in an environment where you could learn, question, and think for yourself. I was encouraged to ask questions so that my curiosity could take me to interesting places. I learned that appropriately questioning myself or others meant I could be comfortable discussing and debating issues in an open fashion. I could deal with conflict in ways that allowed me to expand my thinking, rather than merely arguing from a rigid viewpoint. Respecting the thoughts, beliefs, and opinions of others allowed me to think critically about what would or would not work for me. It was a path to learning in order to acquire knowledge—and ultimately wisdom.

My parents tried to protect me in every way they could, yet the culture taught me the value of being positive, resilient, and able to do for myself, even in difficult times. When I was 16 years old, I took my first job, at a McDonalds. It got boring very quickly, so I had to invent mind games to keep myself focused on the work. I stayed with that job for two years before finding something more challenging. By learning this type of commitment and integrity on the job, I built the foundation for a successful and meaningful professional life.

I grew up with the value of treating all people equally. Even when I was young, I always thought it was wrong to be prejudiced, given that prejudice gave rise to the Holocaust. Therefore, how could I engage in the same kind of thinking? During the 1967 Detroit riots, when many parts of the city burned down within a week and the Michigan National Guard was called in to bring order to the city, I held no fear of African American people. Later, I was concerned that Asians, as their numbers grew, were being shunned through prejudice just because they were smart and hard-working.

In college, some African American students chose to be violent and militant; most were not. Terror and violence were, to me, unacceptable ways of dealing successfully with life. In my view, these militants had had the same opportunities that my parents did to make a life for themselves. Both parties had experienced socio-economic disadvantages. If they chose a path of violence, this was a self-determining choice which was morally wrong, an excuse for not learning how to live responsibly.

While I received many positive inspirations from Judaism, I also developed a strong sense of guilt. This, too, was embedded in our culture because of the way we were raised as first-generation Americans, with our parents having the highest expectations of us. If one did not live up to their expectations, even if those were not always achievable, one was at fault and in the wrong. Our guilt often drove us to try even harder the next time.

But there was a silver lining to all that guilt. I learned to live life with a sense of humility and a constant desire to improve things. My guilt never allowed me to think of myself as being either good enough or too good for this world. It did allow me to strive to achieve a better outcome the next time; it gave me a sense of resiliency. I lived life then, as I do now, knowing that I owe more to life than life owes me. It was always my responsibility to figure out my purpose and path. Learning, succeeding, and failing were all worth it knowing I could somehow make a difference. Through it all, I knew if my parents could make it after all they had experienced, then I could make it as well.

Our Jewish faith allowed us to build bonds with family and the community; it shaped our values, thoughts, and actions. It strengthened our connections with one another so we could grow and thrive in America. The religious community helped us to never forget our common history and kept us focused on our ancient roots while we integrated into American culture. Our faith created our framework for a better life after so much had been lost in the Holocaust.

Surviving the Holocaust took an act of faith; creating a new life in a new nation in the aftermath of such an unthinkable, organized genocide took optimism and hope. The resilience of our people could only have come from the values generated through Judaism. This vibrant way of life gave my parents and other survivors the will and desire to persevere and succeed in spite of the loss of so many family members. We embraced the values that kept us centered in our struggle to live life and find joy in each day.

It is hard to imagine anyone surviving the Holocaust without their having found the strength to endure and to bring meaning to the everyday sadness that existed during and after that time. Somehow, they had to establish meaningful goals that could get them through their everyday hardships. Then, as now, they had to identify their own special purpose for surviving, something which allowed them to rise above the devastating losses they experienced. Today, more than ever, it is crucial to find that wellspring of strength deep within the human spirit and, most importantly, to maintain a strong sense of connectedness to one another in order to nurture our own ability to thrive.

Our belief in God and the values which developed over time allowed our people to fight social wrongs when our sense of fairness had been shaken. Even when life was good, the need for justice, equality, and freedom held true. Our purpose in life has always been to strive to change things for the better—to repair the hurts and fractures of the world and to create joy and happiness wherever possible.

This sense of purpose, strength, and connectedness are central to Judaism. Throughout our history, the Jewish people have experienced times of exile and lived in far-flung lands. Yet, over the millennia, while other civilizations disappeared, the Jewish people survived. This is because our faith was centered on a body of adaptive laws which created a foundation of values capable of surviving even the harshest conditions.

I would like to take you on a journey to search for the source of these life-giving values. In conducting my own personal exploration and research, I discovered a gift. I fell back in love with my Jewish way of life. I am proud of what it stands for, what it represents in our history throughout the centuries, and ultimately, what it has contributed to the world today.

When I grew up, I never went to Hebrew school like many children. I loved the sound of the Hebrew prayers and songs in synagogue, but I never learned the language so I could not understand them. For that reason, most of the stories I learned from the Hebrew Scriptures were the ones connected with popular Jewish holidays.

Over the course of my lifetime, I had never actually read the Hebrew Scriptures until I began studying ancient Jewish history and how it linked to the antecedents of the Holocaust.

When I started researching the centuries leading up to the Holocaust and the values (or lack of values) which allowed antisemitism to exist and culminate in this tragedy, I learned stories about ancient Israel and the Jewish people. I had unexpected moments of discovery through a better understanding of our history. I read the Hebrew Scriptures and other historical books about Judaism with fresh eyes, with a profound sense of wonder, and with a level of interpretation that can only come with the wisdom of maturity and experience.

It is this history and these stories, I came to realize, that generated the foundational values which allowed the Jewish people—my parents in particular—to survive the Holocaust.

We are driven to achieve goodness in this world. By striving to understand God and standing by our beliefs and values, we bring meaning to our lives. Seeking a greater purpose in the service of others and humanity is what Judaism charges us to do today, directing us on a journey of discovery in an attempt to create a better world. No matter how perceived, God will always encourage to us a higher aspiration.

This book is about understanding the values from the ancient stories of Torah, Tanakh, and ancient Israelite history. Values must adapt over time to remain relevant and to teach us how to live in a changing world. How can we bring our ancient stories alive again, given today's conflict and change? How can we think about these values in a world focused on money, political infighting, and rapidly developing technology? Granted this, how can we learn from these values to better shape the future?

Revisiting our history allows us to view our biblical stories with fresh eyes, and in doing so, live our lives with grace and purpose, and transform our values in ways that can help us successfully navigate a changing world. The usual approach to studying these stories and teachings is to focus on individual values and morals by which we live. Instead, our emphasis will be on societal needs and how history is linked to the changes that a people and a nation must inevitably bring about. From this vantage point, we begin to see cyclical patterns of evolving values, beginning with an early emergence of core values, a growth phase as they take root, and a period of institutionalizing such values, in order to create permanence.

Once a peak is reached, a period of decline begins, as ossified institutions no longer allow us to successfully meet new challenges. As the downward cycle progresses, a paradigm shift is required. We attempt to apply former solutions to oncoming challenges, but this only seems to further accelerate the pace of decline.

We first discover this pattern during the time of Abraham and the Patriarchs, as values of *free will and responsibility* through faith first appear and are then strengthened. These values become institutionalized as *family*, complete with all its trials and tribulations. But conditions eventually deteriorated until the Hebrews, who had expanded into the twelve tribes in Egypt, fell into slavery.

Once the people were freed by God and Moses, and underwent the Exodus, the laws received in Sinai became the template for building a society based on a new set of emerging core values—justice and mercy. This value set grows, first as self-governance under the Judges in the land of Israel, then into the *political institution* of centralized rule under Kings. Eventually, decline sets in as the monarchy becomes corrupted, requiring a paradigm shift based on messages conveyed to the people by the Prophets. This decline leads to the end of the First Temple Period as northern Israel is conquered by the Assyrians, and the Southern Kingdom of Judah by the Babylonians.

A new pattern of emerging core values becomes evident during the Second Temple Period while the Hebrews were subjects of the Persian Empire. Beginning with the Jewish return from the Babylonian exile back to Jerusalem, an *internalized faith in God* emerges as the *Sages teach* and the *people learn* the laws. The Jews integrate their faith and its principles into their daily lives.

During the Hellenist period, learning and living out the values of faith further develop through new levels of governance, and eventually become institutionalized through faith-based education. But under Roman rule, sectarianism ultimately arises, causing a breakdown in Israelite society. This ends with the destruction of Jerusalem and the Temple by the Romans and the removal of the very name—Judea—from Roman maps.

As new values ebb and flow, earlier values become transformed and integrated, allowing the Jewish people to navigate more complex and turbulent periods in their history. In the great diaspora, the Jews had to embrace new values, transmitted through *study and scholarship*, which emphasized *peace*, thereby allowing for their survival. Similar values became the basis for the spread of universal monotheism in Western civilization. Through the microcosm of Israelite history and ancient texts, we can view the transformational pattern of values in society over time. This can also help us understand how our values evolved to the present time.

Today, governance and economic structures within the United States are undergoing turbulent changes based on the polemics of an established political system and the threat of the coronavirus pandemic. Science and technology are moving us at an ever-faster pace into unfamiliar territory. Society is becoming secularized. We must somehow make sense of this new world where circumstances often overwhelm us. We no longer feel in control. Relationships through social media seem ever more superficial rather than being founded on deep conversations. Materialism and consumerism have become our primary driving forces.

The ability to create and innovate in life-affirming ways is predicated on exercising free will while balancing responsibility with a compassionate understanding of humanity's needs. Our responsibility now is to identify and steer a course which will help humanity thrive as we shape appropriate uses for science, technology, and information systems.

What new core values will be necessary to shape the future and steer the course of innovation? What new institutions will be required to protect these values? I believe that *co-creativity driven by compassion* will provide the right combination of values to guide us into the future. We have the ability to create and innovate in ways that will make a difference in this world. We must strive toward greater co-operation and harness competition for the good. The goal is to generate abundance for all, rather than focusing on scarcity and competition for resources.

Material wealth is certainly helpful but is secondary to the journey of achieving outcomes which can help humanity on a local and global basis. Wealth and economics must support the endeavor to create prosperity for people, but not be the sole motivator of our achievement. If scarcity through competition is our mindset, then the few will accumulate greater wealth while the larger masses go without.

It is the teachings of the Torah and the scriptures that can help guide our path into the future, not by the simple application of literal interpretations of ancient writings, but by deriving a more complex and meaningful set of values which will resonate for today.

The stories and history developed in this book will not be the typical stories or interpretations most of us think of when reading the Tanakh or when recalling historical events in ancient Israel, but the ones that better contribute to identifying those values which relate to today's changing global society and a world of violence that is exploding in serious and unexpected ways. Our goal is to discover those values which might help shape the world, our communities, and the people around us so as to achieve a successful path forward.

By sharing these stories in this light, the intent is for us to believe in the possibility that, one by one, and as a society, we can carry forward those values that will lead to a tipping point of creating greater goodness in this world. I believe we can make a difference together, for our future, by understanding how we might better influence our world today.

Faye Lincoln
Salt Lake City
October 14, 2020

Notes on Text

alues That Shape the World refers to *Tanakh* and Hebrew Scriptures interchangeably. Tanakh, which stands for *Torah*, *Nevi'im*, and *Kethuvim* (Torah, Prophets, and Writings), generally corresponds to the Old Testament. The Torah encompasses the first five books of the Hebrew Scriptures, also called the Pentateuch.

Quotes from the Tanakh are taken from Tanakh: The Holy Scriptures, The New JPS Translation According to the Traditional Hebrew Text, published by The Jewish Publication Society, 1985. Bible quotes come from The New English Bible with the Apocrypha, edited by Samuel Sandmel, Jack Suggs, and Arnold J. Tkacik, published by Oxford University Press, 1976, except where indicated.

Transliterations and translations of names and terms can vary widely in everyday usage, especially those originating in languages that do not map exactly to English orthography. For example, the founder of Islam can be spelled Muhammad, Mohammed, Mohamed, and so on. The great Israelite king: Solomon, Suleiman (not to be confused with Suleiman the Magnificent), Shlomo, and so on. To avoid confusion, we have standardized all spellings in the text to the best of our ability except when quoting a source text directly and in the bibliography.

Part I

Foundations

Chapter 1:
Beliefs That Change Our Worldview

In the city of Ur, along the Euphrates River and part of Lower Mesopotamia, there was a man by the name of Terah, a direct descendant of Noah. Terah had two sons, along with a third, Abram. One day, Terah decided to leave the city of Ur. Terah had determined that there was a better life than the one he was experiencing in the city-state of Ur. So he packed up his family and possessions and traveled to Canaan. They traveled as far as Haran to the north, where Terah lived out the rest of his life.

> Terah took his son Abram, his grandson Lot, the son of Haran, and his daughter-in-law Sarai, the wife of his son Abram, and they set out together through Ur of the Chaldeans for the land of Canaan; but when they had come as far as Haran, they settled there. The days of Terah came to 205 years; and Terah died in Haran. (Genesis 11:31–32)

What conditions might have encouraged Terah to leave Ur? In the ancient Semitic world, man operated within a polytheistic worldview and worshiped a pantheon of gods. Man was dependent on and at the mercy of these gods, all of whom were believed to be in control of natural forces and conditions on earth. Kings ruled city-states as representations of these deities on earth. Temples were erected to worship the gods, mediated by priests. Power rested in the hands of the gods, the priests, and the kings.

Very simply, if people worship gods, they believe themselves to be at the mercy of such external deities. These forces control the rains, the water, the rivers, and the crops. If the gods are merciless, they will cause drought and famine. If the gods are good or benevolent, they will bless the people with rain and water to grow crops and raise herds of animals. Man's loyalties are confusingly divided among many deities, never quite sure which god is in charge. Are these gods moral and benevolent, or amoral and hostile? If the gods are moral and benevolent, then life runs smoothly. If they are amoral and hostile, then life is full of constant confusion.[1]

Man needed some way to intervene with the gods during times of suffering because men saw themselves as being weaker. Individuals and families had their own personal deities, which were represented by idols and statues that they could pray to as intermediaries to these gods. Through wailing and lamentation, the people had some semblance of having their voices heard but they clearly were not in control of their own destiny.[2]

Kings who ruled over local regions could also choose to be just and righteous, merciful, and compassionate in support of the people.[3] As with most rulers, however, eventually they tended to fall victim to their own power and greed. Wars erupted as one king decided to conquer another, leading to the need for armies. The king's needs and desires stripped resources from the people, leading to oppression. When peace returned, it was difficult to revert to a model of justice and prosperity.[4]

Under these conditions, people will not decide to think about how to change their lives based on truth and honesty, or how to improve conditions for others, which could bring a thousandfold return. This is because they are never really in charge of their own lives; something or someone else is always in charge. They live a life that is fatalistic, hoping for the best, acting in ways that allow them to believe that their gods will do something good on their behalf.

If the hierarchy is such that gods are over kings, then kings are equivalent to lesser gods. Any man who is not wealthy is a mere servant to the whims of the gods and the king. Life becomes amoral and oppressive. Little in the way of action or thinking makes a difference. It may be easier to live life for the moment. The gods have immortality; man knows only death.[5]

It is only a small step from fatalism to the desire for instant gratification through gluttony, drink, passions, theft, corruption, violence, and killing. The focus is materialistic in nature for the wealthy few and oppressive for everyone else. If the gods in control can act in this manner, the people have little impact on their own destiny. Only lamenting to the deities may make a difference for those who suffer.[6]

When Terah made the decision to choose a different life, he gave himself a chance to step back and reevaluate whether there was a better way to live. Most likely during this time, multiple city-states were warring against each other. Terah passed a legacy on to his son, Abram, and it became solidified in his faith, belief, and relationship with the Lord through a covenant.[7]

Abram became the patriarch of the descendants of the People of Israel. He listened to the voice of the Lord, and believed, unlike his father, that there were not many gods in the world, but only one, who was both just and merciful. Abram decided that if he listened to the voice of the Lord and did as he was instructed, his world would somehow be good and right.

But something more important came out of this change in belief around 1800 BCE. If one chose to live a certain way based on the moral values of honesty, integrity, family, and good deeds, one could become successful. One could, in fact, direct one's own destiny.

In the case of Abram, God reached down to infuse man with spirit and man detected the presence of the Lord. God created a covenant with Abram; Abram chose to follow the path of the Lord toward his destiny.

> *The LORD said to Abram, "Go forth from your native land and from your father's house to the land that I will show you.*
>
> > *I will make of you a great nation,*
> > *And I will bless you;*
> > *I will make your name great,*
> > *And you shall be a blessing.*
> >
> > *I will bless those who bless you*
> > *And curse him that curses you;*
> > *And all the families of the earth*
> > *Shall bless themselves by you." (Genesis 12:1–3)*
>
> *At seventy-five years of age, Abram took his wife Sarai and his brother's son Lot, left his father in Haran, and set out for the land of Canaan. When he reached Shechem, the Canaanites were then in the land. The LORD assigned the land to Abram's offspring. Abram traveled on to Bethel, then journeyed by stages south into the Negeb. (Genesis 12:4–9)*

This is the beginning of Abram listening to the word of the Lord as he was making his way into the world and becoming a great patriarch. This gave birth to monotheism as we know it today. This was a new way of living and worshipping because it diverged from the polytheism of the times.

This is where the power and choice of free will was created, through the relationship between Abram, the Lord, and his following of God's covenant. This was a new, emerging step toward a self-determined life. As an individual, one could choose to accept responsibility and direct one's own destiny toward spiritual goodness. An individual could build a relationship with God, as Abram had, and choose to accept the covenant.

Abram trusted in the Lord and strengthened the value of family over time. He and Sarai traveled to Canaan, but experienced drought and famine. He eventually moved on to Egypt where the famine was not so severe. Abram offered up Sarai, who was beautiful, to Pharaoh, in order to assure protection for their family.[8]

When Abram entered Egypt, the Egyptians saw how very beautiful the woman was. Pharaoh's courtiers saw her and praised her to Pharaoh, and the woman was taken into Pharaoh's palace. And because of her, it went well with Abram; he acquired sheep, oxen, asses, male and female slaves, she-asses, and camels.

But the LORD afflicted Pharaoh and his household with mighty plagues on account of Sarai, the wife of Abram. Pharaoh sent for Abram and said, "What is this you have done to me! Why did you not tell me that she was your wife? Why did you say, 'She is my sister,' so that I took her as my wife? Now, here is your wife; take her and begone!" And

Pharaoh put men in charge of him, and they sent him off with his wife and all that he possessed. (Genesis 12:14–20)

The Lord compelled Pharaoh to give Sarai back to Abram. God taught Pharaoh and Abram that the relationship between husband and wife was sacred and so too began the new foundation of building and honoring family.

Abram again became wealthy and even more successful, with large herds to tend. He traveled back to Canaan with Sarai and Lot, the son of his brother Haran, who was also successful with many herds of animals. Abram and Lot had so many resources between them that they needed more land. So, Lot chose to go east beyond the Jordan River and eventually settled in the town of Sodom. It is here that Abram demonstrated his commitment and strong sense of honor to family as well as his self-directed goodness through honesty.

The lesser kings of Sodom, Gomorrah, Admah, Zeoiim, and Bela had served under King Chedorlaomer for twelve years, but in the thirteenth year, these kings rebelled against him in the Valley of Siddim (now the Dead Sea). King Chedorlaomer and four other allied kings in turn invaded the lands of Sodom and Gomorrah.

Now the Valley of Siddim was dotted with bitumen pits; and the kings of Sodom and Gomorrah, in their flight, threw themselves into them, while the rest escaped to the hill country. [The invaders] seized all the wealth of Sodom and Gomorrah, all their provisions, and went on their way. They also took with them Lot, the son of Abram's brother who had settled in Sodom, together with all his possessions.

A fugitive brought the news to Abram the Hebrew, who was dwelling at the terebinths of Mamre the Amorite, kinsman of Eshkol and Aner, these being Abram's allies. When

Abram heard that his kinsman had been taken captive, he mustered his retainers, born into his household, numbering three hundred and eighteen, and went in pursuit as far as Dan. At night, he and his servants deployed against them and defeated them; and he pursued them as far as Hobah, which is north of Damascus. He brought back all the possessions; he also brought back his kinsman Lot and his possessions, and the women and the rest of the people.

When he returned from defeating Chedorlaomer and the kings with him, the king of Sodom came out to meet him in the Valley of Shaveh, which is the Valley of the King. And King Melchizedek of Salem brought out bread and wine; he was a priest of God Most High. He blessed him, saying,

> *"Blessed be Abram of God Most High,*
> *Creator of heaven and earth.*
> *And blessed be God Most High,*
> *Who has delivered your foes into your hand."*

And [Abram] gave him a tenth of everything.

Then the king of Sodom said to Abram, "Give me the persons, and take the possessions for yourself," But Abram said to the king of Sodom, "I swear to the LORD, God Most High, Creator of heaven and earth; I will not take so much as a thread or a sandal strap of what is yours; you shall not say, 'It is I who made Abram rich.' For me, nothing but what my servants have used up; as for the share of the men who went with me—Aner, Eshkol, and Mamre—let them take their share." (Genesis 14:10–24)

Here we have Abram defending his family values and fighting off the kings who stole the possessions of Sodom and captured Abram's nephew Lot and his family. Not only did Abram risk his life, the lives of others, and his personal resources for family, but he also refused to take possession of Sodom's wealth. Abram fought in order to save and defend his family, not to attain personal gain. His honesty and integrity did not permit him to accept the spoils of war. More importantly, he honors the priest, King Melchizedek, with one tenth of the stolen resources he had recovered. Abram, by now, has proven his worthiness, sense of goodness, and righteous spirit.

God blessed Abram with the promise of offspring for upholding the new values of will directed through self-determination, honoring family, and his belief in the one Lord. Since Sarai could not bear children, early on she offered Abram her maidservant, Hagar. Abram's firstborn with Hagar was Ishmael, who became the founder of the descendants of nations related to Islam.

God then blessed Abram and Sarai, now in their advanced years, with the gift of their own child, who they named Isaac.

When Abram was ninety-nine years old, the LORD appeared to Abram and said to him, "I am El Shaddai. Walk in My ways and be blameless. I will establish My covenant between you and Me, and I will make you exceedingly numerous."

Abram threw himself on his face; and God spoke to him further, "As for Me, this is My covenant with you: You shall be the father of a multitude of nations. And you shall no longer be called Abram, but your name shall be Abraham, for I make you the father of a multitude of nations. I will make you exceedingly fertile and make nations of you; and kings shall come forth from you. I will maintain My covenant between Me and you, and your offspring to come, as an everlasting covenant throughout the ages, to be God to you and to your offspring to come. I assign the land you sojourn in to you and your offspring to come, all the land of

Canaan, as an everlasting holding. I will be their God."
(Genesis 17:1–8)

And God said to Abraham, "As for your wife Sarai, you shall not call her Sarai, but her name shall be Sarah. I will bless her; indeed, I will give you a son by her. I will bless her so that she shall give rise to nations; rulers of peoples shall issue from her." (Genesis 17:15–16)

The covenant with God was not only to be passed down through the successive generations of family, but also to be made stronger over time. Keeping family together was crucial to the safekeeping of the new covenant. Family conveyed the values of will and self-determination in exchange for freely accepting the obligation of acting in accordance with right behavior.

Abraham's children would not truly inherit the land for many generations. Faith, over successive generations, both emphasized and amplified the growth of these values. God's wishes were for Abraham to strive for something greater than himself by acting with purpose out of a sense of humility and to pass on this destiny to his family and his children's children.

Abraham's deepest desire was fulfilled by God. The Lord blessed Sarah and brought her and Abraham their first child together, Isaac.[9] Isaac married Rebekah, who gave birth to Esau and then Jacob. Isaac, on his deathbed, blessed Jacob who continued the covenant. Jacob fell in love with Rachel, but was tricked into first marrying Leah, the eldest daughter, as was the custom, followed by seven years of labor for her father. Their firstborn was Reuben. Jacob then married Rachel after another seven years of labor. Jacob and Rachel conceived both Joseph and Benjamin. As the eldest of the two, Joseph would become the favored son of all the children. The

Lord blessed Jacob and renamed him Israel. He became successful and the father of the twelve tribes of the Israelites through his sons.

When Joseph was seventeen years old, his dreams signified that he would become a prophet of the Lord. Because of these dreams, as well as Joseph being their father's favorite son, the older brothers became envious of him. So, they sold him to a group of Ishmaelites, who then sold him to a courtier of Pharaoh in Egypt. As Joseph grew up, he developed an ability to interpret visions and dreams. One day, Pharaoh had a dream that no one could interpret.

Pharaoh dreamed that he was standing by the Nile, when out of the Nile there came up seven cows, handsome and sturdy, and they grazed in the reed grass. But presently, seven other cows came up from the Nile, close behind them, ugly and gaunt, and stood beside the cows on the bank of the Nile; and the ugly gaunt cows ate up the seven handsome sturdy cows. And Pharaoh awoke.

He fell asleep and dreamed a second time. Seven ears of grain, solid and healthy, grew on a single stalk. But close behind them sprouted seven ears, thin and scorched by the east wind. And the thin ears swallowed up the seven solid and full ears. Then Pharaoh awoke; it was a dream!

Next morning, his spirit was agitated, and he sent for all the magicians of Egypt, and all of its wise men; and Pharaoh told them his dreams, but none could interpret them for Pharaoh. (Genesis 41:1–8)

As Pharaoh had heard that Joseph could interpret signs and dreams, he sent for him. When Joseph heard them, he said:

Immediately ahead are seven years of great abundance in all the land of Egypt. After them will come seven years of famine, and all the abundance in the land of Egypt will be forgotten. As the land is ravaged by famine, no trace of the abundance will be left in the land because of the famine thereafter, for it will be very severe. As for Pharaoh having had the same dream twice, it means that the matter has been determined by God, and that God will soon carry it out. (Genesis 41:29–32)

Pharaoh then asked the capable Joseph to establish a plan to protect the people of Egypt against this famine. He put Joseph in charge of his entire court in order to direct it. He made Joseph the lord of all the land and people in Egypt, with no one superior to him but Pharaoh himself. In the seven good years of abundance, Joseph stored and saved much grain for the upcoming famine. When the years of famine came, all the lands experienced hunger and privation except the land of Egypt, where there was food thanks to Joseph's planning and Pharaoh's trust in him.

Since the famine had reached Canaan, Joseph's father, Jacob, directed his sons, Joseph's brothers, to go down to the land of Egypt to bring back grain for bread. This they did and met with Joseph. The brothers who had originally sold Joseph to the Ishmaelites as a young boy did not recognize him, but Joseph recognized them. The brothers paid Joseph for the grain and Joseph not only gave them grain in exchange, but also hid in the grain sacks double the amount of money they had brought to take back to their father, Jacob. Joseph only asked that the youngest brother, who had been left at home, return to Egypt with the other brothers. This son would have been Benjamin, the second son born of Jacob (Israel) and Rachel.

When Jacob opened the sacks of grain back in Canaan, he found double the amount of money that he had sent to pay Joseph in the grain sacks. He was told of the kindness of this lord over the land of Egypt and of Joseph's request for the youngest son, Benjamin, to return with the brothers to Egypt. Jacob let Benjamin travel to Egypt. Jacob also returned all the money that was given to him by the lord of Egypt, as he thought the money might have been given to him in error. Truth and honestly was a virtue important to Jacob and valued by the Lord. Just because the gift had come from someone in another nation was no reason to be dishonest.

Eventually, the sons learned that the lord of Egypt under Pharaoh was really Joseph, their long-lost brother. Because of the famine, Joseph requested that his father, Jacob, along with all the sons, come to live in the region of Goshen in Egypt, where everyone could be near Joseph and where he could provide for them during the famine. Joseph, having forgiven his brothers, brought the family together so they all could survive.

Joseph lived to be one of the greatest leaders of his time, from the generations beginning with Abraham down through Isaac and Jacob. The value and tradition of self-directed will to do good, coupled with his talents, allowed Joseph to create good fortune in Egypt during a time of abundance and establish a plan which allowed all in the land of Egypt to survive during the seven years of hardship. Throughout the known world, others died of starvation. The value of self-directed will allowed Joseph to not only be successful, but also to forgive the travesty of his brothers having sold him into slavery.

Joseph was not in control of his own fate when he was younger because of his brothers' vengeful actions. But he actively chose to fulfill his destiny when Pharaoh called for him to interpret the dreams. Through Joseph's living out God's covenant in thought and action, he not only saved his family, but also saved a nation. Individuals, families, and society can amplify values as they are passed down through the generations.

The Lord created the covenant through the original patriarch, Abraham. The values of will and self-determination were carried out by the descendants of Abraham; Joseph's honoring the covenant generated a thousandfold return to his family and the people of Egypt. Joseph's actions enabled future generations of Abraham's family to carry out the covenant of the Lord.

Family becomes the backbone for growing the values of free will and self-determination. It is the foundation of ethical responsibility for teaching honesty, practicing integrity, and exercising forgiveness. This culminates in the leadership of one man, Joseph, who saved a nation for the benefit of successive generations. His leadership saved his family and established the future line of the twelve tribes of Israel.

In today's world of instant gratification, the importance of patience, achievement, saving for tomorrow, and enjoying family and friends all too easily fall by the wayside. The covenant between God and Abraham gave direction to a future that was not focused on "me," but instead emphasized the pursuit of higher achievements in life with the greatest values being placed on raising families, caring for the land, maintaining faith, and passing it on to the next generations. Joseph's brothers sold him out of jealousy, but his willingness to forgive them brought them support and solidarity.

Truth and honesty build integrity, something not always high on everyone's list; but these virtues have never been more important in terms of who we are as people, family, and friends supporting one another and building a future. We must remain socially connected, honor our commitments, and work toward something that is greater than ourselves. We must aspire toward a higher purpose which serves us both individually and collectively. We have a responsibility to teach our children these same basic values so that they may teach them to their children and carry them forward in society.

We must remember that in helping others and focusing on achievements which stand for a greater purpose, we will build faith, patience, and grace, based on a higher, aspirational power. We will act as appropriate role models for others. We must also realize that no matter how much we accomplish for ourselves, unless we can live faithfully, we cannot strive toward achieving greater good in our world.

Abraham fulfilled his covenant with God, changing the course of history for his family and future generations. Based on a story of solidarity that led to survival, Joseph too fulfilled his destiny to both family and nation. Today, we are obligated to establish a legacy by amplifying right values and passing them on to successive generations.

Chapter 2:
The Exodus—Faith in God

At the end of Genesis, Joseph said to his brothers: "I am about to die. God will surely take notice of you and bring you up from this land to the land that He promised on oath to Abraham, Isaac, and to Jacob." So, Joseph made the sons of Israel swear, saying, "When God has taken notice of you, you shall carry up my bones from here." Joseph died at the age of one hundred and ten years; and he was embalmed and placed in a coffin in Egypt. (Genesis 50:22–26)

It would be another four generations before Moses was born and God would again speak to the Israelites.[1] The Israelites lived in the region of Goshen in the land of Egypt, where they had settled at Joseph's invitation during the years of famine. During their good years, they multiplied to become a large community. Eventually, a new Pharaoh came to power. He oppressed them and placed them into bondage. And yet, they grew even larger as a group.

> A new king arose over Egypt who did not know Joseph. And he said to his people, "Look, the Israelite people are much too numerous for us. Let us deal shrewdly with them, so that they may not increase; otherwise in the event of war they may join our enemies in fighting against us and rise from the ground." So, they set taskmasters over them to oppress them with forced labor; and they built garrison cities for Pharaoh: Pithom and Raamses. But the more they were oppressed, the more they increased and spread out, so that the [Egyptians] came to dread the Israelites.

The Egyptians ruthlessly imposed upon the Israelites the various labors that they made them perform. Ruthlessly they made life bitter for them in harsh labor at mortar and bricks and with all sorts of tasks in the field.
(Exodus 1:8–14)

Pharaoh tried to limit the number of Israelites, not only through harsh labor, but also by decreeing that all newborn Israelite boys be killed. The midwives, who feared God, would not follow Pharaoh's orders. As the Israelites continued to multiply, Pharaoh turned away from the midwives and then ordered his own people to kill all the newborn boys by throwing them into the Nile. They were to allow the girls to live.

A certain man of the house of Levi went and married a Levite woman. The woman conceived and bore a son; and when she saw how beautiful he was, she hid him for three months. When she could hide him no longer, she got a wicker basket for him and caulked it with bitumen and pitch. She put the child into it and placed it among the reeds by the bank of the Nile. And his sister stationed herself at a distance, to learn what would befall him. (Exodus 2:1–4)

Many know the story from here. Pharaoh's daughter found the baby, named him Moses, and raised him as her own, but she must have known him to be a child of the Israelites, because she looked among them for a nurse. Moses was raised and educated in Pharaoh's household, but when he was older, he realized the plight of his oppressed people. One day, Moses witnessed an Egyptian beating one of his kinsmen, and Moses killed the Egyptian. He then fled to Midian, where he met his future father-in-law, Jethro, and future wife, Zipporah. It was during his exile in Midian that the Lord came to him from the burning bush at Mount Horeb, the Mountain of God:

> *"Moses! Moses!" He answered, "Here I am." And He said, "Do not come closer. Remove your sandals from your feet, for the place on which you stand is holy ground. I am," He said, "the God of your father, the God of Abraham, the God of Isaac, and the God of Jacob." And Moses hid his face, for he was afraid to look at God.*

> *And the* LORD *continued, "I have marked well the plight of My people in Egypt and heeded their outcry because of their taskmasters; yes, I am mindful of their sufferings. I have come down to rescue them from the Egyptians and to bring them out of that land to a good and spacious land, a land flowing with milk and honey, the region of the Canaanites, the Hittites, the Amorites, the Perizzites, the Hivites, and the Jebusites. Now the cry of the Israelites has reached Me; moreover, I have seen how the Egyptians oppress them. Come, therefore, I will send you to Pharaoh, and you shall free My people, the Israelites, from Egypt.* (Exodus 3:4–10)

Thus begins the well-known story of Exodus. This is the history of the Israelites' release from slavery, of God's gifting of the Ten Commandments, and of their journey through the desert to the land of Canaan as promised by the covenant between God and Abraham. This is what the Jewish people celebrate each year at the festival of Passover. This is also a story of a people remaining together as a community and overcoming the hardships of slavery experienced in Egypt through their faith in the Lord.

Exodus, however, is not just a narrative of events but a description of how God inspired a permanent faith in the twelve tribes of Jacob. This was accomplished first through the powerful miracles from God witnessed by the people, and then through the impact of the Ten Commandments. But what most do not realize is that when Moses led the Israelites out of Egypt, they were not a cohesive people. Therefore, this is the story not only of their journey through the desert over forty years, but also about how such adversity helped to unify and bind the Israelites together.

At Mount Horeb, God directs Moses to communicate his commands to Pharaoh. But Moses is fearful of doing so, claiming to be slow of speech. So, God has Moses's brother Aaron, a Levite, speak on behalf of Moses. They go to Pharaoh to ask for the release of the Israelites—and Pharaoh refuses. The Lord demonstrates through Moses and Aaron that God is more powerful than Pharaoh.

Moses and Aaron offer proof to Pharoah that God wants his people released: Aaron takes Moses's staff and turns it into a serpent. Pharaoh's wise men, sorcerers, and magicians are able to perform the same feat, but Moses's serpent is stronger and swallows all the others. Pharaoh remained adamant. The Lord, through Moses and Aaron, then turned the waters of the Nile into blood, killing all the fish. Pharaoh's advisors followed and did the same. The Lord then released frogs throughout the land and Pharaoh's men repeated this act. The Lord struck the dust of the earth and vermin came upon man and beast; all the dust of the earth turned to lice throughout the land of Egypt. Pharaoh's magicians could not repeat this. Still Pharaoh refused to let the people go.

The Lord then caused swarms of insects to be released over all the people and land, except for the Israelites who were living in Goshen, to demonstrate that the Lord was more powerful than Pharaoh and could protect God's people from harm. The Lord then struck dead all the livestock of the Egyptians, sparing the Israelites' animals. The Lord then caused all Egyptian men and beasts to have boils on their skin. The Lord rained down heavy hail which killed all the Egyptians and livestock that were struck. The Lord brought swarms of locusts into the land to invade the fields and palaces. The Lord then brought darkness over the land for three days and three nights while the Israelites experienced light. Still, Pharaoh would not free the Israelites.

God then revealed to Moses the purpose for all these actions.

> [T]he LORD said to Moses, "Go to Pharaoh. For I have hardened his heart and the hearts of his courtiers, in order that I may display these My signs among them, and that you may recognize in the hearing of your sons and of your sons' sons how I made a mockery of the Egyptians and how I displayed My signs among them—in order that you may know that I am the LORD." (Exodus 10:1–2)

Why did the Lord take so many actions, knowing that Pharaoh would not release the Israelites? The oppression of slavery had bound the Israelites as a separate community whose numbers had threatened Pharaoh. But once they were released, these people would need a new set of instructive and inspiring stories to help remind them of the Lord's power. Their freedom was to act as the seedbed of the Israelites' faith.

The Lord's final act would be successfully releasing the Israelites from Pharaoh's bondage. The Lord instructed the Israelites to mark the doors of their homes. That evening, families ate a "hurried dinner" which included roasted lamb and unleavened bread with bitter herbs. The Lord then passed over all the land of Egypt, striking down all the firstborn children of the Egyptians, including Pharaoh's son. This act arose out of Pharaoh's earlier order that all newborn

Israelite boys be killed at the time of Moses's birth. Pharaoh is defeated in every way and finally releases the Israelites.

Clearly, God wanted the Israelites to witness these powerful miracles in order to bolster memories which would inspire their faith. This also supplanted any belief in Egyptian gods that they might have assimilated. The first critical step in building a community was believing in one Lord, God.

To create an enduring culture, unity must be based on a purpose which transcends a group's basic needs. Such cohesiveness must be built on a resilient and commonly shared foundation of beliefs, values, and ethics. Without this, civilizations will and do fall apart.

When my husband and I visited Israel in 2010, we also traveled to Petra, Jordan. Petra is famous for the treasure caves that appear in *Indiana Jones and the Last Crusade*. The Nabateans built some of the most magnificent royal tombs of their times. They developed trade routes throughout the lands of what are today Saudi Arabia, Egypt and the Mediterranean, Jordan, Syria, Lebanon, Iraq, Iran, and India.

Our tour guide, who was Jordanian, theorized as to why he thought the Israelites lived for millennia as a people while the Nabateans ultimately disappeared. The Nabateans maintained pride in their skills for trade and systems of administration. However, they had no binding value-based history that shaped their culture. Ultimately, they died out as a people. But the Israelites have persisted and thrived since the days of Abraham, enabled by their values and faith.

The Lord sets the foundation of unity by working miracles that the people can see for themselves and recall as they journey out of Egypt toward the land of Canaan. The next step was to ensure that the power and might of the Lord continued to remain visible.

> *[T]he Israelites went up armed out of the land of Egypt. And Moses took with him the bones of Joseph, who had exacted an oath from the children of Israel, saying, "God will be sure to take notice of you; then you shall carry up my bones from here with you."*

> *They set out from Succoth, and encamped at Etham, at the edge of the wilderness. The LORD went before them in a pillar of cloud by day, to guide them along the way, and in a pillar of fire by night, to give them light, that they might travel day and night. The pillar of cloud by day and the pillar of fire by night did not depart from before the people.* (Exodus 13:17–22)

The Lord appears to the Israelites in the visible forms of a "pillar of cloud" and a "pillar of fire" so they can see, believe, and maintain faith in the unity of one God.

As the Israelites escape the Egyptians, the Lord shields them from the Pharoah's armies. The Lord creates further miracles to assure their safe passage, which the Israelites witness.

> *The angel of God, who had been going ahead of the Israelite army, now moved and followed behind them; and the pillar of cloud shifted from in front of them and took up a place behind them, and it came between the army of the Egyptians and the army of Israel. Thus, there was the cloud with the darkness, and it cast a spell upon the night, so that the one*

could not come near the other all through the night.
(Exodus 14:19–20)

Here, God appears to the people as the "pillar of cloud" to protect the Israelites by preventing the Egyptian army from attacking them at night. Moses then holds out his arm over the sea, and splits it with the water acting as walls, so that the Israelites can travel over dry land to the other side.

> *The Egyptians came in pursuit after them into the sea, all of Pharaoh's horses, chariots, and horsemen. At the morning watch, the Lord looked down upon the Egyptian army from a pillar of fire and cloud and threw the Egyptian army into panic. He locked the wheels of their chariots so that they moved forward with difficulty. And the Egyptians said, "Let us flee from the Israelites, for the Lord is fighting for them against Egypt."* (Exodus 14:23–25)

Then Moses waved his arm over the sea and the waters came together, with the Lord hurling the Egyptian army into the sea. The Israelites saw the Lord come forth in a "pillar of fire and cloud" to create these miracles. More importantly, they personally understood the Lord's strength and powers at work. For as the people came to observe the Lord's actions, they would have faith in the one God.

Why were these additional visible acts of power so central to the story of Exodus? Remember, the Israelites had lived in Egypt for four generations. Over the centuries, while in the region of Goshen, distinct from the Egyptians, the Israelites were within a civilization which practiced sorcery and magic, one which paid tribute to Pharaoh's gods, priests, and idols. During this time, one has to think that the Israelites might have taken up some of the Egyptians' practices, their monotheistic faith notwithstanding. After all, the Lord had not spoken to the Israelites for more than four generations.

So, God created miracles in order to reinforce the people's belief. These miracles made God real for them. The goal was to strengthen the Israelites' faith in God through a common history based on having been freed from slavery and sharing the experience of miracles.

After forty-five days of journeying, the Israelites suffered hardships in the desert because of hunger. The community began complaining. Once again, as a "cloud," the Lord became present to the people. God then worked the next miracle through the creation of quail for meat and "manna" for bread. These sustained the Israelites throughout their ordeal. More complaints arose because of lack of water. So, the Lord provided for water from the rocks as further evidence of power.

After three months (three full moons), Moses and his people entered the land of Sinai and set up camp by the mountain. God now prepares to meet with Moses on the mountaintop:

> The LORD called to [Moses] from the mountain, saying, "Thus shall you say to the house of Jacob and declare to the children of Israel: "You have seen what I did to the Egyptians, how I bore you on eagles' wings and brought you to Me. Now then, if you will obey Me faithfully and keep My covenant, you shall be My treasured possession among all the peoples. Indeed, all the earth is mine, but you shall be to Me a kingdom of priests and a holy nation. These are the words that you shall speak to the children of Israel."
> (Exodus 19:3–6)

God also states to Moses:

"I will come to you in a thick cloud, in order that the people may hear when I speak with you and so trust you ever after." (Exodus 19:9)

The Lord is about to bestow through Moses the greatest gift God can give humankind: the ethical law that will guide the Israelites in living together as a community. The people have clearly seen God's powers in action on their behalf. They will be mindfully faithful to the Lord, rejecting the many gods worshiped in other lands. They must become a unified people in order to bring the law to the new land. If the Israelites do not survive, the law will not survive. If the people were to scatter rather than live together in one land, the new ethical law would disappear.

On the third day, as morning dawned, there was thunder, and lightning, and a dense cloud upon the mountain, and a very loud blast of the horn; and all the people who were in the camp trembled. Moses led the people out of the camp toward God, and they took their places at the foot of the mountain.

Now, Mount Sinai was all in smoke, for the LORD had come down upon it in fire; the smoke rose like the smoke of a kiln, and the whole mountain trembled violently. The blare of the horn grew louder and louder. As Moses spoke, God answered him in thunder. (Exodus 19:16–20)

Moses climbed the mountain; there he spent forty days and forty nights. The Lord inscribed the new law of the Ten Commandments on two tablets. The Lord spoke to Moses about the additional laws that the people must follow.[2] Thus imparted, we have the birth of a new set of ethical laws which would serve to guide a people, build a nation, and would eventually become the foundation for Western civilization.

The miracles they had witnessed led directly to the Israelites seeing and believing in the Lord as they accepted the new laws God revealed at Mount Sinai. These laws instructed the people in a new way of living together. The first five of the Ten Commandments are the positive foundational values which establish the covenant between God and the people.

> I.   *I the Lord am your God who brought you out of the land of Egypt, the house of bondage: You shall have no other Gods besides Me.*[3]
>
> II.   *You shall not make of yourself a sculptured image, or any likeness of what is in the heavens above, or on the earth below, or in the waters under the earth. You shall not bow down to them or serve them.*
>
> III.   *You shall not swear falsely by the name of the Lord your God.*
>
> IV.   *Remember the sabbath day and keep it holy. Six days you shall labor and do all your work, but the seventh day is a sabbath of the Lord your God: you shall not do any work.*
>
> V.   *Honor your father and your mother, that you may long endure on the land that the Lord your God is assigning to you.* (Exodus 20:2–12)

In Genesis, the Lord gives Abraham and his descendants the gifts of will and self-determination so that they might direct their own lives and destinies in faithfulness to the Lord. Now we have the Lord essentially saying to the people that if they follow in God's ways, their will and self-determination will fashion the destiny of a nation that will survive throughout the ages. The first commandment emphasizes the importance of keeping faith in one God.

The second commandment directs that the people will not bow down to or worship any image of God or idols. Instead, the people are to accomplish such worship through their thoughts and actions, through their hearts and minds, and through an ongoing relationship with God.

The third commandment prohibits one from bearing a false oath in God's name and forbids taking God's name in vain. Oaths are to be solemn, offered in good faith, and with a higher purpose in mind.

The fourth commandment recognizes both the need for work and self-discipline, but also the importance of a day of rest and reflection.

The fifth commandment teaches us that to honor our mother and father is to protect the family unit so that it can pass on lessons to future generations. The family unit is the core of society, and in turn, society must protect the role of families.

God is saying to the people that if they keep these commandments, they will bring the light of goodness to the world for all to see and follow. This goodness is the foundation and motivation of living peacefully with family and neighbors.

The last five commandments prohibit actions that are harmful to society.

    VI.   *You shall not murder.*
    VII.   *You shall not commit adultery.*
    VIII.   *You shall not steal.*
    IX.   *You shall not bear false witness against your neighbor.*
    X.   *You shall not covet your neighbor's house; you shall not covet your neighbor's wife, or his male or female*

slave, or his ox or his ass, or anything that is your neighbor's. (Exodus 20:13–14)

Emotions and actions motivated by the darker side of human nature can easily spin out of control, wreaking chaos on a people, a community, and a nation. These five commandments protect against these effects. Hatred and vengeance, as well as a disdain for the value of life, create the conditions for killing and violence that arise from the darker elements of temperament. The sanctity of life is a gift from God, always to be honored. Note, however, this commandment does not prohibit killing in defense of oneself or a nation; it does deny purposeful murder.

Lust, greed, dishonesty, and envy also comprise the foundation for the final five commandments. People honor their spouses in marriage by not committing adultery. They deal with greed by not stealing from others. People honor each other by not lying or acting dishonestly. The last of the darker emotions envy, or coveting what belongs to another, results in undermining a peaceful society.

The Ten Commandments set a foundation for living in accordance with goodness. It instructed the people to turn away from the darker aspects of human nature. The Israelites are to strive to obey these commandments, and exemplify these laws in their lives and teachings, imparting them to the generations.

People can choose to live in two different ways. One will lead to evil, while another will strengthen them as a people living in goodness. God's intent is to teach the Israelites how to live appropriately and successfully, bound together by the covenant and the Law.

The Lord next provides Moses with laws for the people to follow. These laws were established over three thousand years ago. If one interprets them literally today, one misses the point, for these laws were understood differently in the context of ancient times. But the actions, intent, and spirit they represent still apply in contemporary society.

These laws have become an integral part of the early framework of Western civilization's criminal and civil laws to protect individuals as they live together. They instruct people to respect everyone and to treat one another well. They prohibit harm, loss, or theft against another, and obligate restitution in place of vengeful actions of retaliation.

They speak of treating those people who are not of the same faith equally and with compassion, just as the Israelites lived amongst the Egyptians in a strange land. This becomes the early basis of equality for all people living in the same land.

The Israelites must care for the poor, widows, and orphans among them. They must lend money with no interest and take no bribes. These last two become the early foundations for charity and the just practice of lending funds to help one's people. They speak to acting with kindness toward others by cultivating the strength of benevolence and avoiding selfishness.

As our Jordanian guide in Petra indicated, a people can have successful tribal communities, systems of trade, and models for governing, but if they are not bound together by values which engender ethical behavior and ultimately moral wisdom, there is no guarantee that what they strive for will be appropriate, fruitful, or good. Without such values, society has an equal chance that its people will tend toward evil, destroy themselves, or disappear as a fallen, corrupt civilization.

The Ten Commandments and their accompanying laws create an instructional foundation for how people should come together as a nation. They direct the emotions and actions of society with the goal of preventing harm to others. The foundation of faith supports these laws, helping a society establish a common heritage, using stories and rituals. This is how communities live together peacefully, equitably, and with honor. The spirit of these foundational laws ultimately promotes civility and disciplined self-control.

Chapter 3:
The Exodus—
Unity Through Adversity

The Book of Exodus reveals God's gifting of the Ten Commandments and the related laws that will ensure the Israelites remain together and achieve societal unity and goodness, along with will and self-determination, as they establish a nation in the new land of Canaan.

By determining how they would live in accordance with these laws, the Israelites had the opportunity to develop a common understanding of the systems they would need to support the successful growth of society. This new law focused on going beyond oneself and working in harmony through others. It would provide the framework from which freedom could thrive for these formerly enslaved people.

In the first five commandments, God is affirmatively telling the people what they must do to live together. The last five inform the people what they should not do when living together. God does not spell out how best to fulfill the promise of this new covenant. This is left to the people to ascertain, and allows room for self-determination as well as further problem-solving, discussion, and debate. This unites a people as they think through such issues together in order to make concrete the laws provided to them for everyday life.

God performed miracles to generate vivid memories for the people, to strengthen their faith, and to induce them to adhere to the foundational laws that were revealed at Sinai.

But even if the Israelites retell their history through tradition, the question arises: is this is enough to guarantee that they will become unified and survive throughout the ages? Apparently not, for as soon as Moses came down from the mountain with the Ten Commandments, even after the Lord had demonstrated so many miracles in their presence, and after only forty days and nights, they had already chosen to ignore God's first two commandments! Not a good sign that God's gifts were so quickly forgotten.

Those people waiting for Moses at the foot of Mount Sinai convinced Aaron, Moses's brother, of their fears as to what might have happened to Moses up on the mountain. They bemoaned not being back in Egypt where everything had been safe, even as Pharaoh had enslaved them. They were proving that they had already lost faith in the Lord's promised protection and support.

The people implored Aaron to build another idol for them to worship. They all donated their gold in order to build a golden calf at the base of the mountain. When Moses came down from the mountain and saw that the Israelites had already forsaken the Lord, he smashed the two tablets on which were written the Ten Commandments.

Moses demanded, "Whoever is for the Lord, come here!" (Exodus 32:26) All the Levites came to him, and they took a sword to over three thousand people, allowing Moses to begin driving out evil from among the Israelites. Then Moses climbed the mountain a second time to implore God to forgive the Israelites, but God brought a plague to further drive out evil from their midst. Finally, Moses met the Lord on the mountain for a third and last time to receive a second set of tablets containing the Ten Commandments to share with the surviving faithful.

The Ten Commandments and the laws that accompanied them were to serve as the basis for the development of a social contract with the people, with the first requirement being belief in the one God and no worship of idols. However, old habits die hard. It was too easy for them to backslide into old ways before embracing the new values and laws.

When a large group of people need to become unified as a community, what better way to accomplish this than to provide them with a significant project where everyone must contribute, collaborate, and focus on the outcome? So God directed Moses to focus the Israelites' efforts on building a Tabernacle, with the Tent of the Meeting to cover the Tabernacle. They were to construct the Ark of the Pact (Ark of the Covenant), to be placed in the Tabernacle, along with a divine golden table, an altar for incense, and an altar for burnt offerings. The Israelites would voluntarily give up gemstones, ram skins, dolphin skins, and goat hair for yarns, gold, silver, and other valuables to be used to build and construct these objects.[1]

The people would have to accomplish this collectively, selecting the best artisans for the most difficult and significant tasks while working together as families and teams. The hope was for the Israelites to accept their God by building a "home" for the Lord so that God would journey with them in their midst into the land of Canaan.

God next provided Moses with a lengthy prescriptive set of procedures, which required the people to procure certain male animals for burnt offerings, offerings of wellbeing, and meal offerings composed of flour and special oils to offer to the Lord. The sacrifices comprise a lengthy and meticulous process which would take place within the Tabernacle under the Tent of the Meeting that would house God's presence.[2]

These offerings were God's way of creating a suitable ritual replacement for the worship of idols and false gods. These sacrifices of animals and food also replaced the sacrifice of human beings, a practice taking place in those times among other peoples. The Ten Commandments clearly spell out a new path, one where life is sacred. Any form of human sacrifice becomes forbidden. However, the people must observe the replacement practices on a regular basis in order to integrate them into their consciousness and belief system. They must focus their faith on the presence and power of the Lord. God indicates this, saying to Moses:

> *Thus, shall you say to the Israelites: You yourselves saw that I spoke to you from the very heavens: With Me, therefore, you shall not make any gods of silver, nor shall you make for yourselves any gods of gold. Make for Me an altar of earth and sacrifice on it your burnt offerings and your sacrifices of wellbeing, your sheep and your oxen; in every place where I cause My name to be mentioned I will come to you and bless you. And if you make for Me an altar of stones, do not build it of hewn stones; for by wielding your tool upon them you have profaned them. Do not ascend My altar by steps, that your nakedness may not be exposed upon it.*
> (Exodus 20:19–23)

A table for incense, an altar for burnt offerings, and a golden table for the meal offerings are placed in the Tabernacle. God further instructs the people to build the Ark of the Pact of acacia wood overlaid with gold, with cherubim on each side, in order to protect the revealed tablets and house the Lord. God would use the Ark of the Pact and the Tabernacle to demonstrate an ongoing, visible presence to the people—as a cloud by day and as fire by night.

Once the people finished the Tabernacle, the Tent of the Meeting, and the Ark, the Lord formally bestowed the priesthood on Aaron and his descendants—the Levites, who would have responsibilities in the service of the priesthood. God also listed procedures for designing Aaron's sacred vestments. These prescribed that there be twelve gemstones for the breastplate and inscriptions for the shoulder plates representing the names of the sons of Israel and the twelve tribes to remind them of their origins after they settled in the land of Canaan. The instructions included two special crystals, Urim and Thummim, to be placed over the heart, inside the breastplate.[3] These Aaron used to enhance visions or messages from the Lord.

In the end, all these efforts could only be a temporary measure in building a lasting unity within such a large group of people. The projects were not enough to be a permanent remedy against the temptation of falling back into their old ways. In order for so many to grow into a future nation, they would have to learn to live by some type of social code, integral to their faith.

In Leviticus, the Lord spends a great deal of time instructing Moses on the meticulous procedures that God requires the priests and the people to follow. While the priestly offerings serve as a reminder to the people to be faithful to the Lord, God's instructions also teach the Israelites how to care for the sick, maintain their health, and keep a diet based on appropriate foods. God instructs them on how to grow grain in order to maximize its yield. Laws spell out how to keep the peace when murder, rape, bribery, or stealing occur. God informs the people about treating wives appropriately and respecting marriage as the core foundation of family.[4]

One might ask why the Lord would go to all this trouble to reveal and establish these laws. Just as the burnt offerings provide for the development of a unified faith and belief system in only one God, the procedures provide support for health and growing crops, all necessary for a large community of people. There is a system to identify disease and control it. God directs the Israelites to share the grain they have harvested with the priests and the poor as part of caring for each other. But having received these procedures, the people still need to apply the laws. This will take further focus, unity, and effort as everyone works out the details together.

By establishing this social contract, God binds a people together for centuries to come. God reminds the people that once they enter the new land, they must not make idols for themselves or set up temples to false gods. They must observe God's laws faithfully so that the fruits of their labor and the Lord's blessings will always be with them.

God finally directs Moses to send out scouts, one from each of the twelve tribes, to view the land of Canaan and report back to Moses and the people.

At the end of forty days, they returned from scouting the land. They went straight to Moses and Aaron and the whole Israelite community at Kadesh in the wilderness of Paran, and they made their report to them and to the whole community, as they showed them the fruit of the land. This is what they told him: "We came to the land you sent us to; it does indeed flow with milk and honey, and the cities are fortified and very large; moreover, we saw the Anakites there. Amalekites dwell in the Negeb region; Hittites, Jebusites, and Amorites inhabit the hill country; and Canaanites dwell by the Sea and along the Jordan."

Caleb hushed the people before Moses and said, "Let us by all means go up, and we shall gain possession of it, for we shall surely overcome it."

But the men who had gone up with him said, "We cannot attack that people, for it is stronger than we." Thus, they spread calumnies among the Israelites about the land they had scouted, saying, "The country that we traversed and scouted is one that devours its settlers. All the people that we saw in it are men of great size, we saw the Nephilim there— the Anakites are part of the Nephilim—and we looked like grasshoppers to ourselves, and so we must have looked to them." (Numbers 13:25–33)

The whole community broke out into loud cries, and the people wept that night. All the Israelites railed against Moses and Aaron. "If only we had died in the land of Egypt," the whole community shouted at them, "or if only we might die in this wilderness! Why is the LORD *taking us to that land to fall by the sword? Our wives and children will be carried off! It would be better for us to go back to Egypt!" And they said to one another, "let us head back for Egypt."* (Numbers 14:1–4)

In spite of God's presence and the miracles, which were performed to build faith and a unified belief system founded on will and self-determination; in spite of the ethical law and rules provided to unify a community of people—God's greatest gifts—the Israelites could not maintain their faith and belief in the presence and protection of the Lord. Their daily offerings, as well as the stories of miracles and rituals, could not convince them that God's strength would overpower the people of Canaan.

So, the Lord acted one final time to teach the people faith. Instead of proceeding on to conquer the land of Canaan, the

Israelites were to wander the desert for an additional forty years. The majority, from twenty years of age on, would die in that wilderness, all except Caleb, son of Jephunneh, and Joshua, son of Nun. The Lord commanded that it would be the next generation who would enter the new land. (Numbers 14:26–35)

This is the heart of the Book of Exodus. The Lord used adversity arising from the harsh conditions of the desert to unify the people. They had to learn how to live together. They had to believe in the Lord and to interpret the laws God had gifted to them. They would have to learn to follow the laws, assimilating and applying what God had laid out for them.

A community based on freedom came together out of slavery, was built up and strengthened by enduring and overcoming shared adversity. God was clear that the older generation would not pass into the land of Canaan; only the next generation, for they would truly come to believe in the Lord and not fall back into the old ways.

During this period, the Israelites would retell their history and stories. Over time, their belief system would mature. Adversity creates a special tension that promotes solutions which become ingrained in social consciousness. Ultimately, adversity builds resilience into a people.

Even more important, parents learn to apply themselves to the care and instruction of their children. Using adversity as a tool to strengthen faith and values which will survive into the next generation, the people develop free will and self-determination as a group. This will also be imparted to their children. Such God-centered living requires them to give up instant gratification in exchange for long-term, value-based needs focused on a higher purpose.

In the story of Exodus, God gave the people values based on belief and faith. These values promote the creation of a higher ethical standard; this then becomes the foundation of justice. Positive ideals and goals should theoretically encourage people to strive toward achievement and community. When any number of dark elements arise, such as hatred, anger, greed, and envy, they will disrupt and ultimately break down the community.

Today, there are dictators and leaders who try to unify their people using the wrong set of conditions and belief systems. Instead of establishing strong beliefs based on faith, self-determination, and ethical values, the true gifts of God, they exploit the darker emotions of hatred, animosity, and vengeance. They enforce extreme oppression on others in order to maintain riches and amass power for the few—just the opposite of what ethical law requires.

Yes, such tyranny can unify a people, but at what cost to the sanctity of life? These conditions are certainly not based on sound belief systems and ethical laws that strengthen a society and help it strive toward goodness. Principles of unification in a nation must promote the greatest good for its citizens. Such principles must direct people toward the light of goodness rather than submit to the arousal of intense, passionate emotions that emanate from the darkness of evil. Societies that turn toward darkness will ultimately fail and destroy themselves.

The Ten Commandments, the laws, and the Israelites' sojourn in the desert for forty years became the early seedbed of the values of justice and mercy, which will be explored in coming chapters. Living together in the desert assured that a new generation not only learned to live in freedom, but also established the foundational framework of societal harmony based on laws that were meant to serve the people.

Chapter 4:
The Books of Judges and Kings—
The Law Treats Everyone Equally

In ancient times, kings conquered lands in order to amass power and resources. People became a means for serving the king's needs. Centralized rule was the norm. As the adage goes, absolute power corrupts absolutely. Kings were above the law; they were a divine representation of the gods on earth. Their whims and desires controlled the people. If kings were just and moral, the people received righteous treatment. If kings were corrupt, the people suffered at their hands.

The law God revealed to the Israelites allowed for a new social order. The twelve tribes divided the land by regions and grew in size. Priests were advisors to tribal chiefs, warriors, and elders, with singular individuals rising up as judges to defend the nation's tribes in its infancy. These judges interpreted the law in a just and merciful manner, aligned with God's expectations.

As time passed, however, the tribes and chieftains felt they were no longer able to defend their lands. The people demanded that a king be selected by God to rule over them. A king could raise larger armies against the enemy. The tribes no longer had to act alone; they could act collectively under centralized rule.

God had freed the Israelites from Pharaoh's slavery in Egypt. But with freedom comes responsibility, both to maintain social order and to live in accordance with the ethical law. For the people to demand that a king be placed over them was in direct conflict with God's power and authority. Tribes could have worked together under common leadership, but the people were antagonistic to such a solution. The Israelites demanded a king. God confronted the people through the prophet Samuel, the last of the Judges.

The Israelites were not convinced. God finally decided to place a king over them but established the expectation that any king would rule in accordance with the law and God's authority. No king was to be above the law or its people, and he would be expected to submit to the authority of God, not take power into his own hands. The king would set the example for the people, and if successful, the king's line of descendants would continue to rule.

In accordance with God's will, Samuel appoints Saul, a Benjaminite, as Israel's first king. But Saul fails to submit to God's directives on behalf of the people. Saul is to defend the tribes but fails to meet God's expectations. Instead, he takes power into his own hands and ignores the requirement to carry out the law. God then has Samuel select David who, at a young age, ascends to the kingship after Saul dies.

The representative tribes of Israel also designate David to become their warrior king, willingly assenting to God's selection. David submits to God's power and authority and becomes a great king. From his line, all future Israelite kings would arise. Initially, everyone respects David's authority and leadership. But even David, as king, stumbles badly. He comes to abuse power for his own desire and takes the law into his own hands.

From Judges to Samuel

Returning now to the time of Joshua's rule, we begin with the growth of the twelve tribes and their attempts to carry out God's law based on justice and mercy. During the period covered by the book of Judges, the law grows erratically under the organization of chieftains and elders.

When the Israelites first entered the land of Canaan, it was necessary for them to settle into designated regions and establish a social order. The Lord selected Joshua as the successor to Moses. Joshua leads the tribes to conquer the land. Having conquered a total of 31 towns and kings, he permits many of the defeated people to remain and live among the Israelites.

Joshua divides the land, each tribe settling into its designated region. In order to accomplish this integration, a more formalized faith had to evolve, along with a system which would support and inform the people how to live within the new law. In other words, the people who wandered the desert had to become a nation. The values learned while traveling the desert for forty years became the means of ensuring that the laws and faith in God would survive. These values would enable the people to thrive as a nation. The new system had to ensure that there would be no return to enslavement.

Therefore, the laws God gifted to the Israelites became not only the origin of future common law, but the seed of early democracy. Tribal chieftains and elders, advised by priests, ensured that the laws would be applied equally to the people and would empower them to live with an inner discipline. The law guided everyone. Equality, based on just and merciful treatment, encouraged individual strength and expression. It would guard against oppression, violence, and exploitation.

Prior to this, kings and pharaohs ruled their lands by fiat. They operated under their own laws and were controlled by a small cadre of people. In many cases, the kings and pharaohs behaved as they saw fit, often for their own benefit. They would force a people to succumb as subjects, servants, or slaves, since the norm often was oppression, violence, and exploitation.

The Book of Judges speaks in terms of tribal rule based on justice and mercy. The generations living during and after Joshua's time witnessed the Lord's strength and power in conquering the region. But for successive generations, these divine interventions ceased.

The Lord left the following nations in the land to test future generations in their faith: the five principalities of the Philistines plus the Canaanites, the Sidonians, and the Hivites of the hill country of Lebanon. The tribes of Israel would fail the test of faith over and over.

Joshua, son of Nun, the servant of the Lord, died at the age of one hundred and ten years, and was buried on his own property, at Timnath-heres in the hill country of Ephraim, north of Mount Gaash. And all that generation were like-wise gathered to their fathers. Another generation arose after them, which had not experienced [the deliverance of] the Lord or the deeds that He had wrought for Israel. And the Israelites did what was offensive to the Lord. They worshiped the Baalim and forsook the Lord, the God of their fathers, who had brought them out of the land of Egypt. They followed other gods, from among the gods of the peoples around them, and bowed down to them; they provoked the Lord. They forsook the Lord and worshiped Baal and the Ashtaroth. Then the LORD was incensed at Israel, and He handed them over to foes who plundered them. He surrendered them to their enemies on all sides, and they could no longer hold their own against their enemies. In all their campaigns, the hand of the LORD was against them to their undoing, as the LORD had declared and as the LORD had sworn to them; and they were in great distress. Then the LORD raised up chieftains who delivered them from those who plundered them. But they did not heed their chieftains either; they went astray after other gods and bowed down to them. They were quick to turn aside from the way their fathers had followed in obedience to the commandments of the LORD; they did not do right. (Judges 2:8–17)

Later generations reverted to their old, errant ways and worshipped other gods. God would then select other groups to attack and conquer the Israelites. But eventually, God would lift up chieftains to become judges, successfully defending the land. As long as the chieftain was alive, the people would live in accordance with the commandments. Once the chieftain died, the people would regress and act basely again.

Then the LORD became incensed against Israel, and He said, "Since that nation has transgressed the covenant that I enjoined upon their fathers and has not obeyed Me, I for my part will no longer drive out before them any of the nations that Joshua left when he died. For it was in order to test Israel by them—[to see] whether or not they would faithfully walk in the ways of the LORD, as their fathers had done— that the LORD had left those nations, instead of driving them out at once, and had not delivered them into the hands of Joshua. (Judges 2:20–23)

God had been testing the Israelites, the generations who had never seen war, to determine if they would remain faithful. For example, when they lived in accordance with God's law, warrior leaders, as chieftains acting as judges, would arise, such as Othniel the Kenizzite, who defeated the King of Aram. After this, the people experienced peace for forty years. Then, the Israelites again offended the Lord with their ways, and God forced them to surrender to another king, Jabin of Canaan. A woman, Jael, wife of Heber the Kenites, killed the Canaanite army commander, Sisera, and destroyed the King of Canaan. This cycle continued with the Midianites, who Gideon won over, and finally with the Philistines, who Samson won over from the tribe of Dan. During this time, there was no king over Israel, and the people chose to follow their own ways and worship other gods.

And so follows the story of Samuel, the last prophet, who was most beloved amongst the people. There once was a man by the name of Elkanah, son of Jeroham, an Ephraimite. He had two wives, Peninnah and Hannah. Hannah was childless. She visited the priest Eli and prayed that if the Lord would allow her to bear a child, she would dedicate this son to God. The son she finally bore was Samuel, and she gave him over to Eli, the priest, who raised him.

Eli acted as the warrior chief for the land of Israel. Later on, Samuel and his two sons led the Israelites into battle against the Philistines who were ruling over them at the time. His two sons took the Ark of the Covenant into battle and the Philistines captured the Ark for a period of seven months.

Then Samuel, as the prophet to the Lord, became the warrior chief over Israel. He gathered the troops to bring back the Ark. He eliminated all alien gods and idols from the land and directed the people's hearts to the Lord. He followed the laws of God, and the Israelites regained the Ark.

Samuel grew old, and he appointed his sons as judges. But Samuel's sons did not follow in their father's ways. They were not fair; they were "bent on gain ... and they subverted justice." (I Samuel 8:3) All the elders of Israel decided to act on their concerns by assembling and confronting Samuel at Ramah. They said to him:

> *"You have grown old, and your sons have not followed your ways. Therefore, appoint a king for us, to govern us like other nations." Samuel was displeased that they said, "Give us a king to govern us." Samuel prayed to the LORD, and the LORD replied to Samuel, "Heed the demand of the people in everything they say to you. For it is not you that they have rejected; it is Me they have rejected as their king. Like everything else they have done ever since I brought them out of Egypt to this day—forsaking Me and worshiping other gods—so they are doing to you. Heed their demand; but warn them solemnly and tell them about the practices of any king who will rule over time."*

> *Samuel reported all the words of the LORD to the people, who were asking him for a king. He said, "This will be the practice of the king who will rule over you: he will take your sons and appoint them as his charioteers and horsemen, and they will serve as outrunners for his chariots. He will appoint them as his chiefs of thousands and of fifties; or they will have to plow his fields, reap his harvest, and make his weapons and the equipment for his chariots. He will take their daughters as perfumers, cooks, and bakers. He will seize your choice fields, vineyards, and olive groves, and give them to his courtiers. He will take a tenth part of your grain*

and vintage and give it to his eunuchs and courtiers. He will take your male and female slaves, your choice young men, and your asses, and put them to work for him. He will take a tenth part of your flocks, and you shall become his slaves. The day will come when you cry out because of the king whom you yourselves have chosen; and the LORD will not answer you on that day."

But the people would not listen to Samuel's warning, "No," they said. "We must have a king over us, that we may be like all the other nations: Let our king rule over us and go out at our head and fight our battles." And the LORD said to Samuel, "Heed their demands and appoint a king for them." Samuel then said to the men of Israel, "All of you go home." (I Samuel 8:5–22)

The Lord, through Samuel, reminded the Israelites of their own history of enslavement under the oppressive rule of Pharaoh in Egypt and of the exploitive rule by many kings within civilizations of their time. Kings oppressed their people. Traditional rule under kings would generate a cruel and violent class system—those smaller numbers who ruled and the majority who became subjects, servants, and slaves. The people would serve under the oppressive authority and violence of a king's rule, forever locked into forced slavery and impoverishment.

Samuel sought to convey warnings explaining that only the Lord could be King in accordance with the value of treating one another in an equitable and respectful fashion. If they lived by God's law, they could avoid the inevitable enslavement to a ruler.

Regional tribal-based consensus became unrealistic as the Israelite nation grew larger. Some functions, such as the conquest of enemies, required tribal coordination. Formulating broader decisions for the common good of the nation needed some centralized oversight. In spite of the fact that a leader and a worthy council representing the different tribes might have accomplished the same outcome, the people demanded a king.

The Anointment of Saul as the First King of Israel

God, through Samuel, assured that the Israelites would elect a king. God has Samuel anoint Saul, who is from the tribe of Benjamin, to be the first king of the Israelite nation. Saul's first rule begins around 1029 BCE.[1]

Saul's monarchy superseded the leadership of tribal clans and communities. The king was to be the servant of God and submit to God's authority, but the king also represented the people in their faith, the law, and as a warrior leader.

Samuel summoned the people to the LORD at Mizpah and said to them, "Thus said the LORD, the God of Israel: 'I brought Israel out of Egypt, and I delivered you from the hands of the Egyptians and of all the kingdoms that oppressed you.' But today, you have rejected your God who delivered you from all your troubles and calamities. For you said, 'No, set up a king over us!' Now station yourselves before the LORD, by your tribes and clans."

Samuel brought forward each of the tribes of Israel, and the lot indicated the tribe of Benjamin. Then Samuel brought forward the tribe of Benjamin by its clans, and the clan of the Matrites was indicated; and then Saul, son of Kish was indicated. But when they looked for him, he was not to be found. They inquired of the LORD again, "Has anyone else come here?" And the LORD replied, "Yes; he is hiding among the baggage." So, they ran over and brought him over there; and when he took his place among the people, he stood a head taller than all the people. And Samuel said to the people, "Do you see the one whom the LORD has chosen? There is none like him among all the people." And all the people acclaimed him, shouting, "Long live the king!"

Samuel expounded to the people the rules of the monarchy and recorded them in a document which he deposited before the LORD. Samuel then sent the people back to their homes.
(I Samuel 10:17–25)

The Israelite community had agreed to the selection of a king. However, until his old age, Samuel represented God and the people. His replacement was a king. How would he be remembered by the Israelites? Would he be forgotten as the line of kings took over? Would he and his sons continue to have a role to play—as part of the tradition of judges aligned with God, or would Saul play a lone hand, with Samuel being relegated to anonymity? Samuel's despair is palpable.

Then Samuel said to all Israel, "I have yielded to you in all you have asked of me and have set a king over you. Henceforth the king will be your leader.

"As for me, I have grown old and gray—but my sons are still with you—and I have been your leader from my youth to this day. Here I am! Testify against me, in the presence of the LORD and in the presence of His anointed one: Whose ox have I taken or whose ass have I taken? Whom have I defrauded or whom have I robbed? From whom have I taken a bribe to look the other way? I will return it to you." They responded, "You have not defrauded us, and you have not robbed us, and you have taken nothing from anyone." He said to them, "The LORD then is witness, and His anointed is witness, to your admission this day that you have found nothing in my possession." They responded, "He is!"
(I Samuel 12:1–5)

Furthermore, Samuel reminds the people that when they saw other kings attempting to invade them, instead of trusting God and Samuel to protect them, the people demanded a king.

> *But when you saw that Nahash king of the Ammonites was advancing against you, you said to me, "No, we must have a king reigning over us"— though the Lord your God is your King.*

> *"Well, the Lord has set a king over you! Here is the king that you have chosen, that you have asked for.*

> *"If you will revere the Lord, worship Him, and obey Him, and will not flout the Lord's command, if both you and the king who reigns over you will follow the Lord your God, [well and good]. But if you do not obey the Lord and you flout the Lord's command, the hand of the Lord will strike you as it did your fathers.*

> *"Now stand by and see the marvelous thing that the Lord will do before your eyes. It is the season of the wheat harvest. I will pray to the Lord and He will send thunder and rain; then you will take thought and realize what a wicked thing you did in the sight of the Lord when you asked for a king."* (I Samuel 12:12–15)

Samuel has stepped down from his role as the prophet of the Lord. He is heartbroken at the people's lack of trust in God. He is saddened at his own unrecognized life of selfless service. Samuel now offers a role for himself which honors the tradition of the judges and the past, which honors God who gave the people their freedom, while ushering in the new reform in governance.

> *"As for me, far be it from me to sin against the Lord and refrain from praying for you; and I will continue to instruct*

you in the practice of what is good and right. Above all, you must revere the LORD and serve Him faithfully with all your heart; and consider how grandly He has dealt with you. For if you persist in your wrongdoing, both you and your king shall be swept away." (I Samuel 12:23–25)

The Lord now demands that the anointed king, Saul, obey God's word, for if the king does not obey God, then the king is not acting as God's servant and will not serve the people of Israel well. If Saul does not honor the demands of God, and commits even small transgressions, this will be his downfall. It takes Saul one step closer to abusing his own authority and power. The king must uphold his honor with integrity and through faith. The king cannot set himself above the law and God's word.

Saul's first demonstration of leadership in battle begins against the Philistines. He is successful with his forces on behalf of the Israelites and all the men rally. God will next test Saul against the Amalekite people.

Recall that in Exodus, the Israelites had requested that the locals allow them to pass through the land safely when they had left Egypt and journeyed through the desert to Sinai. Instead, the Amalekites chose to make war against the Israelites. Therefore, "… The LORD will be at war with Amalek throughout the ages." (Exodus 17:6) God, through Samuel, now commands Saul to his next battle. This will be a test of Saul's commitment to God.

Samuel said to Saul, "I am the one the LORD sent to anoint you king over His people Israel. Therefore, listen to the LORD's command!

"Thus said the LORD of Hosts: I am exacting the penalty for what Amalek did to Israel, for the assault he made upon

them on the road, on their way up from Egypt. Now go, attack Amalek, and proscribe all that belongs to him. Spare no one, but kill alike men and women, infants and sucklings, oxen and sheep, camels and asses!" (I Samuel 15:1–3)

With the Lord's power and strength, Saul and his men overtook Amalek. The Lord prohibited Saul from allowing the men to take anything for themselves. Instead, Saul violated God's commands and made his own decision to keep the "best of the sheep, the oxen, the second-born, the lambs, and all else that was of value. They would not proscribe them; they proscribed only what was cheap and worthless." This angered God!

The word of the LORD then came to Samuel: "I regret that I made Saul king, for he turned away from Me and has not carried out My commands." Samuel was distressed and he entreated the LORD all night long. Early in the morning Samuel went to meet Saul. Samuel was told, "Saul went to Carmel, where he erected a monument for himself; then he left and went on down to Gilgal."

When Samuel came to Saul, Saul said to him, "Blessed are you of the LORD! I have fulfilled the LORD's command." "Then what," demanded Samuel, "is this bleating of sheep in my ears, and the lowing of oxen that I hear?" Saul answered, "They were brought from the Amalekites, for the troops spared the choicest of the sheep and oxen for sacrificing to the LORD your God. And we proscribed the rest." Samuel said to Saul, "Stop! Let me tell you what the LORD said to me last night!" "Speak," he replied. And Samuel said, "You may look small to yourself, but you are the head of the tribes of Israel. The LORD anointed you king over Israel, and the LORD sent you on a mission saying, 'Go and proscribe the sinful Amalekites; make war on them until you have exterminated them.' Why did you disobey the Lord *and swoop down on the spoil of the* Lord*?" Saul said to Samuel, "But I did obey the* Lord*! I performed the mission on which the* Lord *sent me: I captured King Agag of Amalek, and I proscribed Amalek, and the troops took from the spoil some sheep and oxen—the best of what had been proscribed —to sacrifice to the* Lord *your God at Gilgal." But Samuel said:*

> *"Does the* Lord *delight in burnt offerings and sacrifices*
> *As much as in obedience to the* Lord*'s command?*
> *Surely, obedience is better than sacrifice,*
> *Compliance than the fat of rams.*
> *For rebellion is like the sin of divination,*
> *Defiance, like the iniquity of teraphim*
> *Because you rejected the* Lord*'s command,*
> *He has rejected you as king."* (I Samuel 15:10–23)

As Samuel turned to leave, Saul seized the corner of his robe, and it tore. And Samuel said to him, "The Lord *has this day torn the kingship over Israel away from you and has given it to another who is worthier than you. Moreover, the Glory of Israel does not deceive or change His mind, for He is not human that He should change His mind.*
(I Samuel 15:27–29)

God's revealed law, "You shall not murder," permits for the defense of an individual from harm, but not killing for individual gain. Kings who abuse power will kill and conquer other lands for individual gain. The Israelites' law would only allow a king to defend his lands—not to take the possessions of others. This would violate God's directive and the law.[2]

Saul chose a course of action that put him above the law. Saul lost favor with God, and in the Lord's eyes, could not continue as king. God's power and strength abandoned Saul for his remaining years.

Instead of following the chain of descendants of Saul, the Lord would identify Jesse's young son, David, the Bethlehemite from the tribe of Judah, to become the future king of Israel. The Lord changed the rule of kingship succession to the one that would be more capable of serving and keeping the faith.

The Ascendency and Reign of King David of Judah

Saul's soul turned to evil after the Lord took the kingship away from him. David, son of Jesse in Judah, entered Saul's service, being a warrior. Saul's forces were in constant battle with the Philistines. Jesse asked David to take food to his brothers and the captain in battle. While there, Goliath of Garth stepped forward to fight for the Philistines. Anyone who could kill Goliath would have the king's daughter in marriage and his father's house would be relieved from having to pay royal taxes.

David informed Saul that he would be willing to go down and fight the Philistine who had defied God. Although he was a boy, David had tended his father's sheep and fought off or killed lion and bear if they came after the flock. David defiantly defended his ability to kill Goliath, and Saul allowed David to fight Goliath in battle.

The Philistine, meanwhile, was coming closer to David, preceded by his shield-bearer. When the Philistine caught sight of David, he scorned him, for he was but a boy, ruddy and handsome. And the Philistine called out to David, "Am I a dog that you come against me with sticks?" The Philistine cursed David by his gods; and the Philistine said to David,

"Come here, and I will give your flesh to the birds of the sky and the beasts of the wild."

David replied to the Philistine, "You come against me with sword and spear and javelin; but I come against you in the name of the Lord of Hosts, the God of the ranks of Israel, whom you have defied. This very day the Lord will deliver you into my hands. I will kill you and cut off your head; and I will give the carcasses of the Philistine camp to the birds of the sky and the beasts of the earth. All the earth shall know that there is a God in Israel. And this whole assembly shall know that the Lord can give victory without sword or spear. For the battle is the Lord's, and He will deliver you into our hands."

When the Philistine began to advance toward him again, David quickly ran up the battle line to face the Philistine. David put his hand into the bag; he took out a stone and slung it. It struck the Philistine in the forehead; the stone sank into his forehead, and he fell face down on the ground. Thus, David bested the Philistine with sling and stone; he struck him down and killed him. David had no sword, so David ran up and stood over the Philistine, grasped his sword and pulled it from its sheath; and with it he dispatched him and cut off his head. (I Samuel 17:41–51)

David put his faith in the Lord for protection against Goliath. From his own experience, David also used leverage against the Philistine and hit him in his weakest spot.

Upon David's return to Saul, all the women were singing and dancing to celebrate the young warrior's success. Saul would take offense since the women praised David for greater successes in battle than he.

The women sang as they danced, and they chanted:
  Saul has slain his thousands
  David, his tens of thousands!

Saul was much distressed and greatly vexed about the matter. For he said, "To David they have given tens of thousands, and to me they have given thousands. All that he lacks is the kingship!" From that day on Saul kept a jealous eye on David. The next day an evil spirit of God gripped Saul and he began to rave in the house, while David was playing [the lyre], as he did daily. Saul had a spear in his hand, and Saul threw the spear, thinking to pin David to the wall. But David eluded him twice. Saul was afraid of David, for the LORD *was with him and had turned away from Saul.*
(I Samuel 18:7–12)

Saul knows that the spirit of the Lord of Hosts is with David; soon David will have the kingship. Saul attempts to murder David on several occasions. Saul's son, Jonathan, and David become close; Jonathan loved David as a brother. He would protect David at all costs from his father.

Saul should be focusing on his God-directed leadership of the Israelites; instead, he allows himself to become consumed with the dark spirit of jealousy and rage. In turn, David's men would offer on several occasions to kill Saul. Never once, however, did David become angry with Saul or desire his death. The Lord's commandment is "You shall not murder." And so, David did not allow anyone to harm Saul, the king of Israel, in spite of Saul's threats to his life.

Saul takes his army of men to the wilderness of Ein Gedi where he hears that David has camped out in exile. Saul goes alone into a cave, where David and his men are hiding, and Saul finds himself vulnerable to attack. When David finds that he is free to take Saul's life, he makes the right choice to honor the Lord and the law that directs his thoughts and actions. But he lets Saul know that he could have taken his life, so why should Saul try to take David's life? David can control his emotions and make wise decisions, unlike Saul—who is still consumed with jealousy.

> David's men said to him, "This is the day of which the LORD said to you, 'I will deliver your enemy into your hands; you can do with him as you please.'" David stealthily cut off the corner of Saul's cloak. But afterward David reproached himself for cutting off the corner of Saul's cloak. He said to his men, "The LORD forbid that I should do such a thing to my lord—the LORD's anointed—that I should raise my hand against him; for he is the LORD's anointed." David rebuked his men and did not permit them to attack Saul.

> Saul left the cave and started on his way. Then David also went out of the cave and called after Saul, "My lord king!" Saul looked around and David bowed low in homage, with his face to the ground. And David said to Saul, "Why do you listen to the people who say, 'David is out to do you harm!' You can see for yourself now that the LORD delivered you into my hands in the cave today. And though I was urged to kill you, I showed you pity; for I said, 'I will not raise a hand against my lord, since he is the LORD's anointed.' Please sir, take a close look at the corner of your cloak in my hand; for when I cut off the corner of your cloak, I did not kill you. You must see plainly that I have done nothing evil or rebellious, and I have never wronged you. Yet you are bent on taking my life. May the LORD judge between you and me! And may He take vengeance upon you for me, but my hand will never touch you." (I Samuel 24:5–13)

David has motive and opportunity to kill the king but does not do it. The next time this occurs, the Ziphites have come to

Saul at Gibran to let him know where David is hiding again, still in exile, in the wilderness of Ziph. Saul and his army commander, Abner son of Ner lay asleep inside a barricade of troops.

Once again, David has the opportunity to slay Saul in order to save his own life but refuses to do so in honor of the Lord. David stealthily comes up from behind Saul and his commander as they sleep. His men want to kill Saul, but David refuses because Saul is the servant of God. Instead, they steal Saul's spear and the water jar by his head to prove to Saul that David could have killed him. (I Samuel 26:6–16)

When David has the opportunity to kill Saul, nothing overrides the fact that David, as servant of God, cannot murder another, even when his own life is at risk. David must remain obedient to the law. In one last stand, Saul fights the Philistines. Tragically, he dies along with all of his men—three of his sons and an arms-bearer among them.

David begins his reign as king over the House of Judah in Hebron in 1007 BCE.[3] However, the people had selected Ish-bosheth, the fourth son of Saul, as king over all of the House of Israel. The House of Saul and the House of David went to war with each other. One day, two company commanders of the House of Saul murdered the king of Israel, Ish-bosheth. This settled the matter of there being only one king over the entire Israelite nation.

When David learns that these two commanders have murdered the king of Israel, even though this act establishes David as king over both Houses, David himself decrees that the two commanders be put to death for violating the law. David upholds the dictum that no man is above the Lord and God's laws—even the king.

And so, all the tribes of Israel come to David and ask that he be made king over Israel. David was thirty years old when he became king, which occurred in 1000 BCE.[4] The Ark of God was moved to the City of David in the House of Judah, where he was ruling. David was known as the warrior king, for he conquered many lands and ruled over a united Israel.

King David built a political system that honored both the Lord and the people. He ruled and fought with humility as the servant of God. David would establish a system of rule. If people could not agree on what was right and good in accordance with the law, they could come to David to have their case assigned. Only the most important cases came to David to be heard.

David is good and honors the Lord in his actions; therefore, the Lord is good to him. David, through the rule of law and his judgments, develops a system which truly enacts the law while honoring the faith and belief system of the Lord of Hosts. David is known for being a great and honorable king. He eventually builds a house of cedar for himself in the City of David. Nathan, God's prophet for communicating with King David, now speaks.

> *When the king was settled in his place and the LORD had granted him safety from all the enemies around him, the king said to the prophet Nathan: "Here I am dwelling in a house of cedar, while the Ark of the LORD abides in a tent!" Nathan said to the king, "Go and do whatever you have in mind, for the LORD is with you."*
>
> *But that same night the word of the LORD came to Nathan: "Go and say to My servant David: Thus said the LORD: Are you the one to build a house for Me to dwell in? From the day that I brought the people of Israel out of Egypt to this day I have not dwelt in a house but have moved about in Tent and*

Tabernacle. As I moved about wherever the Israelites went, did I ever reproach any of the tribal leaders whom I appointed to care for My people Israel: Why have you not built Me a house of cedar?

"Further, say thus to My servant David: Thus said the LORD of Hosts: I took you from the pasture from following the flock, to be ruler of My people Israel, and I have been with you wherever you went, and have cut down all your enemies before you. Moreover, I will give you a great renown like that of the greatest men on earth. I will establish a home for My people Israel and will plant them firm, so that they shall dwell secure and shall tremble no more. Evil men shall not oppress them any more as in the past, ever since I appointed chieftains over My people Israel. I will give you safety from all your enemies.

The LORD declares to you that He, the LORD, will establish a house for you. When your days are done and you lie with your fathers, I will raise up your offspring after you, one of your own issue, and I will establish his royal throne forever. I will be a father to him, and he shall be a son to Me. When he does wrong, I will chastise him with the rod of men and the affliction of mortals; but I will never withdraw My favor from him as I withdrew it from Saul, whom I removed to make room for you. Your house and your kingship shall ever be secure before you; your throne shall be established forever. (II Samuel 7:1–16)

The Lord speaks through Nathan. King David and his descendants will reign. God will not take away the rights of kingship as with Saul. David was the servant of God; David ruled the people with justice; and none of his actions and judgments were above the law.

All kings over the Israelites are servants of the Lord and of the people. This demands a certain level of humility from David, which, in turn, assures that the king serves his people fairly and dispenses judgment wisely based on the interpretation of the law.

David is at the height of his service to the Lord. At the turn of the year, David sent his officers and men out to battle the Ammonites.

David remained in Jerusalem. Late one afternoon, David rose from his couch and strolled on the roof of the royal palace; and from the roof he saw a woman bathing. The woman was very beautiful, and the king sent someone to make inquiries about the woman. He reported, "She is Bathsheba daughter of Elian [and] wife of Uriah the Hittite." David sent messengers to fetch her; she came to him and he lay with her—she had just purified herself after her period—and she went back home. The woman conceived, and she sent word to David, "I am pregnant." Thereupon David sent a message to Joab, "Send Uriah the Hittite to me;" and Joab sent Uriah to David. (II Samuel 11:1–5)

David requested that Uriah go back to his home and be with his wife. But Uriah refused and instead remained on guard at the royal palace, in loyalty and protection for the king. This continued for several days, at which time David finally made a decision.

In the morning, David wrote a letter to Joab, which he sent to Uriah. He wrote in the letter as follows: "Place Uriah in the front line where the fighting is fiercest; then fall back so that he may be killed." So, when Joab was besieging the city, he stationed Uriah at the point where he knew that there were able warriors. The men of the city sallied out and attacked Joab, and some of David's officers among the

troops fell; Uriah the Hittite was among them that died.
(II Samuel 11:14–17)

When Uriah's wife heard that her husband Uriah was dead,
she lamented over her husband. After the period of
mourning was over, David sent and had her brought into his
palace; she became his wife and she bore him a son.
(II Samuel 11:26–27)

The deed had been done. Uriah the Hittite warrior had been faithful to David. But instead of respecting another man's life and his wife, David proceeded to order his commander to send Uriah to his death in order to make Bathsheba one of his wives. Therein, David broke three commandments: You shall not murder; You shall not commit adultery; and You shall not covet your neighbor's house: you shall not covet your neighbor's wife … or anything that is your neighbor's.

No king was to be above the law. The king was to act as the servant of the Lord. The king was to act justly and mercifully on behalf of the people. God had just determined that David's line of descendants would rule Israel; God would never take away this line of ascension.

The LORD was displeased with what David had done, and the
LORD sent Nathan to David. He came to him and said,
"There are two men in the same city, one rich and one poor.
The rich man had very large flocks and herds, but the poor
man had only one little ewe lamb that he had bought. He
tended it and it grew up together with him and his children:
it used to share his morsel of bread, drink from his cup, and
nestle in his bosom; it was like a daughter to him. One day, a
traveler came to the rich man, but he was loath to take
anything from his own flocks or herds to prepare a meal for

the guest who had come to him; so, he took the poor man's lamb and prepared it for the man who had come to him."

David flew into a rage against the man, and said to Nathan, "As the LORD lives, the man who did this deserves to die! He shall pay for the lamb four times over, because he did such a thing and showed no pity." And Nathan said to David, "That man is you! Thus said the LORD, the God of Israel: 'It is I who anointed you king over Israel, and it was I who rescued you from the hand of Saul. I gave you your master's house and possession of your master's wives; and I gave you the House of Israel and Judah; and if that were not enough, I would give you twice as much more. Why then have you flouted the command of the LORD and done what displeases Him? You have put Uriah the Hittite to the sword; you took his wife and made her your wife and had him killed by the sword of the Ammonites. Therefore, the sword shall never depart from your House—because you spurned Me by taking the wife of Uriah the Hittite and making her your wife.' Thus said the LORD: 'I will take your wives and give them to another man before your very eyes and he shall sleep with your wives under this very sun. You acted in secret, but I will make this happen in the sight of all Israel and in broad daylight.'" (II Samuel 12:1–10)

No king shall be exalted in his power to take from others just because he is wealthy, and they are poor. No king shall treat his people as slaves to his desires. The king sets the role model for everyone; he must treat everyone fairly and not be above the law. David recognized this and genuinely regretted his error.

David stumbled badly. He fully repented his transgressions. The Lord forgave David because he was sincere. David would forever be the warrior king. David wanted to build a house for the Lord, but he would never be able to do so. The child of the union of David and Bathsheba would die. But Bathsheba would have a second son by David, Solomon, whom the Lord would favor. Solomon would build the House of the Lord and become the king of peace. The House of David would fall. He would love his wives and children. But the Lord had promised never to take away the reign of King David's descendants; this was the gift God kept to the people of Israel.

God wanted Israel's king to lead in ways that were just and faithful. No king could be above the law; the king was only servant to the Lord, as the Lord was truly the King of the people. Given this expectation, no king could enslave or unjustly shackle any of his subjects. The king of Israel could not create an exploited class caste or slave system. It was necessary to guard that the law applies equally to the king and the people, ensuring that Israelite kings would truly act with humility, in the service of God and God's people.

Chapter 5:
Embedding the Law in the Economic and Political System

Solomon became king in 970 BCE and reigned through 928 BCE.[1] His purpose was to uphold the faith of the Israelites and honor the Lord, to firmly embed the ethical law within a successful political and economic system, and to treat everyone, through wisdom and understanding, on a just and fair basis. Solomon integrated monotheism with the evolving ethical law that God gifted to the Israelites. Faith and the law could not exist without each other. But to make these enduring, they had to be effectively institutionalized.

King David, prior to Solomon, built a military and political system which protected the people, the faith, and the law. He strengthened the law by supporting tribal judges who also were responsible for carrying out the administrative interpretation of justice. He developed the economics of the nation by creating a strong army to bring regions together in defense of the Israelites. David transitioned the land of Israel from one functioning as twelve separate tribal regions to a nation of centralized rule for strength and coordination of all the people.

Solomon would continue to strengthen the nation of Israel with the goal of further unifying the Israelites through a focus on social law and justice. He would be responsible for developing a stronger political system of monarchy and for creating one of the most prosperous economic systems in the region. Peace would be his strategy for unifying the tribes.

Solomon first created an alliance with Egypt by marrying Pharaoh's daughter and bringing her to the City of David. He next was concerned with how he could most wisely rule his people. So, Solomon called upon the Lord to seek divine guidance for this challenging and complex task.

The Lord appeared to Solomon in a dream by night; and God said, "Ask, what shall I grant you?" Solomon said, "You dealt most graciously with Your servant my father David, because he walked before You in faithfulness and righteousness and in integrity of heart. You have continued this great kindness to him by giving him a son to occupy his throne, as is now the case. And now, O Lord my God, You have made Your servant king in place of my father David; but I am a young lad, with no experience in leadership. Your servant finds himself in the midst of the people You have chosen, a people too numerous to be numbered or counted. Grant, then, Your servant an understanding mind to judge Your people, to distinguish between good and bad; for who can judge this vast people of Yours?"

The Lord was pleased that Solomon had asked for this. And God said to him, "Because you asked for this—you did not ask for long life, you did not ask for riches, you did not ask for the life of your enemies, but you asked for discernment in dispensing justice—I now do as you have spoken. I grant you a wise and discerning mind; there has never been anyone like you before, nor will anyone like you arise again. And I also grant you what you did not ask for—both riches and glory all your life—the like of which no king has ever had. And I will further grant you long life, if you will walk in My ways and observe My laws and commandments, as did your father David.

Then Solomon awoke; it was a dream! He went to Jerusalem, stood before the Ark of the Covenant of the LORD, and sacrificed burnt offerings and presented offerings of well-being; and he made a banquet for all his courtiers.
(I Kings 3:5–15)

Early in his reign, the Lord granted Solomon the wisdom to understand his people, and to judge wisely with both ethical and moral wisdom. Solomon kept an inner discipline to support self-determination for individuals and tribal communities through the administration of justice. He put God and the service of his people first, instead of power and riches.

Later, two women gave birth during the night in the same house. One woman's child died, and this woman accused the other of stealing her son for her own. The two fought in front of King Solomon as they brought their case before him.

The king said, "One says, 'This is my son, the live one, and the dead one is yours; and the other says, 'No, the dead boy is yours, mine is the live one.' So the king gave the order, "Fetch me a sword." A sword was brought before the king, and the king said, "Cut the live child in two, and give half to one and half to the other."

But the woman whose son was the live one pleaded with the king, for she was overcome with compassion for her son. "Please, my lord," she cried, "Give her the live child; only don't kill it!" The other insisted, "It shall be neither yours nor mine; cut it in two!" Then the king spoke up. "Give the live child to her," he said, "and do not put it to death; she is its mother."

When all Israel heard the decision that the king had rendered, they stood in awe of the king; for they saw that he possessed divine wisdom to execute justice.
(I Kings 3:23–28)

Solomon came to be known as one of the wisest rulers of all the nations. He based his system of justice on the ethical law that God had established. It became the foundation for a great political system to righteously serve the people of the nation.

King Solomon ruled over all of Israel by building an effective system of governance. He had a cadre of officials working around him which included priests, scribes, and recorders. He had a chief over his army, a chief over the twelve prefects, a priest who became companion to the king, as well as an official over the palace and one over labor in Jerusalem. He also assigned twelve prefects over the various regions of the land to coordinate resources and administer to the people. Solomon's political system was strong, and it resulted in righteous government. All the people were content.

The LORD endowed Solomon with wisdom and discernment in great measure, with understanding as vast as the sands on the seashore. Solomon's wisdom was greater than the wisdom of all the Kedemites and all the wisdom of the Egyptians. He was the wisest of all men: [wiser] than Ethan the Ezrahite, and Herman, Chalkol, and Darda the sons of Mahol. His fame spread among all the surrounding nations. He composed three thousand proverbs, and his songs numbered one thousand and five. He discoursed about trees, from the cedar in Lebanon to the hyssop that grows out of the wall; and he discoursed about beasts, birds, creeping things, and fishes. Men of all peoples came to hear

Solomon's wisdom, [sent] by all the kings of the earth who had heard of his wisdom. (I Kings 5:9–14)

Solomon strove to unify his people through one major goal—building the House of the Lord in Jerusalem where the Ark of the Covenant would reside. This would become the central place of worship for burnt offerings, meal offerings, and offerings of well-being. It would replace the numerous local shrines which still existed throughout the nation. This would be the First Temple, which would replace the portable Tabernacle.

Building the House of the Lord would be challenging. Following the death of Saul at the hands of the Philistines, the kingdom had split into two—the House of Saul, supported by the northern Israelites; and the House of David, supported by the Tribe of Judah. David united the two regions and their inhabitants. Solomon would further solidify this unification by building a permanent House of the Lord, centering the people's faith.

Solomon oversaw the building of the First Temple 480 years after the Israelites left Egypt. It took him eleven years to build it and thirteen years to build his palace. King Solomon required wood and stone for the construction of the House of the Lord. He negotiated with King Hiram of Tyre in Phoenicia for cedar and cypress in exchange for food that sustained King Hiram's household. One of Israel's first treaties was based on this trade relationship, a mutually beneficial one which allowed both nations to flourish. (I Kings 5:21–26)

Solomon first developed much of his economic system in order to construct the House of the Lord and, later, to build his royal palace. David built the City of David; Solomon built the city of Jerusalem. When he had completed the House of the Lord and the royal palace, Solomon began rebuilding other cities in the land of Israel. People from all over the region and other lands came to visit Solomon, to see the Temple, and to bring riches honoring the king and the land.

The builders constructed a three-story structure with side chambers for the Great Hall and Shrine of the House of the Lord. They finished it with stones cut at the quarry of King Hiram in Tyre, using no hammer, axe, or tool to avoid sound as they built the House. They lined the walls with planks of cedar and the floors with planks of cypress. They carved the doors of the entrance to the Temple out of olive wood, overlaid in gold, and engraved with cherubim, palms, and calyxes.

The interior Holy of Holies, which would house the Ark of the Covenant, was twenty cubits by twenty cubits by twenty cubits, overlaid in solid gold.[2] Carved out of olive wood and also overlaid with gold, two winged cherubim hovered over the ark, as if to protect it. Each wingspan was five cubits, with one wing of each cherubim touching the wall and the second protecting the ark overhead and touching each other's wings, like a protective canopy for a total span of twenty cubits.

And Solomon made all the furnishings that were in the House of the LORD: the altar, of gold; the table for the bread of display, of gold; the lamp stands—five on the right side and five on the left—in front of the Shrine, of solid gold; and the petals, lamps, and tongs, of gold; the basins, snuffers, sprinkling bowls, ladles, and fire pans, of solid gold; and the hinge sockets of the doors of the innermost part of the House, the Holy of Holies, and for the doors of the Great Hall of the House, of gold.

When all the work that King Solomon had done in the House of the LORD was completed, Solomon brought in the sacred donations of his father David—the silver, the gold, and the vessels—and deposited them in the treasury of the House of the LORD. (I Kings 7:48–51)

The priests and the Levites brought up the Ark of the Covenant from the City of David and placed it under the cherubim in the Holy of Holies. King Solomon, the elders of the twelve tribes, and the whole community of Israel assembled before the Ark. It contained "the two tablets of stone which Moses placed there at Horeb, when the LORD made [a covenant] with the Israelites after their departure from the land of Egypt." (I Kings 8:9)

When the priests came out of the sanctuary—for the cloud had filled the House of the LORD and the priests were not able to remain and perform the service because of the cloud, for the Presence of the LORD filled the House of the LORD— then Solomon declared:

> *"The LORD has chosen*
> *To abide in a thick cloud:*
> *I have now built for You*
> *A stately House,*
> *A place where You*
> *May dwell forever."*

Then, with the whole congregation of Israel standing, the king faced about and blessed the whole congregation of Israel. (I Kings 8:10–14)

Solomon next consecrated the Temple with a lengthy prayer. Finally, he directed attention to the covenant made between God and his father David.

Solomon stood before the altar of the LORD in the presence of the whole community of Israel; he spread the palms of his hands towards heaven and said: "O LORD God of Israel, in the heavens above and on the earth below there is no god like You, who keep Your gracious covenant with Your servants when they walk before You in wholehearted devotion; You who have kept the promises You made to your servant, my father David, fulfilling with deeds the promise You made— as is now the case. And now, O LORD God of Israel, keep the further promise that You made to Your servant, my father David: 'Your line on the throne of Israel shall never end, if only your descendants will look to their way and walk before Me as you have walked before Me.' Now, therefore, O God of Israel, let the promise that You made to Your servant my father David be fulfilled. (I Kings 8:22–26)

Many years later, upon completion of the House of the Lord and the royal palace, and everything else that Solomon had set his heart on, the Lord came to Solomon once again:

The LORD said to him, "I have heard the prayer and the supplication which you have offered to Me. I consecrate this House which you have built, and I set My name there forever. My eyes and My heart shall ever be there. As for you, if you walk before Me as your father David walked before Me, wholeheartedly and with uprightness, doing all that I have commanded you [and] keeping My laws and My rules, then I will establish your throne of kingship over Israel forever, as I promised your father David, saying, 'Your line on the throne of Israel shall never end.' [But] if you and your descendants turn away from Me and do not keep the commandments [and] the laws which I have set before you, and go and serve other gods and worship them, then I will sweep Israel off the land which I gave them; I will reject the

House which I have consecrated to My name; and Israel
shall become a proverb and a byword among all the peoples
..." (I Kings 9:3–7)

During this time, Solomon did not abuse his position—he
was not above the law; rather, he became the role model
necessary to lead the political and economic growth of a
successful nation. He ensured that all the people were able to
contribute to the building of the House of the Lord, as well as
to share in good fortune as his economic system led to
prosperity. Solomon involved both individuals and tribes in
the continuing construction of Jerusalem which further
encouraged economic and spiritual development.

Solomon's greatest reform would be to bring abundance
to the people based on a foundation of peace and trade, rather
than conquering other lands. Solomon's wisdom and vision
brought the light of goodness to a nation and its people.
Solomon did not use war to exploit the resources of other
lands. Instead, he created a system of trade and wealth based
on mutual interests and cooperation.

Kings in Israel were servants of the people and of the Lord.
Other kings, such as the pharaohs in Egypt, or the Assyrian
and Babylonian kings, considered themselves to be divine
embodiments of gods on earth. Kings descended from gods
and demanded to be treated as such. They could easily abuse
power by accumulating riches and using people as slaves and
servants. Kings had a place on earth—to be in control. People
had a place on earth—to either serve the king (a smaller
number) or to be slaves to the king (the larger masses). Kings
could oppress their people, and usually did so violently.

Never before had a king ruled based on a covenant with
God, in order to serve God and to serve God's people. Solomon

pursued peace with other kings. In every other case, rule was about obtaining power and wealth at the expense of the people while protecting the ruler for as long as possible. Rulers employed power's darkest forces to enlarge their position at the expense of others. Such power can easily turn to evil.

The Israelites had come from oppression and slavery in Egypt. So, when the people of Israel, under the prophet Samuel, requested a king for their land, they also expected that king to receive divine inspiration, serving the Lord first, as well as the people.

Once Solomon built the Temple for the Lord, his reputation spread throughout the land. He traded with the Queen of Sheba. He built an alliance with King Hiram of Tyre, bringing in gold from Ophir, and wood for the House of the Lord for decoration. Solomon received gold from the traffic of tradesmen, from all the kings of Arabia, and the governors of the region.

Solomon built up a stable of chariots and horses procured from nearby lands. Chariots purchased from others would then be exported to other kings. He created items of silver and gold in Jerusalem. He accumulated vast riches and wealth, just as God had promised, as long as Solomon abided by God's laws and rules. Would wealth and fame now become Solomon's prime motivator and ultimate downfall?

King Solomon loved many foreign women in addition to Pharaoh's daughter—Moabite, Ammonite, Edomite, Phoenician, and Hittite women, from the nations of which the LORD had said to the Israelites, "None of you shall join them and none of them shall join you, lest they turn your heart away to follow their gods." Such Solomon clung to and loved. He had seven hundred royal wives and three hundred concubines; and his wives turned his heart away. In his old age, his wives turned away Solomon's heart after other gods, and he was not as wholeheartedly devoted to the LORD his God as his father David had been. Solomon followed Ashtoreth the goddess of the Phoenicians, and Milcom the abomination of the Ammonites. (I Kings 11:1–5)[3]

Solomon had in fact now turned away from God. Wealth, materialism, and power had become his primary values and motivations. This would eventually lead to the demise of his kingdom.

The LORD was angry with Solomon, because his heart turned away from the LORD, the God of Israel, who had appeared to him twice and had commanded him about this matter, not to follow other gods; he did not obey what the LORD had commanded. And the LORD said to Solomon, "Because you are guilty of this—you have not kept My covenant and the laws which I enjoined upon you—I will tear the kingdom away from you and give it to one of your servants. But, for the sake of your father David, I will not do it in your lifetime; I will tear it away from your son. However, I will not tear away the whole kingdom; I will give your son one tribe, for the sake of My servant David and for the sake of Jerusalem which I have chosen." (I Kings 11:9–13)

No king could use his position for his own benefit if it harmed the people; no king was above the law. And in so understanding his position, by extension, any king not only had to respect the people he served, but he also had to apply the law even-handedly. He had to ensure that the law would survive by developing a congruent political and economic system which was at the same time unifying for the people. Developing such a system must be based upon royal humility.

Solomon had to remain focused on serving God and the people, in keeping the law and rules of the Lord. The priority for just governance needed to remain uppermost in his mind. Once economic riches and other trappings became the prime motivators, just governance and representation could no longer exist. Instead, Solomon's rule becomes governance by self-interest, to generate more wealth at the expense of the people. Moral corruption sets in. The king abuses power and oppresses the people.

The vast wealth that Solomon amassed was a personal test. The riches that Solomon acquired and the women he loved lured him away from the value of goodness. The stage was set by God through the prophet Ahijah for Solomon's downfall.

Jeroboam, son of Nebat, an Ephraimite of Zeredah, the son of a widow whose name was Zeruah, was in Solomon's service; he raised his hand against the king. The circumstances under which he raised his hand against the king were as follows: Solomon built the Millo and repaired the breach of the city of his father, David. Jeroboam was an able man; and when Solomon saw the young man was a capable worker, he appointed him over all the forced labor of the House of Joseph.

During that time, Jeroboam went out of Jerusalem and the prophet Ahijah of Shiloh met him on the way. He had put on a new robe; and when the two were alone in the open country, Ahijah took hold of the new robe he was wearing and tore it into twelve pieces. Take ten pieces," he said to Jeroboam. "For thus said the LORD, the God of Israel: I am about to tear the kingdom out of Solomon's hands, and I will give you ten tribes. But one tribe shall remain his—for the sake of My servant David and for the sake of Jerusalem, the city that I have chosen out of all the tribes of Israel. For they have forsaken Me; they have worshiped Ashtoreth the goddess of the Phoenicians, Chemosh the god of Moab, and Milcom the god of the Ammonites; they have not walked in My ways, or done what is pleasing to Me, or [kept] my laws and rules, as his father David did. However, I will not take the entire kingdom away from him but will keep him as ruler as long as he lives for the sake of My servant David whom I chose, and who kept My commandments and My laws. But I will take the kingship out of the hands of his son and give it to you—the ten tribes. To his son I will give one tribe, so that there may be a lamp for My servant David forever before Me in Jerusalem—the city where I have chosen to establish My name ..." (I Kings 11:26–36)

Solomon had transgressed the ways of the Lord and the law. Now, the descending line of rule from King David, after Solomon's death, would turn to the House of Israel instead of the House of Judah.

Faith in the Lord, while basing justice on compassion and moral wisdom, had to be Solomon's primary driving force and vision. Values must drive effective political and economic systems which serve to unify the twelve tribes. Otherwise, wealth, power, and fame, when misused, can lead to moral corruption.

Positive values must be compelling to a society and its people so that the collective whole can achieve greatness. They have to be active, living values which are translatable into visions, creating unity for the entire people and serving them well in times of adversity. The values must also create the right balance between individual rights and needs within tribal communities and the nation as a whole. Such balance is a key element of evolving political systems. Building the House of the Lord represented a unifying achievement for all.

Initially, Solomon's priorities were the values of faith and God's law. He administered justice righteously and with wisdom. Then he established an effective system of administration so that all the people shared equally in justice and prosperity. Solomon was the servant of the divine, and he was a model of wisdom for the people he served. Solomon was not above the law. His political system of monarchy institutionalized these values, based on peace rather than war.

All kings who would rule over the land of Israel or the Kingdom of Judah, by extension, had the obligation to protect not only the rights of people as individuals for the common good, but also to protect the human rights of all people in society.

The king must exhibit both humility and strength of leadership in order to assure survival of the kingdom. King David built the faith and protected the people, the tribes, and the nation from foreign conquerors. He developed a judicial political system to interpret the law when disagreements arose among the people of the nation. He initiated an economic system built on an army that defended the land. This served to unify the tribes of Israel and Judah. David was a warrior king, and a champion of the people.

Solomon, in contrast to David, developed the political system by strengthening spiritual faith in the Lord and striving to fulfill a vision in building the House of the Lord, the Temple, and the Holy of Holies as the sanctuary for the Ark of the Covenant. His wisdom strengthened the political system by institutionalizing the law.

Today, there are populations with little or no control over their wellbeing, environment, or social class mobility that might allow them to create a better life for themselves, their families, and their communities. Their lives become hopeless when all is servitude, drudgery, and violence. Does this not sound like people ruled by monarchs, dictators, or leaders in the Middle East who are steeped in radical fundamentalism?

Those rulers with access to oil revenues, who retain most of the wealth for themselves while leaving the majority of their people poor, oppress their populations by prohibiting free movement and education of their women. Such rulers are like the kings of old, who chose to be driven by a desire for vast material riches, leading to their moral corruption, decay, and abuses of power, instead of developing a humane rule of law and political system.

Individuals, especially the young, are left in an economic void with no jobs or hope to provide a future for their families. A spiritual vacuum sets in, which sweeps them up into passionate radical causes built on a foundation of hatred and vengeance against others. Hope is found in achieving greatness in the eyes of God, allowing one to attain rewards in the afterlife. Becoming a suicide bomber and martyr is one path toward this destiny. These nations condone murder and suicide to attain the afterlife instead of supporting the protection of life.

Such dictators base their economic systems on oil. Wealth flows mainly to the small number of people who are in control of the monarchy or dictatorship and their extended families. They give little to the people so they can improve their standard of living. There is no way out.

Money disseminates slowly, if at all, to the masses—just enough to satisfy them temporarily, but not enough to allow them any routes to self-determination. Oppression ensures obedience and control over the people. It minimizes the risk of dissension. When rebellion does arise, wholesale war and slaughter are the result.

The monarchs and dictators of the Middle East command political systems integrated with religion, which arises from the Qur'anic ethic of melding mosque and state. Social control is maintained by the imposition of obedience, shame, and fear. These political systems do not protect the rights of the people or allow them an environment in which to develop. Rather, they keep the people under control, unemployed, and sometimes suicidal. With few exceptions, this has been quite effective in keeping such rulers and monarchs in power.

Shari'a is the fundamentalist Islamic religious law embedded within the political structure practiced by a religious community. The origins of the word Shari'a arise from the phrase "the clear, well-trodden path to water."[4] It has failed to adapt to modern times in the Middle East. Dictators impose laws and interpretations, sometimes on a whim, to keep themselves in power, with few rules truly serving the people.

Democracy tries to promote political systems which strengthen empowerment and equality of the people, which provide necessary freedoms that encourage people to direct their own lives. Democracy promotes creativity and innovation. Leaders are responsible for guiding the masses rather than controlling them through oppression and forced obedience. The system is not perfect, but ideally it is an open, dynamic one which is fluid and adapts to change.

Democracy generally goes hand in hand with a free market economy. When the system is first established and grows, it works based on fair and representative principles of governance and fair trade. It brings peace and prosperity to a nation, creating greater abundance over the long run.

People have the freedom to choose their religious faith without being threatened or shamed into thought or action. Economics supports the ability to raise families and children, to promote interests that generate wellbeing and to help people thrive. Such systems promote lifestyles which create newfound levels of freedom for all who choose to work and support values which can be directed for the good of the whole.

The ethical rule of law that respects everyone is the basis of the rule of equality. It grounds the political system and assures that the law honors individual rights as well as the collective rights of its people. Nations that maintain such laws, generally democracies, sometimes make wrong decisions about how to solve their problems, and outcomes may not be good. But that is the system the people have chosen, and they have the opportunity to correct their mistakes over time.

Sometimes, political systems can push outcomes toward the farthest ends of the spectrum, but most systems are self-correcting. In one case, a political system controlled by a small group with a centralized monarch or dictator does not allow the pendulum to swing at all, and in the other case, the values of choice and self-determination give people the opportunity to push the pendulum in another direction.

If you could choose a system, which would you prefer? One based on the value of choice, equality, and ethical law? Or a system where the ruler has control, which incites fear and obedience, with no opportunity for people to practice self-determination and free choice? Would you prefer an open, dynamic system or a closed, oppressive, and static one?[5]

Would you rather live in a society focused on goodness, giving people a choice—enjoying greater periods of wellbeing with some periods of turbulence? Or would you rather live in a system focused on power, control, and greed—generally ensuring that people live in terror and fear, enslaved by violence and abused by those in power?

God offers the gift of faith and ethical laws. Political and economic systems evolved which embody these values. They protect individuals, safeguard society, and build a nation. These systems encourage a value: that individuals might embrace self-determination. The collective whole of a people evolved into humane and judicious societies built on a foundation of just and stable laws.

As such a nation grows, the system should inspire people to treat and judge one another impartially—given that no one is better or above the law that God established—not the community, not its judges and leaders, not kings or the prophets of the Israelites. Applied justice meted out emphasizes our evolving values of human rights and compassion on behalf of the people. This, of course, is the most enduring and substantial basis of today's democracies and civil law protections for everyone.

Yet, as in the case of Solomon's kingdom, the primary objects of pursuit become riches and wealth instead of righteousness, justice, and equality. Capitalism within today's economic system has grown to the point where the pursuit of materialism is now the main driver. This is creating a new set of problems which is stimulating a decline for many of our institutions and society. Economic policies have become focused on short term gain at the expense of effective long-range planning.

America's pursuit of wealth has superseded every other value. As the economy has grown and become more complex, it has spawned tremendous inequality between the small percentage of the wealthy and the rest of the people. The middle class has diminished in size and number. The economy has commoditized life. If everything can be had for a price, then the most important value, the value of life, falls victim to the drive for money.[6]

Even with so much prosperity and abundance, many fall behind, and decline is evidenced at every turn. In the face of such great economic wealth, how can so many families and individuals find themselves living on the edge? Until the COVID-19 pandemic emerged, most people worked hard yet felt vulnerable in a rapidly accelerating global economy. Democracies were feeling the heavy hand of special interest groups, big money, and political grandstanding at the expense of people's long-range needs in an ever more inequitable economy. Now, the situation has worsened.

Yes, combined democratic and free market economies, given the right conditions, function successfully in their infant, adolescent, and adult phases of development. But eventually, systems that become extremely large, complex, and unwieldy require new dynamics using a transformed set of values and solutions. The reality is that decline may set in first, before there are new solutions, as occurred in Solomon's pursuit of riches which inevitably led to the decline of kings in Israel.

Chapter 6:
The Inevitable Decline of Kings

King Solomon's political system reached the height of its glory and kept the Kingdoms of Judah and Israel united. Solomon ruled for a total of forty years. His pursuit of trade led to the inclusion of people from other nations. Such inclusiveness allowed Solomon to become familiar with numerous belief systems. Later, however, in direct opposition to the commandments of the Lord, he pursued wealth instead of wisdom, leading to a downward cycle. This cycle continued over a period of 350 years, beginning in 928 BCE (the latter part of Solomon's reign) and ending in 586 BCE, with the Babylonian conquest of Jerusalem.

In reality, Solomon's later focus on riches and pleasures led to the moral corruption of that ancient society, much like the focus on materialism today that is failing so many people, both nationally and globally. Interventions, either through governance or economics, can slow the inevitable, but will rarely stop the trend. Traditional beliefs and practices as well as social systems are failing, leaving a vacuum which is creating disillusionment and resentment among people.

As time progresses and as former values remain in place, more appropriate, transformed value systems must emerge as the means for guiding nations into the future. These new values will eventually allow for new institutions and social systems to arise, thus encouraging societal renewal. Without meaningful and aspirational goals, civilizations are destined to decline and possibly disappear.

After Solomon's death, his son Rehoboam became king of Israel. Jeroboam, who was advocating for the rights of the Israelite people upon returning from exile in Egypt, approached Rehoboam. This story continues to emphasize that kings must treat the Israelites properly. People had a right to be treated fairly, or they could exercise their option to leave.

> Rehoboam went to Shechem, for all Israel had come to Shechem to acclaim him as king. Jeroboam, son of Nebat, learned of it while he was still in Egypt; for Jeroboam had fled from King Solomon and had settled in Egypt. They sent for him; and Jeroboam and all the assembly of Israel came and spoke to Rehoboam as follows: "Your father made our yoke heavy. Now lighten the harsh labor and the heavy yoke which your father laid on us, and we will serve you." He answered them, "Go away for three days and then come back to me." So, the people went away.

> King Rehoboam took counsel with the elders who had served his father Solomon during his lifetime. He said, "What answer do you advise [me] to give to this people?" They answered him, "If you will be a servant to those people today and serve them, and if you respond to them with kind words, they will be your servants always." But he ignored the advice that the elders gave him and took counsel with the young men who had grown up with him and were serving him. "What," he asked, "do you advise that we reply to the people who said to me, 'Lighten the yoke that your father placed upon us'?" And the young men who had grown up with him answered, "Speak thus to the people who said to you, 'Your father made our yoke heavy, now you make it

lighter for us.' Say to them, 'My little finger is thicker than my father's loins. My father imposed a heavy yoke on you, and I will add to your yoke; my father flogged you with whips, but I will flog you with scorpions.'" (I Kings 12:1–11)

Servants and slaves became the means of accomplishing tasks in ancient times, although nowhere were such individuals treated more fairly than in the Israelite kingdom. Rulers in other lands routinely oppressed, exploited, and abused slaves. In contrast, there were servants in households of the Israelites who were considered domestics, part of the family, since according to the law, all people were to be treated fairly and with respect.[1]

While the Israelites seldom became slaves because of their history in Egypt, when a debt required security, they might become indentured servants, serving for a limited period of time. Israelites might become slaves as punishment for thievery, but they nonetheless enjoyed protection under the law and rarely had to engage in heavy labor. After seven years of work, they regained their freedom based on the rules God had established. According to Leviticus, they enjoyed the status of a "visitor or a wage-earner and [were] not to be made to do the work of a slave."[2]

King Solomon had used forced labor, slaves, and hired servants to build the House of the Lord, his palace, and future towns in the kingdom. In keeping with God's law, the Israelites under Solomon's reign did not serve as slave labor but worked in service to the king as officials and officers, warriors, attendants, commanders of his chariotry and cavalry, as well as foremen over work sites. Foreigners, such as the Amorites, Hittites, Perizzites, Hivites, and Jebusites living on the land, were the actual slaves. (I Kings 9:20–23).

Rehoboam did not heed the advice of the elders. Instead, he conveyed the message of the young men to Jeroboam and the Israelites that he would tighten the people's yoke. In doing this, he broke the compact between the king and the people.

When all Israel says that the king had not listened to them, the people answered the king:

> *"We have no portion in David,*
> *No share in Jesse's son!*
> *To your tents, O Israel!*
> *Now look to your own House, O David."*

So, the Israelites returned to their homes. But Rehoboam continued to reign over the Israelites who lived in the towns of Judah. (I Kings 12:1–17)

The king did not listen to the people, as the elders advised. The king did not serve the people's needs under the law. This lack of respect motivated the people to voluntarily abandon their ruler. The ten tribes of the Northern Kingdom of Israel instead chose Jeroboam to become their king. With his protectors, Rehoboam tried to go after them to return them to Jerusalem, but to no avail since God informed him:

> *"You shall not set out to make war on your kinsmen the Israelites. Let every man return to his home, for this thing has been brought about by Me." They heeded the word of the LORD and turned back, in accordance with the word of the LORD.* (I Kings 12:24)

Unfair treatment by King Rehoboam led the people from the Northern Kingdom to split from the Southern Kingdom and abandon him, returning to their homes. The tribe of

Judah remained loyal to the House of David, with Rehoboam reigning over Jerusalem.

Both Jeroboam and Rehoboam enraged the Lord; throughout their reigns, they encouraged the worship of false idols and many gods. Since the central location of the House of the Lord was in Jerusalem, Jeroboam was worried that the northern Israelites would want to return there to live and worship God. So, Jeroboam constructed two golden calves and placed them in the northern towns of Bethel and Dan. He also appointed priests from the ranks of people who were not of the Levitical line. (I Kings 12:27–31)

Rehoboam built "shrines, pillars, and sacred posts" in both the Southern Kingdom and Jerusalem, imitating all the practices that the Lord had despised and destroyed before the Israelites arrived in the land. (I Kings 14:21–23). Over time, these alternative practices became more numerous in Jeroboam's northern Israelite kingdom. It is most likely that the people actually practiced the worship of the Lord side by side with the more abhorrent practices of revering false gods and idols.

A series of six kings ruled the northern Israelite kingdom, each continuing their illicit religious practices. Their reigns ranged in length from seven days to twenty-four years, beginning with Jeroboam in 928 BCE, who ruled for twenty-two years. King Omri, the sixth king, founded Samaria as the capital of the Northern Kingdom in 877 BCE.[3]

King Ahab, Omri's son, became the seventh king of the Israelites in 871 BCE and was the worst of these kings. King Ahab married Queen Jezebel, who was the daughter of King Ethbaal of the Phoenicians. Together they elevated the worship of false gods and idols and they introduced the worship of the Phoenicians' god Ba'al. Queen Jezebel had most of the prophets of the Lord murdered, although some went into hiding. (I Kings 16:29–34; I Kings 18:4–5).

As scripture reveals, the prophet Elijah communicated God's abhorrence of all that King Ahab had done by not adhering to the commandments of the Lord. By this time, Elijah was the only prophet of God left in the Northern Kingdom, while the prophets of Ba'al had reached four hundred fifty in number.

In I Kings, Elijah challenges Ahab and the prophets of Ba'al to a ritual offering duel between God and Ba'al at Mount Carmel in the Jezreel Valley. They each set up altars of burnt offerings. All day, the prophets called up Ba'al to accept the ritual offerings, but to no avail. Then Elijah called upon the Lord to receive his ritual offering, and God accepted.

> *When it was time to present the meal offering, the prophet Elijah came forward and said, "O LORD, God of Abraham, Isaac, and Israel! Let it be known today that You are God in Israel and that I am Your servant, and that I have done all these things at Your bidding. Answer me, O LORD, answer me, that this people may know that You, O LORD, are God; for You have turned their hearts backward."*
>
> *Then fire from the LORD descended and consumed the burnt offering, the wood, the stones, and the earth; and it licked up the water that was in the trench. When they saw this, all the people flung themselves on their faces and cried out: "The LORD alone is God, the LORD alone is God!"*
> (I Kings 18:36–39)

This action on God's part was crucial to prove to the people the importance of their returning to worship the one Living God and to help them recognize the sanctity and dignity of life. The people must retain these beliefs in thought and practice under the political system of kings. Otherwise, the risk of their losing touch with the law would be too great.

When our family visited Israel, we hired a guide, who has since become a great personal friend. We were standing on top of Har (Mount) Megiddo, overlooking the vast, green plains of the Jezreel Valley. This area was the ancient crossroad between the lands to the north, the east, and the coast of the Mediterranean Sea, symbolizing the wealth of trade from traveling caravans, as well as the location of the so-called final battle of Armageddon.

We came to the ruins of an ancient fortress that Solomon built. Solomon had maintained a stronghold on this strategic location to coordinate the trading of goods between different lands. As we walked the ruins, our guide shared this ancient story representing the nadir of kingship in Israel under Ahab, and the need for kings to serve God and treat the people equally.

In the story, Jezebel tries to encourage Ahab to steal the vineyards of his neighbor in order to obtain some of the best land for himself. Jezebel has Naboth, the landowner, murdered so that Ahab can steal his land. The king transgresses God's law and places his needs ahead of the people by acting above the law.

Naboth the Jezreelite owned a vineyard in Jezreel, adjoining the palace of King Ahab of Samaria. Ahab said to Naboth, "Give me your vineyard, so that I may have it as a vegetable garden, since it is right next to my palace. I will give you a better vineyard in exchange; or, if you prefer, I will pay you the price in money. But Naboth replied, "The L<small>ORD</small> *forbid that I should give up to you what I have inherited from my fathers!" Ahab went home dispirited and sullen because of the answer that Naboth the Jezreelite had given him: "I will not give up to you what I have inherited from my fathers!" He lay down on his bed and turned away his face, and he would not eat. His wife Jezebel came to him and asked him, "why are you so dispirited that you won't eat?" So he told her, "I spoke to Naboth the Jezreelite and proposed to him, 'Sell me your vineyard for money, or if you prefer, I'll give you another vineyard in exchange'; but he answered, 'I will not give my vineyard to you.'" His wife, Jezebel said to him, "Now is the time to show yourself king over Israel. Rise and eat something and be cheerful; I will get the vineyard of Naboth the Jezreelite for you." (I Kings 21:1–7)*

God's tenth commandment is: *"You shall not covet your neighbor's house ..."* (Exodus 20:14) Here, Ahab's actions constitute an abuse of power based on greed, one that does not respect his neighbor's property, family, and belongings. Jezebel demands that the king demonstrate his right to act above the law in order to selfishly improve their own position.

So, she wrote letters in Ahab's name and sealed them with his seal and sent the letters to the elders and the nobles who lived in the same town with Naboth. In the letters she wrote as follows: "Proclaim a fast and seat Naboth at the front of the assembly. And seat two scoundrels opposite him and let them testify against him. 'You have reviled God and king!' Then take him out and stone him to death."

His townsmen—the elders and nobles who lived in his town—did as Jezebel had instructed them, just as was written in the letters she had sent them: They proclaimed a fast and seated Naboth at the front of the assembly. Then the two scoundrels came and sat down opposite him; and the scoundrels testified against Naboth publicly as follows: "Naboth has reviled God and king." Then they took him outside the town and stoned him to death. As soon as Jezebel heard that Naboth had been stoned to death, she said to Ahab, "Go and take possession of the vineyard which Naboth the Jezreelite refused to sell you for money; for Naboth is no longer alive, he is dead. When Ahab heard that Naboth was dead, Ahab set out for the vineyard of Naboth the Jezreelite to take possession of it.

Then the word of the LORD came to Elijah the Tishbite: Go down and confront King Ahab of Israel who [resides] in Samaria. He is now in Naboth's vineyard; he has gone down there to take possession of it. Say to him, 'Thus said the LORD: Would you murder and take possession? 'Thus said the LORD: In the very place where the dogs lapped up Naboth's blood, the dogs will lap up your blood too.'"

Ahab said to Elijah, "so you have found me, my enemy?" "Yes, I have found you," he replied, "Because you have committed yourself in doing what is evil in the sight of the LORD, I will bring disaster upon you. I will make a clean sweep of you, I will cut off from Israel every male belonging to Ahab, bond and free. (I Kings 21:8–21)

King Ahab does not follow the divine law. He violates not only the Tenth Commandment, but also the Fifth and Ninth respectively, "You shall not murder," and "You shall not bear false witness against your neighbor." (Exodus 20:13) He is by far the worst king; he is greedy, he abuses his power to control and oppress, he enslaves the people.

The cycle of values focusing on will and self-determination under God's divine laws supports rightful living. These values serve to sanctify life, honor family, and respect members of the nation. These values must then guide developing political structures and economics of trade from which society will benefit. This applied to families as well as servants and slaves who were to be treated with honor and respect as members of the family; a practice well beyond other civilizations of the time and one that preserved rights for all Israelites.

A political system evolved which institutionalized these values at the peak of Solomon's early reign. But once Solomon had completed the construction of the House of the Lord, and the palaces and towns, this value system declined because of disobedience to God. King Ahab and Queen Jezebel flagrantly ignored and disdained the ethical law. The Northern Kingdom of Israel continued to decline until it was conquered and destroyed.

The Israelites needed a new set of values, not only to replace the old, but also to integrate and adapt the original ethical law to their changing society. These new values would support rightful living.

God revealed that destruction was coming for the great nation of the northern Israelites and that ten of the tribes of Israel would be abolished. And in the year 722 BCE, under the rule of Hoshea, King Shalmaneser conquered the Northern Kingdom. At first, King Hoshea paid tribute to this king of Assyria. But Hoshea betrayed him by aligning with King So of Egypt, and the Northern Kingdom was ultimately destroyed.

This happened because the Israelites sinned against the
Lord their God, who had freed them from the land of Egypt,

from the hand of Pharaoh king of Egypt. They worshiped
other gods and followed the customs of the nations which
the LORD had dispossessed before the Israelites and the
customs which the kings of Israel had practiced. The
Israelites committed against the LORD their God acts which
were not right: They built for themselves shrines in all their
settlements, from watchtowers to fortified cities; they set up
pillars and sacred posts for themselves on every lofty hill
and under every leafy tree; and they offered sacrifices there,
at all the shrines, like the nations whom the LORD had driven
into exile before them. They committed wicked acts to vex
the LORD, and they worshiped fetishes concerning which the
LORD had said to them, "You must not do this thing."
(II Kings 17:7–12)

King Shalmaneser conquered the ten tribes, exiling and scattering them throughout the lands of Assyria.

He settled them in "Halah, along the Habor [and] the River
Gozan, and in the towns of Media" and were never heard
from again. [This happened] because they did not obey the
LORD their God; they transgressed His covenant—all that
Moses the servant of the LORD had commanded. They did not
obey, and they did not fulfill it. (II Kings 18:11–12)

Their faith and unity as a people, given their faltering belief system, were no longer strong enough to survive the siege. The Northern Kingdom of Israel would lose the memories of the miracles God performed to bring about the Exodus from Egypt and God's gifting of the law at Sinai. Further, the people would forfeit their unity as a nation based on the faith in the one Lord.

Chapter 7:
King Josiah and the Survival of the Israelites

The House of Judah fell. King Nebuchadnezzar and the Babylonians conquered both the Southern and Northern kingdoms in 586 BCE. Despite this fall, the people of the House of Judah survived their exile, during which time their faith became stronger and more resilient. The people did well for themselves as the community remained cohesive and thrived in Babylonia until many returned to Jerusalem to rebuild the Temple.

Why did the House of Judah survive when the Northern Kingdom of Israel did not? The Northern Kingdom suffered an overwhelming defeat. The Assyrians carried them off into exile. This undermined their faith and destroyed their society, made worse by their geographical displacement to Assyrian lands. The people did not have the will to persevere in their new environment. Once forced into exile, they were assimilated, a common occurrence amongst the conquered people of Assyria.

But let us look more closely at what happened in the southern kingdom of Judah, where the people survived the travails of exile. Following Solomon's and Rehoboam's reigns, the kingdom of Judah experienced nineteen kings between 928 BCE and 586 BCE. Over time, most of these kings, along with the people, worshipped many foreign gods and idols. Most likely, they did so alongside their worship of the one Lord, God. However, as documented in I and II Kings, there were some Judean kings who were more effective in including the people in newly established religious reforms.

According to II Kings, the worst ruler in Judah was Manasseh. He became king when he was twelve years old in 698 BCE and reigned for fifty-five years.[1] Manasseh oversaw the House of Judah, Jerusalem, and the Temple. He worshipped idols and foreign gods. He built altars to Ba'al, just as King Ahab had done, and placed idols in the House of the Lord. He even sacrificed his own sons. The book of Kings states that Manasseh "put so many innocent persons to death that he filled Jerusalem [with blood] from end to end ..." (II Kings 21:16). Ultimately, he enraged the Lord one time too many, and God foretold of the banishment of the House of Judah and the exile of the people.

> *Therefore, the* LORD *spoke through His servants the prophets: "Because Manasseh of Judah has done these abhorrent things—he has outdone in wickedness all that the Amorites did before his time—and because he led Judah to sin with his fetishes, assuredly, thus said the* LORD, *the God of Israel: I am going to bring such a disaster on Jerusalem and Judah that both ears of everyone who hears about it will tingle. I will apply to Jerusalem the measuring line of Samaria and the weights of the House of Ahab; I will wipe Jerusalem clean as one wipes a dish and turns it upside down. And I will cast out the remnant of My own people and deliver them into the hands of my enemies. They shall be plunder and prey to all their enemies because they have done what is displeasing to Me and have been vexing me from the day that their fathers came out of Egypt to this day." (II Kings 21:10–15)*

Given the abhorrent practices of the Southern Kingdom, God used Nebuchadnezzar to conquer the people of Judah in 586 BCE. As with the Northern Kingdom, they should not have survived except for one reason. The House of Judah had a wise and powerful ruler, King Josiah. This king reformed and strengthened the Israelites of the House of Judah. He created a new and more enduring value system, one that the people could take with them as they went into Babylonian exile, where learning, aligned with their own internalized discipline of faith, began to develop.[2]

Josiah became king at the age of eight and he reigned in Jerusalem for thirty-one years. He was a great king who served his people and honored God, always following in the best ways of his forebear, King David. As Josiah grew older, he concluded that he needed to abolish the idols and false gods the people worshipped in Jerusalem, as well as in the Northern Kingdom. Societal reform was necessary. But in order to bring this about, he needed to integrate the demands of the mosaic law and faith with the political governance structures of Judah.

Recall that the kings of Israel were to be servants to the Lord and to act on behalf of the people. For centuries, the people were obedient to the law. So how should social and political reform reflect the people upholding the covenant?

Most of the Israelite kings, along with many of the people, worshiped other gods and idols as they saw fit. In order for the people to return to the one Lord, Josiah would need to convince them of the necessity for reform. II Kings (22–23) helps us piece together many of the events that led to this reformation.

In the eighteenth year of King Josiah's reign (621 BC), he repaired the Temple, as it had been desecrated under the rule of prior kings.[3] Josiah coordinated this effort with the high priest, Hilkiah. He took the silver that had been collected from the people, which had been stored in the House of the Lord, and properly paid those who would work on the First Temple's renovation. These included "the carpenters, the laborers, and the masons." He paid for the purchase of wood and quarried stones for repairing the House. (II Kings 22:3–7)

During this reconstruction effort, the high priest Hilkiah, along with the scribe Shaphan, brought to King Josiah's attention the discovery of a unique scroll of the Teaching of Moses in the House of the Lord. The scroll emphasized the threat that if the people did not follow the laws revealed to them at Mount Sinai, God would conquer Israel.

Upon this discovery, Josiah sent Hilkiah and his scribes to meet with the prophetess Hulda, who also revealed God's intent to destroy Judah because of Manasseh's abominations. Josiah then fully understood the consequences of not following in the ways of the Lord, and he dedicated himself to promoting reform. Josiah was intent that Hulda's prophecy would not come to fruition during his reign.

King Josiah and Hilkiah called together the elders and the people. Josiah would read the scroll to the people, so that, for the first time, they would come to hear the words with their own ears and learn the Teachings of Moses. The people were awed by the discovery of such a scroll and its contents.

King Josiah took personal responsibility for the law. His expectation was for everyone to understand and learn the law of God.

At the king's summons, all the elders of Judah and Jerusalem assembled before him. The king went up to the House of the LORD, together with all the men of Judah and all the inhabitants of Jerusalem, and the priests and prophets—all the people, young and old. And he read to them the entire text of the covenant scroll, which had been found in the House of the LORD. The king stood by the pillar and solemnized the covenant before the LORD: that they would follow the LORD and observe His commandments, His injunctions, and His laws with all their heart and soul; that they would fulfill all the terms of this covenant as inscribed upon the scroll. And all the people entered into the covenant. (II Kings 23:1–3)

The people were in great wonder at what they heard. They took it so seriously that they were willing to change their ways and cease the worship of their many gods and idols. Then the king removed all the false gods, idols, altars, and posts from the Temple as well as from both the Southern and Northern Kingdoms. Others claimed that King Josiah would have at least first cleared the false idols from the House of the Lord before having read the Teaching of Moses to the people. However, the discrepancies in the order of these events are less important than the outcome. Once the people realized the perils of their ways, they became willing to abide by any additional reforms that King Josiah put forth.

This was the first step in the development of a new self-directedness for the people of Judah. The people had to decide for themselves how to develop a new inner discipline for practicing the law, instead of being directed by a king to follow the law.[4]

The people studied the document through readings and discussions and thereby determined how best to apply it to their daily lives. King Josiah's leadership inspired the people to develop a self-commitment to these new teachings. This is what enabled the House of Judah to survive the ultimate destruction of Jerusalem in 586 BCE and their subsequent exile from their land.

But how were the people convinced in the first place to follow God's laws? The faith which traveled with the people to Babylonia took on a different form altogether, based on practices no longer Temple-dependent. The new inner discipline enabled the people to thrive, and subsequently, many returned to Jerusalem to build the Second Temple.

Max I. Dimont, in his book *Jews, God and History*, discusses the finding of this scroll and why this new scroll compelled the people to change their ways of worshipping. This scroll was supposedly a newly-discovered version of the Teaching of Moses, which summarized God's teachings before the Israelites entered the land of Canaan, and before Moses died at Mount Nebo. This "newly discovered" scroll became the book we know today as Deuteronomy.[5] It is the history of this book that is so fascinating.

Dimont outlines that in the ninth century BCE, the Judean scribes wrote the first scrolls of the Teachings of the Lord and the Teaching of Moses, known as the J documents. J stands for YHWH, which is the unpronounceable name of God in the Scriptures, also referred to as a Tetragrammaton. The Hebrew reference for Lord, "Adonai," replaced the sacred four letters. Sometime later, after the creation of the first J scroll, the northern Israelite kingdom came forward with its own set of scrolls referred to as the E scrolls, with E referring to God as "Elohim."[6]

The scroll that King Josiah's scribes had discovered was believed to have been a combined document called the JE scroll. It may have taken the translation of Lord and God from the two separate scrolls, and brought them together in this new, combined scroll. Today, Deuteronomy refers to God as the "Lord, God" in most places, a combination of Adonai and Eloheinu (from Elohim). The books of Exodus, Leviticus, and Numbers all use the translation of only "the Lord" throughout most of the writings.[7]

Dimont focuses on the strong possibility that King Josiah had the high priest, Hilkiah, commit what he calls "pious fraud" by having Hilkiah and his scribes combine these two sets of scrolls. Scholars do not believe that scrolls of these books (either in whole or in part) existed before the ninth century BCE. So Dimont also explains that the scrolls could have been written during the time of King Solomon and hidden in the Temple all this time.[8] But if the scribes had combined the J and E scrolls, Dimont hypothesizes, this would have enabled Josiah to merge the religious and political reforms in Judah and Israel. This also may have been the way that Josiah symbolically reunited the two kingdoms.

Did the scrolls come from the time of Josiah or from Solomon's day? The evidence points to the possibility that the high priests and scribes, during King Josiah's time, "recreated" the scrolls. Whether Josiah orchestrated this before his eighteenth year, or whether the high priests first originated it, and then arranged it with Josiah as a vehicle to rebuild the faith, is certainly a question, but not critical to its ultimate relevance.

First, alongside the JE version combining "Lord, God" together in the book that would become Deuteronomy, the writing appears different from the earlier four books. The writing is clearer and the listing of the laws more concise in

Deuteronomy than in Exodus and Leviticus. It is as though the laws had been extant, the content coalescing over time.

Second, based on what appears to be some creative additions and redactions to the document, Deuteronomy includes some interesting statements which might indicate that the writing came from a later period, all of which were more attributable to the period during Josiah's reign than Solomon's. This first quote below references the selection of a king, as well as the prohibition that the king shall not take many wives and not focus on acquiring riches.

> *If, after you have entered the land that the LORD your God has assigned to you, and taken possession of it and settled in it, you decide, "I will set a king over me, as do all the nations about me," you shall be free to set a king over yourself, one chosen by the LORD your God. Be sure to set as king over yourself one of your own people; you must not set a foreigner over you, one who is not your kinsman. Moreover, he shall not keep many horses or send people back to Egypt to add to his horses, since the LORD has warned you, "You must not go back that way again." And he shall not have many wives, lest his heart go astray; nor shall he amass silver and gold to excess.* (Deuteronomy 17:14–16)

This section seems to signify that there was a later addition to the Teaching of Moses. According to I Samuel, the people should not have desired rule by kings because of their history of slavery to Pharaoh, and because God was to have been their supreme King. This reference to kings in Deuteronomy also has no similar source in either Exodus or Leviticus. This would make more sense only if a later king or priest had added these references to the JE scroll, rather than its having been added prior to the Israelites' arrival in the land of Canaan.

Furthermore, this cited passage prevents the king from going back, or aligning with Egypt. But King Solomon's marriage to his first wife, the daughter of a Pharaoh, created an alliance for peace and trade with Egypt. We know that if King Solomon had adhered to the laws of God, he would have abstained from having many wives and from amassing material riches. Had this section been written or in existence during Solomon's time, he would probably have institutionalized God's laws as the accepted standard within the political and economic structure of the time. Therefore, it is more likely to have come from the time of a later king, such as Josiah.

Another section which could have also been added to this scroll at a later time includes the following reference to kings:

> When he is seated on his royal throne, he shall have a copy of this Teaching written for him on a scroll by the Levitical priests. Let it remain with him and let him read in it all his life, so that he may learn to revere the LORD, his God, to observe faithfully every word of this Teaching as well as these laws. Thus, he will not act haughtily toward his fellows or deviate from the Instruction to the right or to the left, to the end that he and his descendants may reign long in the midst of Israel. (Deuteronomy 17:18)

Again, if Deuteronomy as it exists today had dated back to the time of Moses, it would not have included such a passage about kings and their responsibility to this Teaching and to the Lord. God was responsible for releasing the Israelites from the oppressions of Pharaoh.

A third section in Deuteronomy refers to kings and references the future exile, none of which aligns with Solomon's time.

The LORD will drive you, and the king you have set over you,
to a nation unknown to you or your fathers, where you shall
serve other gods, of wood and stone. You shall be a conster-
nation, a proverb, and a byword among all the people to
which the LORD will drive you. (Deuteronomy 28:36–37)

Exodus and Leviticus do not anticipate the institution of kings. This section's reference to the king once again conflicts with the earlier commands of the Lord to the prophet Samuel, wherein he tries to dissuade the Israelites from having a king to rule over them.

There are several additional references to the Lord, God, scattering the people to the other nations where they will worship other gods of wood and stone. (Deuteronomy 28:49–57 and 28:64–68). In a later section, we have this reference to the exiled people:

When all these things befall you—the blessing and the curse
that I have set before you—and you take them to heart
amidst the various nations to which the LORD your God has
banished you, and you return to the LORD your God, and you
and your children heed His command with all your heart
and soul, just as I enjoin upon you this day, then the LORD
your God will restore your fortunes and take you back in
love. He will bring you together again from all the peoples
where the LORD your God has scattered you. Even if your
outcasts are at the ends of the world, from there the LORD
your God will gather you, from there He will fetch you. And
the LORD your God will bring you to the land that your
fathers possessed, and you shall possess it; and He will make
you more prosperous and more numerous than your fathers.
(Deuteronomy 30:1–5)

This section, coupled with other references to the Lord scattering the people, would seem to focus on the exile of the people of the House of Judah, and their return to Jerusalem. Again, this would seem to come at a later date rather than appearing in a scroll hidden during the time of Solomon.

Although these are merely my own interpretations of Deuteronomy, Dimont strongly argues that "pious fraud" may have occurred, and more likely during the time of King Josiah. I, too, lean toward this position.

King Josiah motivated the people of Judah not only to learn the Teaching of Moses, but also to internalize these teachings. On their own, the people were willing to follow the ways of the Lord, but they were not literate. This was among the first times in history that priests, scribes, and the king were involved in directly teaching the people the readings so that they could learn how to live according to the ethical law.

This new inner discipline and learning was the key to ensuring that the Israelites from the House of Judah would survive the Babylonian conquest in 586 BCE. The belief system became so strong that it survived until the Israelites finally returned to Jerusalem in 538 BCE under the Persian rule of King Cyrus.

The faith and beliefs of the ten tribes from the Northern Kingdom of Israel did not survive the Assyrian invasion, while the southern kingdom of Judah, being more resilient with its inner discipline, did so. King Josiah initiated a new value system alongside the continued centralized practice of ritual offerings in the Temple. It would eventually become strong and adaptable enough so that the faith would endure without a centralized place of worship.

Practicing an internalized faith, now based on a form of unified learning, was the start of a new value system. It occurred close to the end of a declining cycle of values from the old system of kings and empires. The institution of the monarchy, which had incorporated the values of self-determination and respect for life, justice, and mercy, and the people being treated fairly, with no king being above God's law, was no longer sufficient to sustain the Israelites as a nation. That system had failed to adapt to the changing times.

The social system would need to revamp and incorporate these former values into a new and higher level of societal development. A new cycle of transformed values would emerge based on an inner discipline of faith and learning. These new values originated during the reign of King Josiah and would allow the Israelites to adapt and survive. They appear today in Deuteronomy.

Chapter 8:
The Israelites in Exile—
Time for a Paradigm Shift

The exile of the Israelites to Babylon was the end of an era. The Israelites had built a nation on their practice of faith, founded on the values of free will through self-determination, and justice with mercy. They learned to live ethically by honoring the dignity and sanctity of life, respecting the rights of others, upholding the proper treatment of family, and working the land.

The nation's political system grew under King Solomon, and, as long as the faith followed the law, or the word of God, the nation grew in strength and resources. Eventually it became too large and split apart. This created a vacuum, allowing different versions of faith to develop. The breakup of the Israelites into separate kingdoms caused disunity, divisiveness, and a weakening from within and between the two kingdoms of Samaria and Judah.

The Assyrians conquered the Israelites of Samaria. The people of the Northern Kingdom had already broken with their faith to the extent that it could not survive the exile in 722 BCE. But under King Josiah in Jerusalem, the faith began to evolve through the instrument of learning. An inner discipline and resolve arose in the people as Josiah and the high priest, Hilkiah, shared the Teaching of Moses.

This new inner faith did not prevent the conquering of the Judean Israelites by King Nebuchadnezzar of the Chaldeans in 586 BCE. He carried the people off to the region along the Euphrates in the area of Babylon. However, the exile of the Judeans to Babylon did force their new inner faith to crystallize, which in turn enabled them to survive and to thrive.

The exile to Babylon forced a unity through adversity. Living in a conquered land would require a new, more resilient form of faith to adapt and evolve in order for the people to survive and flourish. As centralized animal sacrifices or ritual offerings were no longer possible as a form of repentance or expiation of sin, something had to replace them.

Since there was no longer a central Temple, the priests could no longer function as intermediaries to the Lord on behalf of the people. There were also no kings to tell them how to interpret the God-given law or to instruct them in living responsibly. This was now, somehow, up to the people themselves to determine. This would truly test their faith during captivity.

A new discipline of prayer and worship of the Lord would replace the ritual offerings at the Temple. Individual faith and prayer would now become the pathway to promote forgiveness of sin. Through the shared adversity of the exile, religion became revitalized for a more mobile people.

The Israelites constituted a community within another empire. Their own beliefs, though changing, remained intact. The prophets, before this time and while in exile, sustained and energized the consciousness of the Israelites through their revelations from God.

Earlier stories of the Hebrew Scriptures and its history are based on a worldview of God acting upon the people as an external force. These stories and history also represented the law being applied to the people by the ruler of a monarchal political system. At some point, however, the system burned out and spiraled into a downward trajectory. People chose not to follow exclusively in God's footsteps; they interpreted God's commands as being expectations for obedience to the law. Their faith did not disappear but lost its integrity by virtue of the worship of false gods and idols. Moral corruption set in, degrading the law's justness.

The people now had to take responsibility for their own faith by moving into a more soulful internalized discipline of worship and belief. The first step in this process would be to relinquish their dependence on ritual. The First Temple had been destroyed. They would need to learn to trust in their own ability to find a path to goodness and alignment with the law.

The prophets would help lead this effort, and the people, once in exile, would heed their warnings and words, finding a new direction for expressing their faith. Isaiah's beautifully expressed words of admonishment addressed the moral iniquities and the ways of the Northern Kingdom that led to the Assyrians' conquest. Jeremiah's words held particular meaning as he predicted the exile, as well as the Lord's expectations when the people returned from it. God's revelations came through the prophets of the time but were not usually accepted as being accurate until the events predicted had come to pass.

Jeremiah's prophecies first spoke of hope through redemption for the people of the Southern Kingdom, if only they would change their behavior, follow God's law, and eschew moral corruption. God would act in forgiveness if the people would turn back from their ways. The Israelites were no longer living up to God's expectations regarding the covenant, and the House of Judah would also go into exile after King Nebuchadnezzar conquered it.

Once matters reached the point of no return, Jeremiah foretold of the destruction of the southern kingdom of Judah. But Jeremiah gave the Judean Israelites hope through his prophecies, telling them that they would be returning from exile.

Thus said the LORD of Hosts, the God of Israel, to the whole community which I exiled from Jerusalem to Babylon: Build houses and live in them, plant gardens and eat their fruit. Take wives and beget sons and daughters; and take wives for your sons, and give your daughters to husbands, that they may bear sons and daughters. Multiply there, do not decrease. And seek the welfare of the city to which I have exiled you and pray to the LORD in its behalf; for in its prosperity, you shall prosper.

For thus said the LORD: When Babylon's seventy years are over, I will take note of you, and I will fulfill to you My promise of favor—to bring you back to this place. For I am mindful of the plans I have made concerning you—declares the LORD—plans for your welfare, not for disaster, to give you a hopeful future. When you call Me, and come and pray to Me, I will give heed to you. You will search for Me and find Me, if only you seek Me wholeheartedly. I will gather you from all the nations and from all the places to which I have banished you—declares the LORD—and I will bring you back to the place from which I have exiled you. (Jeremiah 29:4–14)

Jeremiah let the Israelite people know that God would encourage them to bring the Lord into their hearts and lives.

They would remain in exile for a period of seventy years. Afterward, they would be free to return to Jerusalem once again to rebuild the Temple. Jeremiah's words would give the people hope, that by using this time during the exile to secure for themselves a new, vibrant faith, they would survive.

> *See, a time is coming—declares the LORD—when I will make a new covenant with the House of Israel and the House of Judah. It will not be like the covenant I made with their fathers, when I took them by the hand to lead them out of the land of Egypt, a covenant which they broke, though I espoused them—declares the LORD. But such is the covenant I will make with the House of Israel after these days— declares the LORD: I will put My teaching into their inmost being and inscribe it upon their hearts. Then I will be their God, and they shall be My people. No longer will they need to teach one another and say to one another, "Heed the LORD," for all of them, from the least of them to the greatest, shall heed Me—declares the LORD.*
>
> *For I will forgive their iniquities,*
> *And remember their sins no more.* (Jeremiah 31:31–34)

For centuries, ritual worship was predicated on external commands and prophecies from the Lord, bound up in the role of priests performing sacrificial offerings in service to God. In the earlier stages of this civilization's development, an external focus of worship centered on unifying a people, enabling them to achieve their potential. The emphasis, first, is on an early set of values based on building tribal unity and building empire through various political and economic structures. Eventually, a downward spiral develops and moves toward a new higher level of cultural complexity with its ensuing values.

For the Israelites, evolving structures of governance were initially responsible for the integration of the law. But after Solomon's reign, the kingdom of Israel split apart, and the people adopted the worship of other gods and idols. Together, with a weakened economic and political system, both the kingdoms of Samaria and Judah eventually fell to conquerors.

A new cycle of values would need to emerge based on a more mature or transformed level of culture. The developing faith would lead to new ways of assimilating the God-given law. This would make the faith more resilient and adaptable by changing its focus from a central location of ritual offerings to a more mobile faith based on prayer, learning, and scholarship in the law.

Jeremiah's visions exemplified the evolution of the people taking personal responsibility for internalizing their beliefs and faith.

> See, I will gather them from all the lands to which I have banished them in My anger and wrath, and in great rage; and I will bring them back to this place and let them dwell secure. They shall be My people, and I will be their God. I will give them a single heart and a single nature to revere Me for all time, and it shall be well with them and their children after them. And I will make an everlasting covenant with them that I will not turn away from them and that I will treat them graciously; and I will put into their hearts reverence for Me, so that they do not turn away from Me. I will delight in treating them graciously, and I will plant them in this land faithfully, with all My heart and soul. (Jeremiah 32:37)

The five books of the Pentateuch view God as having opposing attributes: wrathful and forgiving, as well as just and merciful. Therein God commands and expects the Israelites to believe and obey His commandments. God shows mercy by letting them know over and over that if only the people would believe and obey, and not turn back to worshipping false idols and other gods, they would be forgiven.

Here is one of the strongest examples of God being forgiving and compassionate. God recognizes that while the exile itself will be difficult, it will enable and energize the Israelites. Remembering the prophecy of forgiveness and return will allow the people to survive their Babylonian captivity. In fact, such a belief system will also become the foundation and pattern for survival when the Persians, Greeks, and Romans subsequently conquer them.

Three waves of migration characterized the several stages of the exile of the people from the Southern Kingdom of Judah to Babylon. The first came after King Nebuchadnezzar conquered Jerusalem during the third year of the reign of King Jehoiakim of Judah, second son of King Josiah, who was taken prisoner to Babylon. The second wave of migration occurred after King Zedekaiah rebelled against the Babylonian empire in the ninth year of his reign, 596 BCE.[1] Then, Nebuchadnezzar conquered Zedekaiah, with Gedaliah replacing him. The third phase took place when Jerusalem fell in 586 BCE, the year of its destruction. Nebuchadnezzar destroyed the First Temple, stole its treasures, and exiled the Israelites to Babylon.

The prophet Ezekiel, who followed Jeremiah, was beloved among the "community of exiles by the Chebar Canal" in the land of the Chaldeans. He was taken to Babylon during the first migration. He was the prophet the Lord chose to speak to the elders. Ezekiel would explain the history of the

Israelites leading up to the exile and communicated how they would return to Jerusalem.

Ezekiel received prophecies from God, then informed the elders of the exile community about the history of their banishment, laying out a path for the future, both for the House of Judah as well as for the House of Israel. He foretold the return of the Israelite people from exile to Jerusalem, and the rebuilding of the House of the Lord. Ezekiel reiterated the Lord's message that if the people would turn back and comply with the laws honoring God, they would be forgiven.

> *Say then: Thus said the LORD GOD: I have indeed removed them far among the nations and have scattered them among the countries, and I have become to them a diminished sanctity in the countries whither they have gone. Yet say: Thus said the LORD GOD: I will gather you from the peoples and assemble you out of the countries where you have been scattered, and I will give you the Land of Israel. And they shall return there and do away with all the detestable things and all its abominations. I will give them one heart and put a new spirit in them; I will remove the heart of stone from their bodies and give them a heart of flesh, that they may follow My laws and faithfully observe My rules. Then they shall be My people and I will be their GOD. But as for them whose heart is set upon their detestable things and their abominations, I will repay them for their conduct—declares the LORD GOD." (Ezekiel 11:16–21)*

Ezekiel's prophecies included instructions about how the people should build the Second Temple upon their return. The prophecies from God not only described the tribe of Judah's return to Jerusalem after seventy years, but also that of the Israelites. God revealed that in keeping the covenant with Jacob, God would honor all the tribes, not just the tribes of Judah, Benjamin, and the Levites.

The word of the LORD came to me: And you, O mortal, take a stick and write on it, "Of Judah and the Israelites associated with him;" and take another stick and write on it, "Of Joseph—the stick of Ephraim—and all the House of Israel associated with him." Bring them close to each other, so that they become one stick, joined together in your hand. And when any of your people ask you, "Won't you tell us what these actions of yours mean?" answer them, "Thus said the LORD GOD: I am going to take the stick of Joseph—which is in the hand of Ephraim—and of the tribes of Israel associated with him, and I will place the stick of Judah upon it and make them into one stick; they shall be joined in My hand." You shall hold up before their eyes the sticks which you have inscribed, and you shall declare to them: Thus said the LORD GOD: I am going to take the Israelite people from among the nations they have gone to, and gather them from every quarter, and bring them to their own land. I will make them a single nation in the land, on the hills of Israel, and one king shall be king of them all. Never again shall they be two nations, and never again shall they be divided into two kingdoms. Nor shall they ever again defile themselves by their fetishes and their abhorrent things, and by their other transgressions. I will save them in all their settlements where they sinned, and I will cleanse them. Then they shall be My people, and I will be their God. (Ezekiel 37:15–23)

During their exile, the Israelites created new purpose by keeping their faith alive and burning in their hearts. A new inner discipline opened them to understanding the law through prayer, through communication with the elders, and through the prophets. The law that the kings and priests had originally administered would now become the living law, which the people would come to understand, engage in, and adapt to their changing times.[2]

The Jews would bring back to Jerusalem their revitalized faith. But how would they maintain it once they had returned? Another seed value also emerged during the exile in Babylon. King Josiah had instituted this value and the people advanced it during their displacement. Together with inner faith, discipline, and prayer, Josiah first introduced the values of *learning and knowledge*. He merged learning with skills of governance and scholarly teaching. This would allow the future Israelites to eventually aspire as a people toward the attainment of moral wisdom.

The messages of the prophets are about how political systems based solely on kings or autocratic rulers can move a society toward moral decline, forcing the need to replace old beliefs with a new set of values. We may be caught in the old while still searching for the new, which generally evolves over time. And while we are caught in that transition, it is hard to see what the new set of transformational values should be for the future. Jeremiah gave hope to the people, while Ezekiel helped to bring that newfound hope and inner faith into being during the exile.

But the real message of these two prophets is that the people were in need of a paradigm change. The new paradigm would transition toward a better understanding of God in the hearts and minds of the people; an internalization of how to make God's words their own in order to advance the covenant.

Today, we find ourselves once again in a significant transition period, a paradigm shift. Our world intensely focuses on external wealth and materialism, not too much different from what the First Temple Period must have been like based on its moral injustices, inequities, and corruption. When life is economically good, we tend to forget what we should be valuing. We become myopic and indifferent to the travesties and social ills that beset so many people around us. Money becomes an end unto itself, and we can lose the path that leads to goodness. We become overly focused on the individual and somehow miss the significance of the collective good.

Science has led to the acquisition of new knowledge and advances in technology. A focus on money, materialism, and consumerism can lead us down an untoward path if we do not guide new technology by the right balance of values that will achieve positive outcomes for our society. We are living in a time of accelerating change that can be disorienting as the world becomes ever more complex and impossible to predict.

Money, materialism, and science are here to stay, but they do not provide answers to everything. Our society is losing sight of what is important. There is no real sense of purpose—of something greater than ourselves to which we aspire—as long as we focus on wealth for its own sake.

We have the ability to create so much good in this world. Never before has humankind had so much knowledge and so many tools available to create solutions for today's existing problems. But as long as we focus on materialism and striving for money, we will miss many opportunities and may even find ourselves walking down the path of evil. We could destroy ourselves. This is not too dissimilar from the period of the destruction of the northern and southern kingdoms of Israel. We must purposely seek out new values and shift our moral compass for the future.

Our goal should be to find a transforming set of values which will actively guide us toward goodness and abundance for the many, not just for the few. We must strive for this, just as Jeremiah sought to communicate God's concerns to the people by giving them a new sense of hope and direction during captivity, and just as Ezekiel, with the help of God, encouraged the people to keep their hope alive while urging upon them an inner faith for a new generation.

Chapter 9:
The Second Temple Era—
Return from Exile

O ver time, an internalized discipline preserved the people and their faith, thereby strengthening the impact of the living law. Unified belief and prayer would keep the nation together, but the spirit of the law was even more crucial to instill in the people during exile, for it would assure their future survival. How could this be accomplished?

Cyrus of Persia became king in 539 BCE.[1] He ruled over one of the largest kingdoms in the region. In his first year, 538 BCE, he issued a decree that all Jews could return to Jerusalem and begin rebuilding the Temple, thus fulfilling Jeremiah's earlier prophecy.[2] The representative people from the tribes of Judah and Benjamin, as well as the Levites, would return to the land. (Ezra 1:1–11)

Cyrus's proclamation also served a more practical purpose for his empire. It ensured that the area of Jerusalem and the former land of Samaria would once again become prosperous and generate greater revenues for the king. It would also have the indirect impact of relocating people to the southwestern border of the Persian empire to protect the kingdom and to prevent uprisings or rebellions.[3]

The royal decree allowed more than 42,000 Jews, and by additional count, their servants, to return to Jerusalem. (Ezra 2:64) Upon resettling, and after several years of building, the returning Jews finally completed the foundation of the Temple of the Lord. When they celebrated, there were both cries of joy and weeping:

> When the builders had laid the foundation of the Temple of the LORD, priests in their vestments with trumpets, and Levites, sons of Asaph, with cymbals were stationed to give praise to the LORD, as King David of Israel had ordained. They sang songs extolling and praising the LORD, "For He is good, His steadfast love for Israel is eternal." All the people raised a great shout extolling the LORD because the foundation of the House of the LORD had been laid. Many of the priests and Levites and the chiefs of the clans, the old men who had seen the first house, wept loudly at the sight of the founding of this house. Many others shouted joyously at the top of their voices. The people could not distinguish the shouts of joy from the people's weeping, for the people raised a great shout, the sound of which could be heard from afar. (Ezra 3:10–13)

Those who remembered the first House of the Lord could recall its glory and wept because the Second Temple would not be as grand. Nevertheless, the formal initiation of the rebuilding had begun.

The process would have starts and stops. There would be uprisings from the Samaritans who now lived in northern Israel. The Assyrians had conquered these people from other lands and had resettled them to this area, mixed with the small number of poor Israelites who had remained in the region after its destruction in 722 BCE. The Samaritans also worshipped God and were desirous of assisting with the building of the Temple. However, the returned exiles would not consent, as the original decree by King Cyrus stated that only the Jews could rebuild the Temple (Ezra 4:1–5). This created animosity between the two groups, which over time delayed construction. It is estimated that the work restarted in 516 BCE, with the urging of the prophets Haggai and Zechariah, and with the approval of King Darius.[4]

When the proclamation to encourage the Israelites to return to Jerusalem came out, not everyone made the journey back to the former land. The largest number of Israelites remained in the Persian Empire in the region of Babylon because of their overall success, affluence, and integration in the new land.[5] Those who did stay behind donated their own personal wealth and material possessions to ensure the success of the returning exiles. (Ezra 1:6)

The completion of the Second Temple was a historic moment in Jewish survival, granted it was done based upon a newfound faith and spiritual discipline. It also restored the role of centralized ritual offerings. That such faith had become more mobile through the agency of prayer, rather than dependent solely on centralized ritual offerings, made for greater flexibility and resiliency.

These two modes of worship persisted side-by-side. It is not unusual for one original tradition to continue in a new form or to combine a former tradition with new practices, for purposes of continuity and acceptance. This is a way to honor tradition as the new practice develops and takes hold.

Ritual offerings and prayer would continue in Israel, even during the Greek and Roman Empires, until the destruction of the Second Temple in 70 CE. Only then did the sacrificial system formally come to an end. Prayer expressing faith is the first major innovation and value that emerged from this period.

"Priest-scribes" brought about the second major innovation with their scholarship concerning the scrolls of the law. To believe in the living law that the Lord provided, the people first had to understand it in ways which would allow them to introduce the law into their daily lives, such that it would become embedded in their hearts. The priest-scribes brought the teachings to the people; learning about of the law would become the new value that the leaders, Ezra and Nehemiah, introduced.

According to the book of Ezra, under the reign of King Artaxerxes, the priest-scribes were the first to acquire learning, knowledge, and scholarship, just as the wealthy had been the first of the Israelites to become capable of translating Hebrew into the Chaldean and Aramaic languages during the exile in Babylon. This facility brought them wealth and success in the trades as well as in governance.

Ezra was a "scribe expert in the Teaching of Moses ..." (Ezra 7:6). Ezra was the great-grandson of Hilkiah, the High Priest in Jerusalem under King Josiah. While he was a known scholar of the Teaching of Moses (which would eventually become Deuteronomy), Ezra had also studied the scrolls of the Teachings of the Lord, which would become the first four books of the Hebrew Scriptures. In later centuries, these became the Five Books of Moses—the Torah.[6]

Ezra requested permission from King Artaxerxes that a second wave of Jews might return to Jerusalem. The king gave approval in a letter to Ezra and the Jewish people. Ezra would lead the second return and lend scholarly strength to the foundation of faith for all of Israel. He would bring with him the scrolls related to the Teaching of Moses and the Teachings of the Lord.

Ezra was joyful when he received the letter from Artaxerxes. He communicated the good news to the Jews residing in the lands of the Babylonian empire. According to the historian Josephus in his book *Antiquities of the Jews*, the communication went out to the tribes of Judah and Benjamin as well as to the Levites in Babylonia where Ezra (Esdras) lived. It also went out to the Jews in Media and "beyond the Euphrates [River] ..." for all to know they were welcome to return to Jerusalem.

When Esdras had received this epistle, he was very joyful, and began to worship God, and confessed that he had been the cause of the king's great favor to him, and that for the same reason he gave all the thanks to God. So he read the epistle at Babylon to those Jews that were there; but he kept the epistle itself, and sent a copy of it to all those of his own nation that were in Media; and when these Jews had understood what piety the king had toward God, and what kindness he had for Esdras, they were all greatly pleased; nay, many of them took their effects with them, and came to Babylon, as very desirous of going down to Jerusalem; but then the entire body of the people of Israel remained in that country; wherefore there are but two tribes in Asia and Europe subject to the Romans, while the ten tribes are beyond Euphrates till now, and are an immense multitude, not to be estimated by numbers. Now there came a great number of priests, and Levites, and porters, and sacred singers, and sacred servants, to Esdras. So, he gathered those that were in the captivity together beyond Euphrates, and stayed there three days, and ordained a fast for them, that they might make their prayers to God for their preservations, that they might suffer no misfortunes by the way, either from their enemies, or from any other ill accident.[7]

The writings of Josephus provide a rare insight and reference to the ten lost tribes, who were "beyond Euphrates till now, and are immense in multitude." Recall that in II Kings 17:6, the Assyrians had conquered the ten tribes of the Northern Kingdom and scattered them. Their settlements were in Halah on the River Habor, at the River Gozan, and in the towns of Media. The town of Halah was located beyond the River Euphrates in ancient times. Also note that Ezekiel prophesied to the Jewish elders that the Lord would reunite all twelve tribes, never to be divided again, after the Israelites from the Southern and Northern Kingdoms returned from exile to Jerusalem (Ezekiel 37:15–28).

Is it possible that many of those in exile from the Northern Kingdom of Israel not only survived the Assyrian conquest but united with the two tribes of Judah and Benjamin under Ezra? Could it be that representatives from each of the twelve tribes returned to Jerusalem, fulfilling Ezekiel's prophecy, with everyone merging into one group led by the House of Judah and the Levites? Could the writers of the books of Ezra and Nehemiah have removed any references to these tribes for the sake of uniting those who returned from exile?

When Ezra returned to Jerusalem, his chief concern was strengthening the unity of the people. He wanted to ensure that everyone observed faith in the Lord God. His first act was to convince the Jews, particularly the Levite priests, to abandon the practice of taking foreign wives and recommit to marrying only those who were Jews. This was not done for the purpose of excluding others. Instead, during ancient times, it was necessary to ensure the survival of the faith, which otherwise would surely be diluted through a return to polytheistic worship. (Ezra 9, 10)

The book of Nehemiah and the story therein is crucial to the understanding of the start of the Second Temple period. Therefore, we will digress briefly from Ezra's history in order to review that of Nehemiah and describe how the accomplishments of these two men converged in time.

Nehemiah was an exiled Israelite and the cupbearer (another term for a butler) to King Artaxerxes I in the royal court. He was concerned about the impoverishment and plight of the Jews in Jerusalem. While successful and growing in number in Babylon and within the Persian Empire, the Jews now residing in the land of Israel needed material and spiritual support. Nehemiah requested to travel to Jerusalem to help his people (Nehemiah 2:1–9).

In the twentieth year of his reign, King Artaxerxes appointed Nehemiah as governor of Jerusalem, in 445 BCE.[8] He was an able governor, gathering the people to rebuild and fortify the protective walls around the city and the Temple. He encouraged the priests, Levites, and Israelites to also move within the city walls once they were rebuilt.

In his role, Nehemiah also lived in accordance with the living law of the Lord. Not charging interest for debts to the Jews was one of God's laws. If a Jew incurred, or took on, debt, then he would gain release after seven years. The effect of this law was to avoid impoverishing the people and to reduce the gap in societal wealth. Many of the Israelites had lost their farmland in order to pay off debts. Some even gave up their sons and daughters to slavery.

There was a great outcry by the common folk and their wives against their brother Jews. Some said, "Our sons and

daughters are numerous; we must get grain to eat in order that we may live!" Others said, "We must pawn our fields, our vineyards, and our homes to get grain to stave off hunger." Yet others said, "We have borrowed money against our fields and vineyards to pay the king's tax. Now we are as good as our brothers, and our children as good as theirs; yet here we are subjecting our sons and daughters to slavery— some of our daughters are already subjected—and we are powerless, while our fields and vineyards belong to others."
(Nehemiah 5:1–5)

Since the Israelites came out of slavery, it seemed contradictory to create the same economic conditions of exploitation which might give rise to a different form of slavery and oppression through indebtedness. Nehemiah tried to set an example for how all people should live righteously by the law of God. He therefore pursued this matter among the nobles and prefects.

It angered me very much to hear their outcry and these complaints. After pondering the matter carefully, I censured the nobles and the prefects, saying, "Are you pressing claims on loans made to your brothers?" Then I raised a large crowd against them and said to them, "We have done our best to buy back our Jewish brothers who were sold to the nations; will you now sell your brothers so that they must be sold [back] to us?" They kept silent, for they found nothing to answer. So, I continued, "What you are doing is not right. You ought to act in a God-fearing way so as not give our enemies, the nations, room to reproach us. I, my brothers, and my servants also have claims of money and grain against them; let us now abandon those claims! Give back at once their fields, their vineyards, their olive trees, and their homes, and [abandon] the claims for the hundred pieces of silver, the grain, the wine, and the oil that you have been pressing against them!" They replied, "We shall give them back, and not demand anything of them; we shall do just as you say." (Nehemiah 5:6–12)

Nehemiah led the way by abolishing any loans that he himself had secured from others. It is important to note that the law the Lord gave, which the prophets interpreted, was a law which was meant to instill justice through righteous actions, based on merciful compassion. The people, together with their leaders, had to internalize and honor their understanding of the law in order to establish a just society.

Earlier, during the period of downfall of the kings, the leaders had failed miserably to internalize their faith in the Lord and in the law. This failure weakened the societies of the two kingdoms and led to both the Assyrian and Babylonian conquests. From a spiritual perspective, the downfall of these kingdoms was linked to the practice of pagan and polytheistic worship, which either replaced the belief in the One Lord, God, or was practiced side-by-side along with belief in the Lord. However, the downfall was in equal measure a result of rich landowners exploiting the poor, with wealth being concentrated in the hands of a minority while the majority of the people remained or became destitute.[9]

Now, the very same phenomenon was recurring in Nehemiah's day. Exploitation was creating distinctions in wealth amongst the people. Upon their return to Jerusalem after the exile, the people once again became impoverished due to their indebtedness to the wealthy. They put their lands up as security for loans. This could only lead to further oppression of the people. This was in direct conflict with the purpose of the living law of the Lord. What better way to exemplify the law's intent but for Nehemiah to forgive all outstanding debts?

Ezra, the priestly scribe scholar, and Nehemiah now converge in their partnership to strengthen the Jews and their faith by directly teaching them about the law. Ezra and the priests, along with Nehemiah as governor, jointly gathered everyone in Jerusalem around the Temple and, standing up high, Ezra and the priests read to the people from the Teachings of the Lord and the Teaching of Moses. The people themselves would hear and learn the living law of the Lord with their own ears, hearts, and minds (Nehemiah 8:1–18). More importantly, the scrolls were read both in the original Hebrew, a language with which the exiles from Babylonia were no longer familiar, and also in their common language of Aramaic. This translation was an innovation that brought clarity of understanding to the people.[10]

Before the exile, the priests in Jerusalem kept the information from the Teachings of the Lord and Moses to themselves. This produced rigidity and inflexibility, enabling a small, elite group to corrupt its meaning and intent. Now, the people took a significant step forward through the process of learning the law. In this way, did they bring it alive for themselves.

Rabbi Dr. Binyamin Lau, in his book *The Sages: Character, Context and Creativity*, states that the role of the priests in the past had been to protect and interpret the law, as well as to transmit it to the people. The priests still continued ritual offerings on behalf of the Israelites to both help expiate sin and to promote forgiveness by God.[11]

The priests were so good at protecting the law in the scrolls for their own benefit that, over the centuries, they neglected to transmit the spirit of the law to the people. The

Israelite community had oral stories and interpretations to go by, but with little insight, the people became estranged from the law and the scrolls. The only remnants resided in the corrupt priesthood and their ritual offerings.[12]

The Israelites reverted to alternatives such as the reintegration of pagan and polytheistic belief systems and practices. During the time of separation between the Northern and Southern Kingdoms, there arose rulers like Josiah who would institute social reforms in faith and governance through learning, internalized faith, and prayer—essentials for surviving the Babylonian exile. But such kings were rare.

The innovation of educating the people in their own language as well as inspiring them to learn and integrate the meaning of the scrolls into their daily lives would now further strengthen their personal, inner belief in God. It also informed their attitudes toward faith, making that faith mobile and flexible. This would encourage the Jews of the future to maintain their freedom to worship privately, without conflicting with the laws and governance of any king in the land. It was a first step in the separation of faith and governance.

Nehemiah then created a foundational document, which he signed and swore to along with the priests, the Levites, as well as the heads of the Israelite people; it was an oath to follow the commandments and laws, as well as to tithe and support the House of the Lord. (Nehemiah 9, 10).

The people began learning the Written Law and its regulations. This was an innovative way of administering the law; it differed from the more traditional, rigidly hier-archical, and controlling structure of kingship. The era of

Israelite kings had come to an end with the Babylonian conquest. Under Nehemiah, however, there arose a whole new governance system. He governed the people based on the laws of faith—which became integral to the people's lives.

The Jews drew insight into their understanding of how to adapt a living law to a new environment and put it into practice. This was extremely empowering for them.

The work of Ezra and Nehemiah provided an opening for great social reform and changes to take place. How better to ensure that people understood the law and put it into practice than to have them learn it for themselves? It is far easier to have knowledge shared widely; this serves to maintain the integrity of the system for all, rather than allowing control by a few who can easily benefit from imposing oppressive and abusive laws.

The living law of the Lord became the foundation for developing human rights for all individuals within society. It assisted in preventing oppression and injustice as well as poverty and slavery. It served to unify the people through righteous administration of justice based on mercy, compassion, and an understanding of others. It was a living law that translated into proper norms and values to support society.

This was the first step toward democratization of the law. It created a new path for a paradigm shift in a changing worldview of God. It is at this point that we began to see the merging of faith that prayer expressed with the study of Jewish law, a virtual joining of the heart and mind.

Chapter 10:
The Sages of the Great Assembly

Exile was initially a sad time for the Jews as it took them away from the land promised by the God of the covenant. It was a period of great adversity which wiped clean the slate of old values in order to establish new ones. Through a more flexible form of worshipping the Lord, based on an internalized faith expressed through prayer, the Jewish people became successful under Babylonian rule, and later, under the Persian kings.

The return from exile to Jerusalem allowed the Jews to further strengthen their faith by placing a new emphasis on learning and knowledge. Ezra became the first scholar of the Teachings of the Lord and the Teaching of Moses. Incorporating the former tradition of centralized ritual, the priests and scribes taught the law without causing conflict with any ruling Persian king. Nehemiah's development of an aligned governance structure assured that such practices would prevail.

This remarkable transformation ushered in a new era known as the period of the Great Assembly. During this time, the priestly scribes and scholars, along with governing officials, worked together with the remaining prophets to compile the final scrolls of the Lord. According to Rabbi Dr. Binyamin Lau in his book *The Sages*, the Great Assembly was a transitional body whose agency replaced the prophetic revelations with the teachings of the scholarly sages.[1]

This period began as Ezra, Nehemiah, and the priests taught the Jewish people to read and understand the scrolls of the first five books of the Hebrew Scriptures. At the start of this period, the scrolls may have been completed, but were not yet canonized.[2] According to Rabbi Lau, the Men of the Great Assembly brought the final scrolls of the Hebrew Scriptures into the public realm, thereby bequeathing them to the nation and its people as a whole.[3] Canonization took approximately fifty years (400 BCE to 350 BCE). The priests, who had earlier been protectors of the law and overseers of the practice of ritual offerings, became sages, scholars, and teachers to the people.[4]

The priests, following Ezra's influence, assumed a dual role: they continued their ancestral duties regarding Temple offerings and began leading the people in the discipline of prayer. Teaching the community along with making offerings allowed for the old and the new to evolve together.

The period of the Great Assembly was also a transition between the last remaining prophets, Haggai, Zechariah, and Malachi, who entrusted the words and meaning of the scrolls of the Five Books of the Lord to the great sages. Ezra was the first sage, and Simeon the Just the last during the time Alexander the Great conquered the land. The Great Sages were various scholars, scribes, teachers, and priests who helped formalize and canonize not only the Torah scrolls, but also the scrolls of Nevi'im (the Prophets). According to Rabbi Lau, the end of the period of the Great Assembly was the time when knowledge and wisdom replaced divine or prophetic inspiration.[5]

It was during this transition period of the Great Assembly that prayers and blessings became standardized and put into practice.[6] It was the compilation of these Books in the

Hebrew Scriptures, the standardization of the prayers and blessings, as well as the acquired learning, knowledge, and moral wisdom, that allowed the Jewish people to survive the later diasporas in the lands of Western Europe, the Near East, and Northern Africa. Over time, the Jews became the first "People of the Book."

This is also the start of a period when the people directed their questions about the living law to the sages and priests for interpretation. The sages studied the questions and then provided an understanding of the written law that applied to societal needs. The sages diligently imparted greater understanding of the law through discourse with the people.

Another lasting gift emerged from this period—the beginnings of monotheism, practiced as we know it today. The accepted belief is that the monotheism we know today originated at the time of the creation of the world and followed an unknown chain through Noah and the later patriarchs, Abraham, Isaac, and Jacob, who then carried it on. But a different, more solid form of monotheism developed during the time of the exile at the start of the Second Temple Period, after the Jews returned to Jerusalem.

Think back to the time of the Israelites, both in the Northern and Southern Kingdoms. Even when they were practicing monotheistic elements in their faith, the people themselves had not learned the living laws—except through the practice of ritual offerings. The priests did not impart teachings to the community but acted as intermediaries between the people and God.

As Rabbi Lau noted, when the priests kept the law to themselves, they denied the spirit of the law to the people, many of whom turned away from worshiping the Lord, God, to pray to other gods, such as Ba'al. Ultimately, the beliefs of the Israelites developed an ebb and flow, progressing forward and then backsliding, between monotheistic and polytheistic practices drawn from other peoples.

Only after the rebuilding of the Second Temple, with Nehemiah and Ezra working together, do we see what appeared to be the start of a transformed monotheism grounded in newer practices, one much closer to the monotheism we know today. The Jews worshipped no other gods. The people learned and lived in accordance with the instructions of the scrolls of the Torah, which laws they adapted to their times. This gave them mobility and resilience, thus returning them to the one and only God that Moses had been urging upon them in Deuteronomy. In fact, as previously noted, they were so committed that they were willing to sign a foundational document attesting to their faith. (Nehemiah 10:1–28)

The priestly scholars and sages teaching the people the values of this knowledge in their daily lives had a democratizing impact on the living law. The priests imparted ethical law concerning social, economic, and political conduct. All of this permitted everyone to internalize the teachings and planted the seed for a more portable faith. This eventually became widespread throughout the Jewish Diaspora and later in Christianity.

If people can rightfully understand and interpret the law in their own daily lives, from an education which permits them to question and think critically, then the foundation of equal treatment and respect under the law prevails for all and leads to democratization. The issue of human rights begins to grow and solidify on a collective basis. More people can hold each other accountable for the way they exercise their free will related to respectful living—and no one, not king, governor, or even a priest, can rule over the people in an oppressive manner.

In contrast to this is the fundamentalist Islamic world of today's Middle East, which bases itself on rigid and rote forms of education and learning, teaching values from an outmoded model. The values of hatred and violence toward those "not like them" are at the core of this system. The fundamentalist approach is rigid and archaic and does not encourage dynamic individual development and critical thinking, skills which are so necessary for living in the modern age. In other words, it is a form of social control and obedience that entrenches society.

In many parts of this region, religious fundamentalism is tightly enmeshed in the educational system. Secular topics may be taught, but only through the lens of rigid, religion-based learning. From this type of teaching, which discourages and even prohibits discussion and debate, people come to develop a belief system which may be based on truth or false information.[7]

If a religion teaches its people and children to hate others, and that killing, terror, and war are acceptable in today's world, then they adopt such a worldview from a young age as the correct and "good" approach. When these children grow up, their hatred only intensifies. More importantly, when they are taught not to question authority, faithfulness through obedience is the given result. Then radical violence against others becomes foremost among this society's unifying values.

The cultural and political structures in which people live serve to reinforce such beliefs. Integrated faith, prayer, and learning can work both ways. They can combine to form a belief system necessary for living in this modern age, one that leads to ethical living and the practice of truth, justice, and goodness. Alternatively, they can combine to strengthen the darker inclinations toward anger, envy, greed, vengeance, and hatred, all of which ultimately lead to war, terrorism, and death. Such teachings blindly ignore the sanctity and dignity of life.

Women have no rights under cultures governed by Shari'a, leaving powerless over half the people of these mostly Middle Eastern nations. Men use women to meet their sexual needs and abuse them if they disobey. Men in certain Arab nations can divorce their wives at will; they isolate and segregate women from other men. Women essentially become prisoners.

Women cannot receive an education in some countries, leaving them illiterate and constrained. They are unable to question anything, especially the dictates of faith. If men are taught that women have no rights, and men control women, then a patriarchal, oppressive society often arises. If there is no way to break out, then what women experience turns into a modern-day form of servitude. With this style of education, its repression of critical questioning and thought, dictators, rulers, and modern-day priests (or imams) are able to consolidate their power, which is their primary and ultimate goal.

When the value of learning based on an interpretation of the law in any faith is too narrow, how do you know if the teachings are good or bad? In fact, how will you know that moral wisdom at the end of the day is based on goodness as opposed to hatred? Within an open, questioning system of learning, goodness will evolve on the values of peace, human rights, and the sanctity of life.

Ironically, the whole concept of violence, war, and terrorism now represents "goodness" from the radical fundamentalist's hate-filled point of view. Such enforced learning is used to generate beliefs, with no comprehension of ethical soundness and little opportunity for the people to think critically for themselves. To base understanding on blind obedience and faith in God ensures that children grow up never questioning authority under the current rule. Children are then taught to project hatred onto others who are unlike them. War, terror, and hatred become integral parts of their accepted worldview.

A dangerous blending of rigid belief systems and political structures creates an environment of valuing "holy" war over peace. War and terrorism become ingrained as right actions. These people believe they are doing the right thing, but through an indoctrination process which teaches them debased values of hatred and vengeance. As a result, they learn to redirect the responsibility for their own serious plight. This does not seem logical—and yet it is exactly what is happening in the world today.

Blending education, political governance, and religion has the unfortunate advantage of keeping current rulers in power and the people in a position of not questioning their authority. Severe repercussions are imposed, which include execution by beheading, stoning of offenders, and other forms of extreme torture—a practice of justice without compassion. This, too, is an integration of faith and governance, but aligned to maintain an unjust system.

Rulers and dictators in many Middle East nations maintain their power and wealth from oil revenues. The people receive just enough money for food, housing, and education to avert uprisings, but this subsistence money is not enough for them to marry, raise families, or achieve social mobility. This leads to a feeling of hopelessness. The minority ruling class accumulates wealth in order to maintain their power and style of living. In countries without oil revenues, the vast majority of the population is impoverished. They see no way out. In both cases, these groups are prime targets for radicalization.

Extremist groups prey upon disenfranchised people and encourage them to become martyrs, performing suicide bombings as a means of honoring the faith they so value. Their families then receive further government rewards and entitlements for these acts of terrorism.

Unifying people by blaming other cultures and religions serves to deflect energy and attention away from their own social inequality, misery, and impoverishment. Generating such conflicts allows the leaders to avoid addressing the severely limiting character and plight of their culture. In fact, this prevents such repressed people from entering the modern world.

Therefore, moderates in the Islamic world who do believe there is a better way cannot easily break free of this rigid learning system which pervades their society, even if such individuals are in the majority. Sometimes, yielding to repression and being passive in the face of such terror and violence is the only way to survive.

The period of the Great Assembly in the land of Israel strengthened the faith and the living law with more flexible forms of governance based on the ethics that the law contained. The people learned their responsibilities regarding faith and everyday life through the new value of study and scholarship. Values can point people toward goodness or evil. It is our responsibility to choose the path society will use to both teach our children and other people to think critically about the laws of goodness and their application.

In their book *Why the Jews? The Reason for Antisemitism*, Dennis Prager and Joseph Telushkin teach that society conveys the balance between good and evil, based on the integration of both faith and ethics.

> Jews must make the world aware of two basic principles: ethics need God and God demands ethics. The Jewish people, in the tradition of ethical monotheism's greatest advocates, the Jewish Prophets, must therefore oppose religionists who advocate God without depicting goodness along with faith as the major concern of God, and likewise oppose secularists who advocate a value system devoid of religious moral values. In the first case, God is rendered morally irrelevant and religion becomes either a superstitious refuge from the moral demands of this world or a proponent of evil … In the second instance (i.e., a value system without God), ethics become relative, rarely transcending personal taste. God without ethics has led to religious massacres from Crusaders to Osama bin Laden; values and ideologies without God have led to the secular massacres of the Gulag and Auschwitz."[8]

Humanism based on philosophy, ethics, and rational thought can ignore a higher purpose of goodness; religion interpreted literally may never adapt in changing times. Faith in God, or some higher aspirational power, links the emotions of the heart with the wisdom of the mind, centered in a spirit of compassion. For without weaving together these fine strands, we lose our moral center.

How do we teach the goodness of the living law which emphasizes the sanctity of life and respect for one another as well as for other societies? How can faith inspire us to achieve a higher transcendent purpose in our lives? How do we create congruency in faith, education, governance, and economics that leads toward beneficial outcomes? In other words: how do we ensure that we are teaching people the values that will enable us to shape the world for the future we desire?

Chapter 11:
The Ptolemaic Empire, Hellenism, and the Jews

Previous chapters have focused on values derived from the stories and history presented in the Hebrew Scriptures, from Genesis through Kings and Prophets. More recent chapters have encompassed the First Temple Period, the period of Babylonian exile, the early return to Jerusalem, and the building of the Second Temple. Forthcoming chapters begin with the Second Temple Period, during which the history and cycle of values originates from other sources in ancient Israel. These chapters also emphasize the lives of Jews as subjects within empires, beginning with the Greeks.

Alexander was the son of King Phillip II of Macedon. After King Phillip died under suspicious circumstances, Alexander, at the age of twenty, succeeded his father to become king. Alexander believed that King Darius III of Persia had commissioned his father's assassination and Alexander's subsequent conquest of the Persian Empire was, in part, retaliation for his father's death. In 335 BCE, he set out to conquer the Persian Empire with an army of 40,000 men. Eventually his empire extended to the shores of India, becoming the largest in this part of the world.

Pollard and Reid's *The Rise and Fall of Alexandria—Birthplace of the Modern World* dramatically tells the history of Alexandria in Egypt, linked to Alexander the Great's conquests. Egypt had been part of the Persian Empire since

525 BCE, when Cambyses first conquered it. The Egyptians despised their Persian rulers, including the last, Darius III.

When Alexander conquered Egypt, however, the people were enthusiastic about him. His first move won the Egyptians' support. He demonstrated respect for ancient Egyptian customs and beliefs by paying homage to the gods of this ancient land. Alexander visited the temple of Ammon, the god of sun and air, in the city of Siwa, and left having convinced the Egyptians that he was the divine son of that god.[1] In this way, he secured ever greater acceptance by the Egyptians.

Egypt was the land of many gods, goddesses, idols, and magic. The people believed they were ruled by living gods such as Horus, the son of Osiris. Divine rule by the gods was ultimately attributed to their Pharaoh. Such a linkage assured nature's order, especially concerning the annual flooding of the Nile. This was how life was prescribed for the people—through the gods who controlled the rhythm of nature and created order.

Alexander and his army established the Hellenistic Empire on an ideological foundation which served to unify diverse groups of people. How did he come to have these ideas? Alexander and his childhood friend, Ptolemy Soter, grew up together in the court of King Phillip II in Macedon. Aristotle, one of the greatest Greek philosophers, tutored them both. These lessons prepared Alexander to conquer the Persian empire with the help of Ptolemy and his generals. Alexander and Ptolemy would learn how to govern diverse groups of people, but it would be Ptolemy who would become instrumental in accomplishing this goal.

The grand triumvirate of Greek philosophers were Socrates, Plato, and Aristotle. Aristotle passed along the great ideas and values that Plato and Socrates taught, which spoke of the ways to rule a nation, develop political systems, and establish economies of trade. Aristotle tutored Alexander and Ptolemy to give both these great students access to knowledge about the development of leadership. Aristotle's teachings would become critical to Ptolemy following the death of Alexander when power would eventually pass to him.

Aristotle taught Ptolemy of Socrates's radical humanistic wisdom, but it was the teachings of Plato that most interested Ptolemy Soter. Plato's premise involved three types of knowledge. According to Diogenes Laertius in the chapter concerning Plato in *The Lives and Opinions of Eminent Philosophers*,

> In the same way, there are also three species of know-ledge. There is one kind which is practical, a second which is productive, a third which is theoretical.[2]

It was this concept that electrified Ptolemy—bringing together the productive, the practical, and the theoretical in one. He defined these three themes as:[3]

1. Productive knowledge—economics of trade and ships
2. Practical knowledge—best and most efficient forms of government and administration
3. Theoretical knowledge—which seeks out the truths of the universe and reaches out for the perfect forms of God and the soul that lie behind the chaos of the everyday world.

From the teachings of Aristotle, Ptolemy believed that an empire focused solely on trade and political systems would eventually collapse. Large empires had a wide diversity of people who required common and unifying values, without which said empires would fail through division, conflict, and rebellion. One had to focus on knowledge and wisdom to bring together a diverse society.

After Alexander died in the city of Babylon at the age of 32, in 323 BCE, the empire came into the hands of Alexander's slow-witted half-brother, Phillip III Arrhideaeus, and a baby son, who became the formal heir. The empire was basically left to his three generals, one of whom was Ptolemy Soter.

Ptolemy wanted to govern Egypt and build it into one of the greatest nations. Ptolemy's rule would encompass the lands of Israel, parts of Syria, Cyprus, the Aegean islands of the Cyclades, and the ancient city of Cyrene, west of Alexandria. Using all that he had learned from Aristotle, he would create one of the greatest centers for knowledge and scholarship in the world by building the port city capital of Alexandria on the Mediterranean. Thus, he would also control all the major trade routes along the sea.[4]

For Ptolemy to merge Egyptian and Greek cultures, he needed a common value of moral and ethical wisdom to unify the people. This foundation would support and promote a flourishing trade and excellence in governance for a growing empire. Hellenistic society did not believe in living gods, as they did not come down to create faith and law for men. Instead, the Hellenists would create their own righteous rule through the unifying values of ideas, scholarship, and knowledge. This governance would exemplify Hellenistic philosophy at its best.

It was important that the Egyptians, though, with their ancient culture and beliefs, first accept Ptolemy as a ruler. To accomplish this, he needed to bring the body of Alexander the Great to Egypt. The Egyptians had already accepted Alexander as divine, the so-called son of the god Ammon. His body was the treasure which would strengthen the divine link for Ptolemy to help solidify his position as the future Pharaoh of Egypt. Ptolemy intercepted the body of Alexander en route to Macedonia, and brought it back to Egypt, to bury it at Memphis, the city of the Pharaohs.[5]

According to Pollard and Reid, Ptolemy next befriended the Egyptian priests in order to become familiar with their history, beliefs, and practices. As a result, he was able to work together with them and demonstrate respect for the Egyptian faith. During this transition, Ptolemy set himself up as the satrap or governor ruling Egypt. He built the city of Alexandria based on a vision, without fear of reprisal from the people.

With time, Alexandria became one of the greatest trade centers in the ancient world for both Greeks and Egyptians. Ptolemy's strategy was to integrate the culture of the Egyptian gods with Greek thought and reason. He accomplished this by creating a new, hybrid religion which allowed him to be crowned divine Pharaoh, and he became sole ruler of the people. It took nineteen years to establish this cult-like faith.

It is important to understand why Ptolemy developed this new, integrated religion; he intended it both as a sign of respect to the Egyptian people and to ensure acceptance by the Greeks, who did not believe in living gods.[6] Egyptians believed that living gods did not just take the forms of men, but also animals, such as Apis the bull. To the Egyptians, the bull representing Apis was the manifestation of a living god, worthy of worship. They also believed in an afterlife, and preparation for it was important during their lives; so the Egyptians collected valuable personal items to take with them into the next world. When King Cambyses of Persia first conquered Egypt in 525 BCE, he did not respect the Egyptian gods, thus breeding animosity in the people. Conversely, Ptolemy and his predecessor, Alexander, showed respect for Egyptian culture and were therefore welcomed as rulers of this nation.

The Greeks and Macedonians believed in a pantheon of gods which existed in a transcendent realm, distant from the people. They felt compelled to seek out truth, beauty, and reason without the assistance of gods. When death occurred, the Greeks believed that people traveled to a bleak afterlife, "a dusty place of regret where the dead looked back in sorrow at what they had and hadn't done in life." Life was to be lived on earth. Life should be about pleasure and learning. It was about living in the now, not in another world after death.[7]

To solidify his rule as Pharaoh, Ptolemy introduced the worship of Serapis, a god who would be suitable for both the Egyptians and the Greeks. Serapis was depicted as a man with a beard, bearing a great resemblance to Zeus and seated on a throne wearing a crown of fertility (as a link to divinity in the afterlife). The three-headed dog of the Greek underworld, Cerberus, crouched at his knee, and he held a staff in his left hand, similar to the one held by Asclepius, the Greek god of healing. For the Egyptians, Serapis was a cross between the Egyptian god of the underworld, Osiris, and the living god Apis, who was depicted both as a bull and as a man with the head of a bull.[8] Serapis represented a living god, accepted by the Egyptians, and a deity in human form for the Greeks and Macedonians.

Ptolemy wanted Alexandria to be the new capital of Egypt and the grandest port city of the Mediterranean. He established opportunities for trade, built a great harbor, and constructed many new roads. The city was divided into three areas—the Egyptians lived in one designated district, the Greeks ruled and lived in a second area of the city, and over 100,000 Jews lived in the third region, many of whom had come to Alexandria as captured slaves after Alexander and Ptolemy had conquered Jerusalem.

Not every ruler took the opportunity to recognize the diversity of people within an empire. Recall the Assyrians conquered the Northern Kingdom of Israel and its capital, Samaria, and immediately broke it up by scattering the people into new areas. The Assyrians took the Cutheans and other people they had conquered and transplanted them into northern Israel. They became known as the Samaritans and mixed with the many poor Israelites who had remained on the land.

The Babylonian and Persian kings took a different approach. When they exiled the Israelites of the Southern Kingdom of Judah to Babylon, these kings allowed the conquered people to practice their faith as long as it did not interfere with their rule. Diverse cultures flourished, with little resistance from rulers.

Ptolemy Soter took control of Egypt and Alexandria in 323 BCE, shortly after Alexander's death, but did not become Pharaoh Ptolemy I until 305 BCE.[9] His next goal was to establish an empire that was based not only on trade and governance but was also steeped in intellectual scholarship as a means of pursuing moral wisdom and justice. He set out to build one of the greatest libraries in the known world—the Library of Alexandria.

Prior to the rise of Alexandria, Athens had been known for its famous academies of learning, and for its philosophers who were disciples of the great master philosophers— Socrates, Plato, and Aristotle. Alexandria, as the new capital of Egypt, shifted the center of culture to the Mediterranean. Central to the city, the great library, along with a museum Ptolemy constructed, became the gathering center for scholars of the ancient world.

Philosophers, scientists, and mathematicians alike arrived to work together and explore new ideas. They created a culture of scholarship and discovery. This intellectual center became the first university-type setting in the known world.[10] The value of knowledge and learning by scholars became the apex of achievement that unified and energized Ptolemy's kingdom.

Demetrius of Phalerum was a great philosopher of the Athenian academy. He had worked with Ptolemy to develop the great library and museum. Demetrius thought the museum should become the "place of the Muses, [of] goddesses of poetry, music, dance, and the liberal arts and sciences, where these subjects should be both taught and all manner of knowledge contemplated."[11] The library eventually became home to over half a million manuscripts and scrolls collected from throughout the known world.[12]

When Ptolemy I died, his son, Ptolemy II (Philadelphus), became Pharaoh, continuing the traditions of his father. The greatest philosophers and scholars of their time gathered in Alexandria. The Greek world believed that if man was the center of the universe, then knowledge and learning would link him to moral wisdom, which would establish a divine connection with the otherworld gods.

Many of the great scientific findings that emerged from the Enlightenment in Western Europe were derived from scholarly work in Babylonia within the Islamic caliphate between 645 CE and 1200 CE. But much of the earliest work came from the time of the Greek philosophers, which originated not only in Greece but in Alexandria, Egypt, during the rule of Ptolemy I and II.

The city of scholarship and knowledge attracted many renowned thinkers of the time. One of the greatest mathematicians, Euclid, became famous for his geometry. Herophilus founded anatomy and physiology in Alexandria, dissecting bodies and first establishing that the heart was the center of the circulatory system. This discovery came long before William Harvey rediscovered it in the 1600s. Erasistratus discovered the root nature of disease and illness.[13]

Aristarchus studied astronomy and was the first to determine that the Sun, not the Earth, was at the center of the solar system, a discovery that Archimedes later referenced in one of his books. This was not accepted at the time, since faith and belief held that the Earth and humankind were the center of the universe. Therefore, the thought that the sun was the center became heretical, just as it would for Copernicus, who published his heliocentric theory shortly before his death in 1543.[14]

Eratosthenes, well-known in his day, helped transform the mathematics of that time. He discovered that the Earth was a sphere, calculating its circumference to within 318 kilometers (198 miles) out of 40,000 km. He calculated the tilt of the earth as the basis of the seasons. He created the first map of Egypt and other geographic areas of the world. He also became the head of the great library.[15]

Archimedes studied in Alexandria and invented the pump now named for him, the "Archimedean screw pump," as a means of bringing water to crop fields. When he returned to his homeland of Sicily, he used the knowledge he gained in Alexandria to develop a way for calculating the purity of gold by its weight.[16]

Alexandria had the largest Jewish population outside of Jerusalem. They arrived in the city in three main groups: those who migrated to Alexandria after the Babylonian destruction of Jerusalem; those whom Ptolemy I had captured; and those who continued to migrate there under the reigns of the Ptolemaic kings because of opportunities for trade.[17]

The Hellenistic culture with its broad knowledge and prevailing polytheism was, for the Jewish people, powerfully seductive. The greatest threat to the Jews was assimilation, which would imperil their faith and way of life. This was a risk not only in Alexandria, but in the land of Israel, where Greek *poleis* developed after invading soldiers settled in small military posts surrounding the area of Jerusalem. These soldiers were encouraged to intermarry with Jewish women as a form of successful cultural integration.[18]

The Hellenistic world focused on humanism, placing man at the center of the cosmos. It was a culture based entirely on free will. This was in direct opposition to the Jewish faith, which based itself on the belief that God had created the universe and humankind; a Living God, not gods created by men. For the Jews, the dynamic interaction was about man acting and living in accordance with God's will, based on an inherent relationship with the divine.

As noted earlier, the Greeks did not have a concept of living gods. Their focus was on the here and now and the way to live life to its fullest. It was about physical strength, beauty, art, and culture. Knowledge, reasoning, and development of the intellect were also at the heart of their aspirations, which resulted in a new period of philosophical pursuit centered on man's search for spiritual fulfillment.

Ultimately, these secular values centered on the pleasure and choices of man alone, rather than aspiring to a higher purpose which integrated the physical world with faith in a transcendent God. A world based solely on secular values ultimately runs the risk of developing self-centeredness and actions grounded in the destructive inclinations of greed and oppressive, tyrannical power.

Many Alexandrian Jews would, of course, pick up the more secular and paganistic values of the Hellenistic world and incorporate some of these beliefs. Others would create a hybrid synergy of faith and living law joined with Greek philosophy and knowledge.

It is against the backdrop of this seductive lure of wealth, materialism, and knowledge that the story of the Greek *Septuagint* appears. The Hellenistic world greatly influenced the Septuagint—the Greek translation of the first five books of the Hebrew Scriptures. This early version became the first seed which spread the Jewish faith and its laws pertaining to ethical righteousness and mercy into the world. Formerly, the Hebrew Scriptures had been restricted to those living in Israel and the earlier Babylonian lands of the exiled within the former Persian Empire.

Chapter 12:
The Legend of the Septuagint

As Alexandria grew in size and power, the Jews there existed successfully within the Ptolemaic empire. However, the seductive pleasures offered by Hellenistic culture threatened their newly internalized belief in God and the living law, especially since they were so far away from the central source of priestly scholarship and learning in Jerusalem. Therefore, the risk of assimilation and loss of faith was high. How could the Jews retain their identity while living in this distant culture?

First, they needed a powerful connection to their fundamental source texts, the Hebrew Scriptures. As Greek speakers, they were no longer fluent in the Hebrew of the texts. This was the purpose of the Septuagint, a Greek translation of the Five Scrolls of Moses (also later referred to as the Torah or the Pentateuch). It was the first time the Hebrew Scriptures had been translated into Greek, outside of the Jewish world, making their lessons available to Alexandrian Jews and to others. It would allow the Jews to retain their faith, while further promoting learning and scholarship.

There is a well-known legend about the origins of the Septuagint, whose name stands for seventy. It is based on the legend of the seventy-two elders who traveled from Jerusalem to Alexandria to translate the Five Scrolls of Moses at the time of the Ptolemaic empire.

Demetrius, the library keeper for Ptolemy I, attempted to gather as many books as possible from throughout the ancient world, one of which was the Septuagint. Ptolemy II Philadelphus was in power from 285 to 246 BCE.[1] He continued his father's tradition of developing the library and maintaining Alexandria as the most powerful city for trade and learning in the Near Eastern world. According to the legend of the Septuagint, Ptolemy I learned of the Jews' scrolls of law. The scrolls, however, were only in Hebrew. Ptolemy II found it desirable to gain access to this book.

There have been many explanations about how the Septuagint came about. The legend is based on Ptolemy II's invitation to the High Priest of Jerusalem to send seventy-two elders to Alexandria to translate the scrolls. The goal may have been for Ptolemy II to seek an understanding of the history of the Jewish faith, with its one God and the basis for the living law, as well as to learn how to rule wisely from such laws. Maintaining positive relationships with the people of Jerusalem and Israel was critical since Ptolemy II's control of this land was located at the most strategic crossroad in the Near East. Integration and acceptance of the Jews as members of the local population was important, much as the integration of the Egyptians into Greek society had been important for Ptolemy I.

Documents from a later time describe a robust legend. The basic premise, first and foremost, was that a translation was completed in Alexandria, under the auspices of the High Priest of the time, possibly Eleazar, son of Simeon the Just. However, other surviving documents bring the legend into question.

Pollard and Reid's *Alexandria* covers the history of this translation, offering two possible versions of how it came about.[2] Sometime after the Roman Wars, Josephus, the Jewish historian, wrote a comprehensive account of this legend based on the lost "Letter of Aristeas," which he quotes extensively in *Antiquities of the Jews.* The Letter was written around 200 BCE, but no complete copies exist.[3]

According to Josephus, the Letter appears to have been composed by a close acquaintance of Ptolemy II, Aristeas, who was initially thought to have been a Jewish historian. The Letter specifically states that Demetrius, head of the great Alexandrian library, suggested to Ptolemy II that he obtain a translation of the Hebrew scrolls.

Josephus describes Ptolemy II first releasing Jews from slavery as a gesture of goodwill, then sending gifts to the High Priest, Eleazar, including gold and silver for the Temple and money to support sacrifices. Ptolemy II then wrote to request a Greek translation of the First Five Scrolls of the Hebrew Scriptures. The High Priest, Eleazar, accepted the king's request and sent seventy-two elders, six representing each of the twelve Israelite tribes, to Alexandria. The seventy-two (often rounded to seventy) elders dined with the king and answered many questions about the living law and its wisdom.

Once settled on the island of Pharos, the location of the great lighthouse, the elders separated into pairs. When completed, the translation of the Hebrew into Greek by each of the pairs of elders was miraculously identical, as if they had been divinely inspired. Once the king received the translation, the elders then traveled back to Jerusalem bearing additional gifts from the king for the Temple and for themselves. This summary is a simplification of the legend that Josephus described, as the actual writing is comprehensive and highly descriptive of the events.[4]

Is the legend of the Septuagint factual in any way? The original version of "Aristeas's Letter" was written around 200 BCE as a pseudepigraphon, a letter about the event but from a much later period than Ptolemy II's reign. It was written by an anonymous writer—not the historian Aristeas. Aristeas could not have known certain facts from later in time, and other assertions were simply incorrect.[5] However, we do know that there was a Greek translation of the Hebrew Scriptures written in Alexandria, probably sometime during the reign of King Ptolemy II.

The Letter of Aristeas has value in and of itself; it was not a forgery of an earlier document, but neither was it written at the time of the event. Someone with intimate knowledge of royal protocol had written it around 200 BCE, attributing it to Aristeas. Although the letter presented itself as ancient literature that served a purpose to an audience, it was something altogether different. It appears to be some type of embellished propaganda describing the event in support of the Ptolemaic kings. During this period of time, great conflict had occurred between the army of the Ptolemaic empire (probably Ptolemy V) to the south, and that of Antiochus III of the Seleucid empire to the north of the land of Israel. The Letter could easily have been written to gain the support of the Jews of Alexandria and Jerusalem for the current Ptolemaic rule.[6]

It is, however, the translation of Philo of Alexandria (25 BCE to 50 CE) that is of greatest interest. Philo was born to one of the wealthiest and most privileged Jewish families in

Alexandria. He became a most erudite Jew who successfully synthesized Greek philosophy with Hebrew scripture and thought. In fact, it was through Philo that the Hebrew Scriptures were first introduced as the Word of God. They have been referenced as such even to the present day.[7]

Philo wrote an explanation of the Septuagint translation almost 300 years after this translation had supposedly occurred during Ptolemy II's reign. Philo presented his version to the Roman embassy in about 39 CE to persuade Rome to exempt the Jewish people from the obligation of emperor worship. His version may be the only one that we can be sure of in terms of accuracy, since Philo of Alexandria, this great scholarly Jewish leader, was aligned with the Greeks as well as the Jews.[8]

Philo's interpretation is preserved by the Christian church as the *De Vita Mosis*. Excerpts from Book II are presented here. Philo's document underscores the respect that Ptolemy II had for the Hebrew law as well as the esteem that the Jews held for the rulers of an empire.[9]

V. That the sanctity of our legislation has been a source of wonder not only to the Jews but also to other nations, is clear both from the facts already mentioned and those which I proceed to state. In ancient times the laws were written in the Chaldean tongue, and remained in that form for many years, without any change of language, so long as they had not yet revealed their beauty to the rest of mankind. But, in course of time, the daily, unbroken regularity of practice exercised by those who observed them brought them to the knowledge of others, and their fame began to spread on every side. For things excellent, even if they are beclouded for a short time through envy, shine out again under the benign operation of nature when their time comes. Then it was that some people, thinking it a shame that the laws should be found in one half only of the human race, the barbarians, and denied altogether to the Greeks, took steps to have them translated. In view of the importance and public utility of the task, it was referred not to private persons or magistrates, who were very numerous, but to kings, and amongst them to the king of highest repute. Ptolemy, surnamed Philadelphus, was the third in succession to Alexander, the conqueror of Egypt ... To put it shortly, as the house of the Ptolemies was highly distinguished, compared with other dynasties, so was Philadelphus among the Ptolemies. The creditable achievements of this one man almost outnumbered those of all the others put together, and as the head takes the highest place in the living body, so he may be said to head the kings.

Philo next described the wisdom of Ptolemy II, who had invited the elders to Egypt. They dined with the king while answering questions and demonstrating their knowledge of the law. They were then situated on the island of Pharos to begin the translation.

VI. In front of Alexandria lies the island of Pharos, stretching with its narrow strip of land towards the city, and enclosed by a sea not deep but mostly consisting of shoals, so that the loud din and booming of the surging waves grows faint through the long distance before it reaches the land. Judging this to be the most suitable place in the district, where they might find peace and tranquility and the soul could commune with the laws with none to disturb its privacy, they fixed their abode there; and taking the sacred books, stretched them out towards heaven with the hands that held them, asking of God that they might not fail in their enterprise. And He assented to their prayers, to the end that the greater part, or even the whole, of the human race might be profited and led to a better life by continuing to observe such wise and truly admirable ordinances.

Philo finally describes the divine intervention which must have taken place to create the final translation of the Hebrew Scriptures into the Greek language.

VII. Sitting here in seclusion with none present save the elements of nature, earth, water, air, heaven, the genesis of which was to be first theme of their sacred revelation, for the laws begin with the story of the world's creation, they became as it were possessed, and under inspiration, wrote, not each several scribe something different, but the same word for word, as though dictated to each by an invisible prompter. Yet who does not know that every language, and Greek especially, abounds in terms, and that the same thought can be put in many shapes by changing single words and whole phrases and suiting the expression to the occasion? This was not the case, we are told, with this law of ours, but the Greek words used corresponded literally with the Chaldean, exactly suited to the things they indicated ... Therefore, even to the present day, there is held a feast and general assembly in the island of Pharos, whither not only Jews but multitudes of others cross the water, both to do honour to the place in which the light of that version first shone out, and also to thank God for the good gift so old yet ever young ...

Philo chronicles the remarkable congruence between the Hebrew Scriptures and the Greek translation, as if these scholars had been collectively inspired.

One can only hypothesize about the impact this translation had on the Jews of Alexandria. Many of these people would have spoken only Greek. There would have been concerns about the assimilation of the Jews into the Hellenistic world, a hedonistic culture of pleasure based on sex, beauty, physical strength, and wealth. This clash of cultures created a conflict for the Jews, who balanced wealth with charity and care of strangers, widows, and orphans. They had learned that justice tempered with mercy and compassion prevented oppression. The Greek gymnasium was the center of learning and education in Hellenistic society. To advance in such a world, one had to enter it at the risk of losing oneself to its pleasures and demands.

The Jews residing in Alexandria faced this challenge: how could they maintain an enduring relationship with their one God, and still feel comfortable following the living laws of social conduct in such a wealthy and materialistic world? The Greek translation of the Septuagint connected the Jews of Alexandria, the largest such population outside of Jerusalem, to the heritage of the teachings in the Hebrew Scriptures.

Translating the Torah into the common Greek language for the Jews was a purposeful and innovative method of ensuring that the people remained connected to Jerusalem and retained a deep respect for and understanding of the faith. It did not guarantee that all Jews living in Alexandria or Jerusalem would not assimilate into Hellenistic culture, but it did assure that a significant number could survive the cultural onslaught, thereby carrying their faith into the future in outlying lands. The fact that Ptolemy II respected the law enough to allow for and support its translation would build pride for the people who practiced it.[10]

The translation would also further strengthen the relationship between the Jews in Jerusalem and the diaspora Jews in Alexandria and Cyrene, North Africa. Between 205 and 201 BCE, the Jews emigrated further throughout Asia Minor into what is today Turkey, as well as Greece, Macedonia, Crete, and Cyprus. In 200 BCE, they also spread to other lands, populating the cities of Antioch and Damascus, as well as Tyre and Sidon. Many relocated from Babylonia to Asia Minor once Antiochus III of the Seleucids forcibly took control of Jerusalem.[11]

As these Jewish communities grew over time, they came together in communal gatherings, assembling in what was possibly the earliest known version of the synagogue. The word derives originally from the Greek roots *sun* and *age* meaning "to bring together." Combined, the word became "sunagōgē," "a gathering." This term, in late Latin and Middle English, eventually became the word "synagogue."[12]

Since central worship could only occur at the Temple in Jerusalem, synagogues were not places of prayer like they are today, but sites for communal gatherings to educate youth, conduct independent courts of justice, and elect officials. They were places of learning and community.[13] The earliest synagogue, circa 225 BCE, was located at Schedia, fourteen miles from Alexandria, with Greek as the common language instead of Aramaic.[14] What better way to help keep the Jewish people from abandoning their faith and integrating into the Hellenistic culture than through the use of the Hebrew Scriptures translated into their own language?

Instead of keeping people together by tying them to a centrally located place of worship, the slowly emerging People of the Book learned from the Five Scrolls of Moses during their extended migration into the Hellenistic world. That set the stage for the future, when the permanent diaspora occurred in 70 CE, with the Roman destruction of the Second Temple.[15]

The Septuagint also secured the wisdom of the law with its emphasis on righteous and just rule, as well as the belief in one God, enabling its spread throughout the empire. It would eventually become the seed for spreading universal knowledge of the living law into the western world. It is believed that the Greek Bible originated from this first Septuagint, although it evolved and expanded over time. This does not detract from or diminish the significance of transferring such knowledge and wisdom of the scrolls to the larger world.

Containing what could be considered an ancient university setting, Alexandria hosted some of the most enlightened scholars of that day. Jewish people living there benefited from their proximity to the great library and museum. Alexandrian Jews were exposed to Hellenism's values of intellectual thought and philosophy. When viewed through the lens of their faith and the living law, such knowledge could develop into moral wisdom. Conversely, the Hellenistic world received the very first seed of universal faith which emphasized better rule and justice.

The Jews would eventually become learned translators of Greek philosophical works. They carried such knowledge with them into the Muslim world after 600 CE into the empires of the Islamic caliphate, when knowledge and scholarship was also blossoming throughout this empire. After the Christians conquered the caliphate, Jewish and Islamic scholars assisted in translating these learned works for Western Christianity. This ultimately contributed to the Enlightenment. It is possible that the Greek writings might have been lost to both the Islamic and Christian worlds had it not been for the unique translating skills which Jews developed during this Hellenistic period.

It may seem as if the values of Hellenism, based on ideas and knowledge, should have served to permanently bind the Greek empire, enabling it to survive. But as we know, their rule only lasted from 323 BCE, starting with Alexander the Great, to 25 BCE when the Romans conquered the Greeks. By then, the Jewish faith had already survived for over 1,500 years.[16]

A value system must be compelling enough to be binding. It must be based on a *shared history*, and it must be resilient enough to adapt with changing times. Philosophy must be bound up in something stronger than just its ideas and knowledge (or the theoretical), as both can be used for good and just purposes, as well as for self-centered ambitions and corruption. Jewish history was instead based on both faith and the one Living God, with its developed literature transmitting divine law for the Jews to follow. The translated Scriptures directed the people toward greater good, generally encouraging them to progress along a path toward righteousness.

The living law, once translated into their own language, helped immeasurably to conserve the people's faith and to broaden their understanding by providing for them access to the foundational material of their Scriptures. It opened them to a communal sharing of responsibility and compassion in their lives. While the Greeks espoused hedonism; the Jews, in contrast, would filter Greek philosophy through the lens of the living law of Torah in order to achieve ethical and just communities.

Chapter 13:
The Struggle for Religious Freedom

B etween the years 440 BCE and 70 CE, the Jews completed the Hebrew Scriptures. This began with the great sages of Jerusalem, known as the Men of the Great Assembly, and ended soon after the destruction of the Second Temple. The Jews created some of the greatest literature of antiquity. The Hebrew Scriptures would help to preserve and drive the faith for centuries to come, to the extent that the Jewish people would come to be identified as the People of the Book.[1]

The scriptures were canonized over time into three books. Collectively, they are known as the Tanakh. The T stands for Torah—the first five Scrolls of Moses or the Pentateuch. This portion was completed in the time of Ezra, during the period of the Persian Empire. It includes Genesis, Exodus, Leviticus, Numbers, and Deuteronomy. This was the written law and the foundational center of the faith.

N stands for Nevi'im (Prophets), which includes the books of Joshua, Judges, I and II Samuel, and I and II Kings. The later book of Prophets included Isaiah, Jeremiah, Ezekiel, and the twelve minor prophets. It would cover the early history of the Israelites and the divine revelations up through the Babylonian exile and was probably completed during the late Persian to early Greek periods.

K stands for Kethuvim (Writings), which are the collective wisdom of the people. These include stories, parables, and poetry illustrative of the faith, the living law of the time, and the moral wisdom derived from allegory, dealing with events in a changing world. The writings contain Psalms, Proverbs, Job, the Five Scrolls (composed of Song of Songs, Ruth, Lamentations, Ecclesiastes, and Esther), and Daniel. Later, Writings included Ezra, Nehemiah, and I and II Chronicles.

It is unclear to scholars if Esther was based on history or was a story. The book of Job was a parable. Ecclesiastes, written by a Hebrew sage and later translated into Greek, shares philosophical thoughts and reflections on life and one's relationship with God. The Kethuvim texts would have been completed by approximately 70 CE, some time before the destruction of the Temple.

With this backdrop of growing biblical scholarship, the Seleucid kings to the north brought on another period of religious persecution. The Seleucid rulers sought to impose Hellenism and idol worship on the people of Jerusalem. The Jews overcame this threat, standing up for their unique set of ideals and values, and defeating the Seleucid army. Judah Maccabee (called the Hammer) led the Israelites to victory in these battles. Today, the holiday of Hanukkah, the Festival of Lights, commemorates this victory.

Why was this such a crucial phase of history for the Jewish people? This is the first time that a group would fight to preserve their faith based on a set of ideals. The earlier wars with Assyria and Babylonia, along with those of the Persian Empire, were still fresh in the minds and hearts of the people. They had learned their lesson well, not to veer off course and return to the ways of worshipping idols and many gods—but to believe in the faith of their One God. To preserve this right became their ideal.

Over time, factions of Jews emerged in the area of Jerusalem and surrounding towns. The economic and intellectual stimulations of Hellenism were attractive to the wealthy Israelite aristocrats and priests. This encouraged many to turn to Hellenism and to assimilate into the culture.

The Hellenistic Jews still believed in One God and central ritual, but began to alter their attitudes, enjoying the pleasures that Greek culture had to offer them. Their beliefs in following the living law became malleable in order to better integrate the mores of Hellenistic society. Most of the time, assimilation, a movement unacceptable to most, meant rationalizing away many of the beliefs and moral values to which the Jews adhered.

Such rationalization separated the Jewish Hellenists from those whose loyalty was strictly to one God. Many wealthy Jews and priests aligned with the Hellenistic kings. Others remained truer to their faith and would, if necessary, lay down their lives for their beliefs. This schism created extreme factions between the Hellenistic Jews in Jerusalem and the more faithful in surrounding towns; so much so that the former would threaten the freedom of the rest of the people. These divisions would lead to conflict, rather than a mutual respect for their differences within society.

Such conflicts provided an opening to oppressive kings, ones who would eliminate the freedom of the Jewish people to worship their God. The ultimate goal of these kings was to exploit the Jews and their Temple's wealth. Where once the Jews were allowed to practice their faith in peace under foreign rule, they were no longer able to do so. Such divisions would ultimately threaten to destroy their world.

Historian Lawrence H. Schiffman, in his book *From Text to Tradition: A History of Second Temple Rabbinic Judaism*, provides insight into the developing Jewish world under the disruptive Seleucid empire.[2] At the time that Ptolemy I Soter ruled Egypt and built Alexandria (323 BCE), a second general under Alexander the Great, Seleucus I Nicator (312 BCE to 280 BCE) took control of the lands of Asia Minor (modern day Turkey) and the eastern portion of the Middle East (Iraq and Iran), which became the Seleucid empire. In 223 BCE, Antiochus III the Great became ruler. Between 221 and 201 BCE, Antiochus III consistently tried to invade Ptolemaic Israel, since this was the land bridge to conquering Egypt. Israel was on the shores of the Mediterranean, an important sea route as well as the passageway to the lands east of Israel. Antiochus III was finally successful in conquering these lands in 201 BCE, and he would remain in power until 187 BCE.

Antiochus III taxed the Jews just as they had been taxed by the Ptolemaic kings. However, one of his early acts was to grant the Jews the right to practice their faith freely within the Seleucid empire. The people were able to continue their central ritual offerings at the Temple under the High Priest, and to maintain central administration of their faith through an assembly of leaders. The body that had been recognized in earlier times as the Men of the Great Assembly had by now evolved into the *Gerousia* (Greek for "Council of Elders").

Probably developing under the kings of the Ptolemaic empire, the priests and leaders of the Jewish aristocracy of Jerusalem made up this council of elders. It represented not only the central source of authority for the faith, but also acted as a quasi-governmental body. The Assembly, which formerly had taught and interpreted the Hebrew scriptures, now also participated in political activities supportive of the Hellenist empire.

The Gerousia would influence the Jews of the Greek diaspora through the shared teachings of the foundational

Hebrew scrolls. It encouraged the people to make pilgrimages and to pay tithes to the Temple, all of which strengthened and emphasized the centrality of the faith in Jerusalem. The Gerousia evolved into the Sanhedrin, the governing body for the faith during the late Second Temple Period under the future Roman Empire.[3]

In 188 BCE, the Romans conquered that portion of the Seleucid Empire which represented Asia Minor under Antiochus III's rule. They already controlled the trade routes between Alexandria and Rome. Following Antiochus III, his son, Seleucus IV Philopater, ruled between the years 187 to 175 BCE. Then Antiochus IV Epiphanes, a second son of Antiochus III, followed as king of the Seleucid Empire (175 to 164 BCE), continuing under Roman rule.[4]

Rome encumbered the Seleucid kings with large retributive payments. This heavy financial burden created an incentive for Antiochus IV Epiphanes to double the tax burden of the Jews of Jerusalem. He would impose greater domination over the people in order to obtain their wealth. He plundered the beautifully designed treasures of gold and silver in the Temple including the tithes that the people sent from the Greek and Babylonian diasporas.[5]

Many of the Jewish aristocracy as well as the priests encouraged further assimilation. The priests and the Gerousia were already aligned with the Seleucid Empire and had been for some time under Antiochus III the Great. When Antiochus Epiphanes took over as ruler, Onias III, who had been the High Priest, stepped down and his brother, Jason, purchased the right to the priesthood from the king. This created the first breach in the succession of High Priests since the time of Aaron. Instead of following the line of descendants from father to son, as dictated by the living law of the Torah or Pentateuch, a brother had purchased the position as if it were a commodity. This change in the law was unacceptable to most people.

As high priest, Jason did not seek to change the central faith of the Jews so much as to reshape the political and commercial aspects of the culture to align them more with Hellenism. Jason built the first gymnasium for learning in Jerusalem, to integrate into Jewish society the Hellenistic secular subjects of education and athletic training. To participate in athletics, Jewish men had to do so naked, which conflicted with their laws of modesty.

Eventually overthrown as High Priest, Jason went into exile; Menelaus became High Priest in 171 BCE. By now, Antiochus Epiphanes was beholden to Rome and paying greater amounts of tribute tax. The wealth from the Second Temple in Jerusalem could help alleviate the burden, and Menelaus was in a better position to meet Antiochus Epiphanes's needs while continuing to drive Jewish culture in Jerusalem closer to Hellenism. Menelaus was one of the sons of Joseph ben Tobias. Joseph was a wealthy patriarch and a Hellenistic Jew who had been politically dominant and aggressive in his role as a tax collector for the entire country on behalf of an earlier ruler, Ptolemy III Euergetes.[6]

Antiochus Epiphanes attempted to conquer Egypt on several occasions in order to increase his resources. He was successful in conquering parts of the empire in his first campaign; then, he turned against Jerusalem and the entire land of Israel to plunder its wealth. After his second Egyptian campaign, Antiochus proceeded to desecrate Jerusalem and the land of Israel. The book of I Maccabees chronicled these events. The original Hebrew text, written around 134 BCE was lost, but a Greek translation, probably written around 100 BCE, was found in the early Greek Septuagint.[7]

This excerpt from I Maccabees describes Antiochus's actions against Jerusalem after the first Egyptian campaign.

After his conquest of Egypt, in the year one hundred and forty-three [169 BCE],[8] Antiochus turned about and advanced on Israel and Jerusalem in massive strength. Insolently breaking into the sanctuary, he removed the golden altar and the lampstand for the light with all its fittings, together with the table for the loaves of offering, the libation vessels, the cups, the golden censers, the veil, the crowns, and the gold decoration on the front of the Temple, which he stripped of everything. He made off with the silver and gold and precious vessels, he discovered the secret treasures and seized them, and removing all of these, he went back to his own country, leaving the place a shambles and uttering words of extreme arrogance.
(I Maccabees 1:20–25, Jerusalem Bible)

The Temple's stolen wealth would support the financial needs of the king and assist with retribution payments to the Romans. The Hellenist Jews, mainly those who were wealthy and had become aligned with Antiochus, had foisted their ways upon the poorer people of Israel, and protests against these leaders were mounting. The tax burden together with this crushed free expression of faith was too much and thus pushed them toward rebellion.

Two years later, in 167 BCE, Antiochus returned a second time to conquer Egypt, but was assaulted by the Romans. Jason, the former High Priest, still in exile, believed incorrectly that Antiochus had been killed in battle. This gave him the opportunity to round up over one thousand discontented men and lead an armed rebellion to overthrow

Menelaus as High Priest and take back Jerusalem, along with his position.

Because of Antiochus's failed second campaign to conquer Egypt, he was humiliated by the Romans. Antiochus learned of Jason's attacks and sent his commander, the Mysian Apollonius, to further pillage the city of Jerusalem. His goal was to destroy the Jews. This would become one of the greatest slaughters in Jewish history.[9]

> *The days passed, and after two years the king sent the mysarch through the cities of Judah. He came to Jerusalem with an impressive force, and addressing them with what appeared to be peaceful words, he gained their confidence; then suddenly he fell on the city dealing it a terrible blow, and destroying many of the people of Israel. He pillaged the city and set it on fire, tore down its houses and encircling wall, took the women and children captive and commandeered the cattle. Then they fortified the City of David with a great strong wall and strong towers and made this their Citadel. There they installed an army of sinful men, renegades, who fortified themselves inside it, storing arms and provisions, and depositing there the loot they had collected from Jerusalem; they were to prove a great trouble.* (I Maccabees 1:29–37, Jerusalem Bible)

Antiochus next decided the best way to defeat the rebels was to destroy the core of the Jewish faith, by creating an "onslaught against the forces that propelled them, the Torah, the commandments, and the culture of the Jewish people."[10] In 167 BCE, Antiochus Epiphanes would reverse his father's decree which had ensured the Jews the right to practice their faith freely under foreign rule.

Jerusalem was to become an assimilated *polis* (city), as ordered by the king. The Hellenistic religion would replace the faith, bringing great strife to the people. After four hundred years, the privilege of practicing their faith quietly was gone.[11]

> *Then the king issued a proclamation to his whole kingdom that all were to become a single people, each renouncing his particular customs. All the pagans conformed to the king's decree, and many Israelites chose to accept his religion, sacrificing to idols and profaning the Sabbath. The king also sent instructions by messenger to Jerusalem and the towns of Judah directing them to adopt customs foreign to the country, banning holocausts, sacrifices, and libations from the sanctuary, profaning Sabbaths and feasts, defiling the sanctuary and the sacred ministers, building altars, pre-cincts and shrines for idols, sacrificing pigs and unclean beasts, leaving their sons uncircumcised and prostituting themselves to all kinds of impurity and abomination, so that they should forget the Law and revoke all observance of it. Writing in such terms to every part of his kingdom, the king appointed inspectors of the whole people, and directed all the towns of Judah to offer sacrifice one after another.*
> (I Maccabees 1:41–54, Jerusalem Bible)

All that Israel and Jerusalem had stood for had been stripped away. Not only was the tax burden on the Jewish people great, especially upon the poor, but the king introduced foreign deities into the Temple, promoting the idolatrous worship of Antiochus Epiphanes. He placed a golden statue of Zeus in the Temple, linking the pagan idolatry of the Greek gods to the king. In I Maccabees 1:54, this was referred to as the "abomination of desolation." He also introduced cult prostitution to the Temple.

Surprisingly, the Hellenized Jews and Menelaus, the High Priest, rationalized their allegiance by interpreting these foreign deities as being equivalent to worshipping the One God of Israel. By decree of the king, they also built altars throughout the land for sacrifices, for further worship of Antiochus. Jews refusing to idolize the king were subject to death. Antiochus's soldiers burned Hebrew scrolls throughout the land.[12]

> *Many of the people—that is, every apostate from the Law— rallied to them, and so committed evil in the country, forcing Israel into hiding in all their places of refuge. On the fifteenth day of Chislev in the year one hundred and forty-five [December 8, 167 BCE] the king erected the abomination of desolation above the altar; and altars were built in the surrounding towns of Judah and incense offered at the doors of houses and in the streets. Any books of the Law that came to light were torn up and burned. Whenever anyone was discovered possessing a copy of the covenant or practicing the Law, the king's decree sentenced him to death. Having might on their side they took action month after month against any offenders they discovered in the towns of Israel. On the twenty-fifth of the month sacrifice was offered on the altar erected over the altar of holocaust. Women who had had their children circumcised were put to death according to the edict with their babies hung round their necks, and the members of their household and those who had performed the circumcision were executed with them.* (I Maccabees 1:55–64, Jerusalem Bible)

Mattathias, of the priestly line of Joarib and head of the Hasmonean family, initiated the revolt against this religious persecution. He left Jerusalem and settled in Modein, known today as Modi'in in Israel. Mattathias had five sons—John (known as Gaddi), Simon (called Thassi), Judah (the Maccabeus), Eleazar (Avaran), and Jonathan (Apphus).

This family dedicated their lives to God and the living law. The Jews of the Hasmonean lineage of priests had not forgotten their history. When the king's commander came to Modein and requested that Mattathias set an example by offering up a sacrifice on the altar outside of the Temple in Jerusalem, he refused.[13]

Mattathias and his men traveled throughout the land of Israel and removed all the desecrating altars. Rather than give up their faith, Mattathias and his sons rebelled. On his deathbed, Mattathias put Judah (the Maccabee) in charge of these rebellions.

As the days of Mattathias were drawing to a close, he said to his sons, "Arrogance and outrage are now in the ascendant; it is a period of turmoil and bitter hatred. This is the time, my children, for you to have a burning fervor for the law and give your lives for the covenant of our ancestors." (I Maccabees 2:49–50, Jerusalem Bible)

Here is your brother Simeon, I know he is a man of sound judgment. Listen to him all your lives; let him take your father's place. Judas Maccabaeus, strong and brave from his youth, let him be your general and conduct the war against the pagans. The rest of you are to enroll in your ranks all those who keep the Law, and to exact vengeance for your people. Pay back the pagans to the full and hold fast to the ordinance of the Law. Then he blessed them and was laid with his ancestors. He died in the year one hundred and forty-six [166 BCE] and was buried in his ancestral tomb in Modein, and all Israel mourned him deeply. (I Maccabees 2:65–70, Jerusalem Bible)

Here we see a group of people fighting for an ideal—the preservation of their right to practice their faith. Up to this point in time, kings fought and conquered one another for land and resources, or in order to expand their empires. Now we see the Jews voluntarily rising up, both individually and collectively, to defend their human rights and freedom.

The Jewish people were willing to put their lives on the line for a faith that had taken them out of slavery from Egypt and enabled them to live peacefully under foreign rule since the Babylonian exile four hundred years earlier. Antiochus IV Epiphanes, however, interpreted any rebellion by the Jews against the Seleucid Empire as a direct threat to his divine authority and his ability to obtain needed revenues.

Judah Maccabee (the Hammer) led the final revolt against the Seleucids in 164 BCE.[14] The Festival of Dedication (Hanukkah) commemorated the freeing of Jerusalem and the cleansing of the Temple of all foreign idols. Once the Temple had been cleared, so the legend goes, Judah lit the lampstand (golden menorah) which is representative of the God-given law and from oil sufficient to last only one day, the lights burned miraculously for eight days.

This very value of religious freedom and tolerance still exists today in our civil laws and democracies of Western Europe and America. These laws not only provide protections to all people but also defend their right to worship. Laws also protected people from oppressive rule, as history reveals about kings who imposed taxes without the people having representation. Political systems have evolved over the centuries for the protection and respect for such freedoms. They have been fought for as fervently and as idealistically as they were by the Jewish people in ancient times.

Given the influx of people who wish to impose their own religious laws and practices on European culture, governments must act in order to protect all of their populations from religious persecution or victimization.

They must guard religious freedom as a right and privilege, and not concede power to those rulers or leaders who seek personal and collective gain. Promoting religious violence against others of a different faith is unacceptable.

There is, today, a fine line between mutual respect of faiths and accepting religious intolerance. Let us not ignore willful violence and persecution against others who have different beliefs. It is not acceptable to turn a blind eye to violent actions and terrorist attacks for the sake of religious tolerance. Diverse faiths must co-exist peacefully within countries which have established righteous and humane forms of law that are just and compassionate.

Chapter 14:
The Book of Daniel

The faith of the Jews would not have survived without their victory against the Seleucids. The Hebrew versions of this history have been lost; the only writings remaining today of this historic event are in versions of Bibles that include the Apocrypha.[1] Does the Tanakh preserve something relative to this time frame?

The Book of Daniel may represent the preserved literature from this period. It is a sometimes confusing but compassionate set of parables, dreams, visions, and prophecies concerning a learned man who held fast to his faith in God. Daniel is a Jewish exile living in the royal court of Nebuchadnezzar, who eventually oversees administrative provinces in Babylon and Persia. Some of the stories are apocalyptic and prophetic to the point of detailing, with incredible accuracy, future events, up to the Roman period.

Is Daniel a prophet or does the Book of Daniel represent something else in ancient biblical history? Nathan Moskowitz, a neurosurgeon and assistant professor of neurosurgery at Johns Hopkins University, published an article in the *Jewish Bible Quarterly* in 2010, which may shed light on this story.[2]

Recall that the Book of Daniel is in the section of the Tanakh known as Kethuvim (Writings), not in the section reserved for prophets. The final version of Daniel was probably written in 164 BCE, just before the events of Judah Maccabee.[3]

According to Moskowitz, this story may have been written to help a certain group of Jews during the time of the Maccabees. The Hasidim, the Righteous or the Learned (not to be confused with contemporary Hasidim), were that group of Jews who non-violently resisted the Seleucids' attempts to forcibly assimilate them. The Hasidim believed that their faith would enable them to be judged after their deaths by God as righteous for their willingness to follow the living law. Despite Antiochus having attempted to force the Jews to convert to Hellenism, these people held true to their beliefs.

The Book of Daniel, Moskowitz hypothesizes, was a theological-political tractate written as a series of stories about a man or legend, Daniel (which in Hebrew means "God is my judge"), which encouraged the people to live in accordance with their faith and the law, without resorting to violence.

This left them no other option but to die at the hands of their oppressors as martyrs or victims of a stronger power. To watch this happen to a group of Jews must have been heartbreaking enough to destroy the people's spirit. Therefore, the stories of Daniel would become the literary encouragement necessary for the Hasidim to continue both to uphold and adhere to the laws of God and to oppose the extremes that Hellenism imposed upon them.

Embedding messages in stories was a style that came out of the Babylonian, Persian, and Greek empires. In this instance, it did not directly focus on Antiochus IV Epiphanes. If the stories had been openly written against Antiochus, he would have surely killed the writers for their opposition. Instead, the storylines provided guidance, comfort, and hope to the Hasidim, who would ultimately prevail.

Moskowitz believes that the Hasidim maintained their Hebrew identity and literacy in a foreign, multi-cultural world. The first section of the Book of Daniel exemplifies this by describing Daniel and three fellow exiles of the tribe of Judah as captives in Babylon who become part of the royal household of Nebuchadnezzar. Daniel and his men hold true to the living laws by following prescribed dietary requirements in their new setting.

Several sections of the book recount the king's dreams, which foretold the fall of the Babylonian, Median, Persian, and Greek empires. For example, Nebuchadnezzar has a dream, which he brings to Daniel for interpretation. Daniel envisions an enormous statue constructed of a head of gold; breasts and arms of silver; belly and thighs of bronze; legs of iron; and the feet of iron and clay—a brittle mix of materials. (Daniel 2:31–45)

This dream symbolized the four empires which had overtaken the land of Israel between 586 BCE and 167 BCE, with the gold head representing Nebuchadnezzar and Babylonian rule. Silver represented the empire of the Medes who had conquered the Babylonians, followed by the bronze of the Persian empire and its kings. Finally, iron represented the conquest of Alexander the Great and the establishment of the Hellenistic Empire.

Iron signifies strength, but the feet and toes, composed of a brittle mix of iron and potter's clay, portrayed the struggle between the two warring empires which followed Alexander's rule: by the stronger Ptolemies to the south in Egypt (the iron), and the two weaker Seleucid kings with Antiochus IV Epiphanes to the north (the clay). This comparison was a sign to the Hasidim that the empire was weak and would eventually break.

How could Nebuchadnezzar's dream be so accurate in its description of the future? According to Moskowitz, it is unlikely that these were true visions; rather, they were stories written contemporaneously with the events of the rule of Antiochus Epiphanes. The known past, then, would become hidden in parables to appear as prophecy which predicted the future.

The story of Nebuchadnezzar's dream would give hope to the Hasidim that this current and final empire of Antiochus Epiphanes and its aggressive Hellenism would come to an end. All empires rise and fall in cycles, as would this one, if only the people would continue to hold fast to their faith. Such was the message in the Book of Daniel.

Antiochus Epiphanes destroyed the city of Jerusalem and denied the Jews the right to practice their faith freely and peacefully, a right given to them by his father, Antiochus III the Great. On pain of death, he forced idolatry upon the people. A golden altar of Zeus was placed in the Temple. This is referred to in I Maccabees as the "abomination of desolation" and in Daniel, the "appalling abomination." (I Maccabees 1:57, The Jerusalem Bible; Daniel 11:31)

The golden altar of Zeus in I Maccabees symbolized the divine rule of Antiochus Epiphanes. The Book of Daniel similarly describes a golden statue of Nebuchadnezzar. Daniel and his advisors were required to pray and pay homage to the statue, lest they be put to death by the king. Instead, they adhered to their Hebrew identity and tradition and refused to do so. (Daniel 3:1–7) This passage, then, is a message for the Hasidim to remain steadfast and refuse to pay homage, keeping their faith only in God.

For failing to participate in idol worship, Daniel's three fellow Judahites were thrown into a "burning fiery furnace," only to live, protected by the grace of God. The Hasidim also experienced this kind of threat of being tortured or killed as martyrs by the mercenaries of Antiochus. This occurred for upholding their beliefs and failing to pay homage to the idol statutes, with Nebuchadnezzar representing Antiochus Epiphanes. (Daniel 3:13–29)

Section 10 of Daniel speaks to the time of King Cyrus of Persia, a friend to the Jews, who allowed them to return to the land of Jerusalem and in accordance with prophecy, rebuild their Temple. Daniel has a great vision of a man whose "body was like beryl, his face had the appearance of lightning, his eyes were like flaming torches, his arms and legs had the color of burnished bronze, and the sound of his speech was like the noise of a multitude." (Daniel 10:6)

The Book of Daniel speaks to this vision and the despair that the Hasidim, lacking in strength and spirit, must have felt during this violent period, wondering if it would ever end. The message being conveyed to the people was to hold strong and wait for the end times when the people would ultimately prevail.

While he was saying things to me, I looked down and kept silent. The one who looked like a man touched my lips, and I opened my mouth and spoke, saying to him who stood before me, "My lord, because of the vision, I have been seized with pangs and cannot summon strength. How can this servant of my lord speak with my lord, seeing that my strength has failed, and no spirit is left in me? He said, "Have no fear, precious man, all will be well with you; be strong, be strong!" As he spoke with me, I was strengthened, and said, "Speak on, my lord, for you have strengthened me!" Then he said, "Do you know why I have come to you? Now I must go back to fight the prince of Persia. When I go off, the prince of Greece will come in. No one is helping me against them except your prince, Michael. However, I will

tell you what is recorded in the book of truth.
(Daniel 10:15–21)

Here we have a direct reference to the Persian and Greek empires in the visions and dreams that Daniel foretold. The reference to the Greek empire is clear, that the people, in their suffering, should remain strong until the angel of mercy, Michael, destroys the Seleucid ruler, Antiochus Epiphanes.

Section 11 of the Book of Daniel symbolically addresses the Syrian Wars between the Seleucid king Antiochus Epiphanes and the southern Ptolemaic empire. It focuses on Antiochus's first conquest of Egypt and his pillage of Israel and the Temple.

> *He [Antiochus] will muster his strength and courage against the king of the south with a great army. The king of the south will wage war with a very great and powerful army but will not stand fast, for they will devise plans against him. Those who eat of his food will ruin him. His army will be overwhelmed, and many will fall slain. The minds of both kings will be bent on evil; while sitting at the table together, they will lie to each other, but to no avail, for there is yet an appointed term. He will return to his land with great wealth, his mind set against the holy covenant. Having done his pleasure, he will return to his land.* (Daniel 11:25–28)

The following section refers to the second Egyptian conquest, when the Romans (referred to as "Kittim") drove Antiochus out of Egypt and humiliated him. Antiochus and his army returned to Jerusalem, where he suppressed the armed rebellion of Jason, the exiled high priest, and destroyed the city. Apollonius, the king's mercenary commander, vanquished the people and desecrated the Temple, after which he abolished their freedom to worship as Jews.

The Hasidim were called to remain strong in their faith, even as they suffered during this time.

At the appointed time, he will again invade the south, but the second time will not be like the first. Ships from Kittim will come against him.[4] He will be checked, and will turn back, raging against the holy covenant. Having done his pleasure, he will attend to those who forsake the holy covenant. Forces will be levied by him; they will desecrate the temple, the fortress; they will abolish the regular offering and set up the appalling abomination. He will flatter with smooth words those who act wickedly toward the covenant, but the people devoted to their God will stand firm.[5] The knowledgeable among the people will make the many understand; and for a while they shall fall by sword and flame, suffer captivity and spoliation. In defeat, they will receive a little help, and many will join them insincerely. Some of the knowledgeable will fall, that they may be refined and purged and whitened until the time of the end, for an interval still remains until the appointed time. (Daniel 11:29–35, Jewish Study Bible).[6]

It is clear that during the time of their revolt against their Seleucid oppressors, many of the Hasidim martyred themselves rather than give up their faith. They needed spiritual encouragement during this period to survive and sought consolation in their time of hopelessness. The promise of reward in the afterlife, through the resurrection of the physical body and the immortality of the soul, gave them strength.[7]

At that time, the great prince, Michael, who stands beside the sons of your people, will appear. It will be a time of trouble, the like of which has never been since the nation came into being. At that time, your people will be rescued, all who are found inscribed in the book. Many of those that sleep in the dust of the earth will awake, some to eternal life, others to reproaches, to everlasting abhorrence. And the knowledgeable will be radiant like the bright expanse of sky, and those who lead the many to righteousness will be like the stars forever and ever. But you, Daniel, keep the words secret, and seal the book until the time of the end. Many will range far and wide and knowledge will increase." (Daniel 12:1–4)

The Book of Daniel may be the preserved literature of the Hasidim, which provided them hope and encouragement during a tragic period. The stories, dreams, and visions are confusing unless understood in their symbolic context. It gives hope to recall that unjust empires come and go, but only God's kingdom prevails, and that the people who retain their faith will be rewarded in the afterworld. The brutality that the Hasidim experienced was only mitigated after they joined forces with Judah Maccabee and the Hasmoneans in armed rebellion.[8] Had both groups not united to fight the enemy's army, the Jews and their faith would not have survived.

Today, people of many nations practice religious freedom because of hard-won struggles. Oppression never endures, even if it briefly appears to do so. Ultimately, as the Book of Daniel documents, oppressive nations rise and fall, brought down by those willing to fight for their rights. We want to believe that peaceful and diplomatic actions will solve all problems, yet at times war is necessary. It is worth fighting to protect our ideals.

Part II

Edifices

Chapter 15:
The Birth of Universal Education

While the Book of Daniel consoled the Hasidim and encouraged them to resist through non-violence, they eventually joined forces with the Hasmoneans to win back Jerusalem and the Temple. However, Judah Maccabee's rededication of the Temple was not sufficient to give people the freedom to practice their faith. Israel would also need to reestablish independence, so as to no longer suffer foreign domination. Although the Jews had freed themselves from religious persecution, the Seleucid empire still controlled them.

At the death of Antiochus IV, his son, Antiochus V Eupator, took control of the empire. He recognized the importance of compromise and ensured that the Jews had the freedom to practice their faith. Until his death in 161 BCE, Judah Maccabee would continue the fight to free the nation. Absent this additional struggle, Seleucid kings would continue to appoint High Priests aligned with Hellenism to rule over the people of Israel.

After Judah's death, his brother Jonathan took over as commander, fought successfully, won the nation's independence, and became the first to assume the position of High Priest. Based on a treaty he worked out with the Seleucid king, Jonathan ruled between the years of 152 to 142 BCE.[1]

Between 142 and 134 BCE, following Jonathan's death, Simon, another of Judah Maccabee's brothers, became High Priest. Simon was the first High Priest and Ethnarch to govern the land of Israel under the Seleucid King Demetrius II Nicator. Demetrius granted the Israelite state both its independence and an exemption from taxation, a status which remained in place until the time of the Roman occupation.[2]

During their reign, Jonathan and Simon loosely combined the roles of High Priest and governing leader. These two positions were not meant to be held by one person but to remain separate in order to preserve the Aaronic line of the priesthood while the most capable ruler would govern the land, independent of the High Priest.

Both Jonathan and Simon also expanded the original lands of Israel, which included Judah and the city of Jerusalem, winning over the surrounding areas of eastern Israel to the town of Jaffa on the Mediterranean coast, the area to the southeast shores of the Dead Sea, as well as what is today the northern part of Jordan.[3]

After Simon died, his son, Jonathan (Yochanan) Hyrcanus, became the first ruler of the Hasmonean dynasty to fashion himself both a true king and High Priest in one centralized role. This became the earliest instance of a governing theocracy in the history of Israel. Subsequently, his first son, Aristobulus I, would succeed, followed by Jonathan's second son, Alexander Janneus (Yannai). These three ruled between the years of 134 to 76 BCE.[4] War and expansion characterized the years of the Hasmonean monarchy. By 76 BCE, these rulers conquered Samaria, the Galilee, all the land in between to the Mediterranean coast, the Golan Heights to the north, as well as Idumea and the ancient lands of the Philistines along the southern coast, down to the Negev desert.

Theocracy corrupted the priesthood, causing great conflict and dissension between the people and the priests.

The Hasmonean descendants became victims of their own power by ultimately realigning with the Hellenists. The Gerousia and the Priesthood had also aligned themselves with their Hellenistic rulers.

King Alexander Janneus's wife Queen Salome became the first female monarch when her husband died. She ruled between 76 BCE and 67 BCE. Although few are aware of her role in history, she became the greatest and most beloved ruler of the Hasmonean dynasty. Queen Salome's leadership helped heal the breach between the people, the monarchy, and the Temple priests.

When Queen Salome came to power, she split the role of governing ruler and the High Priesthood. She recognized the corruption that resulted by combining these dual roles into one, which had skewed the interpretation of the living law and the faith to meet the needs of the ruling king. Queen Salome was also able to alter the role of the Gerousia so that it better represented the people and their faith.

The historian Kenneth Atkinson documented the history of Queen Salome in his book about her.[5] He notes that as a female ruler of Israel, she could not hold the position of High Priest as part of the Levitical male succession: so, by default, she split these roles in accordance with the original Written Law. This served to immediately reconcile numerous conflicts among the common people and created a separation of power in the governance structure between monarch and High Priest. She was also a warrior queen who successfully defended Israel and led the troops. But as long as she protected her borders, she had no need to conquer more lands as had her husband. Queen Salome oversaw a much-needed period of peace for the land of Israel.

Queen Salome's vision also provided support to the group that would lead the Gerousia, called the Pharisees, thereby allowing education to flourish within synagogues throughout the land. This would increase the availability and begin the institutionalization of learning for all children. The value of learning would grow among the people, thus helping the faith to survive, and initiating the birth of universal education.

To understand the importance of the unity Queen Salome brought to the faith, one must first gain some perspective on the sectarian differences which existed between the Sadducees and Pharisees, incited by the ongoing corruption introduced by earlier Hasmonean monarchs and the priesthood.[6] Only then can one begin to understand Queen Salome's full impact on the people.

Following Israel's hard-won independence, the Hasmonean monarchs ultimately realigned with wealthy Hellenists, siding once again with the Seleucid kingdom and generating further conflict. This disunity, a result of the combined centralized power of the king and High Priest, led to the rise of the Sadducees, who followed the more traditional line of centralized worship at the Temple in Jerusalem.

The Sadducees oversaw Temple offerings and the Gerousia, representing the priesthood and the wealthy, while the Pharisees interpreted the law on behalf of the common people. The Sadducees followed the Written Law strictly. They would not allow for any adaptations to help people cope with changing times, in contrast to the great sages, who taught the people to learn the law for themselves, which brought greater meaning to their lives.[7]

Additionally, the Sadducees did not believe in an afterlife. Instead, in their view, humans were in total control of their choices, for good or for evil, with no intervention from God. The soul perished with the body at death. There were no resulting rewards or punishments for living by a certain standard or following the laws of social or ethical conduct. Believing man to be the center of the universe, rather than God, the Sadducees mirrored the egocentric Greek model of values and pleasures.

The Sadducees and what they represented, in their break from the traditional descendant line of priests, created so much societal conflict that one group split off to become the Essene sect, located at Qumran on the southwest shores of the Dead Sea. The Essenes were associated with the Dead Sea Sect, who adhered to the position that there was a directly-descended priestly line based on the law and that the offices of high priest and king could not be combined.[8]

According to Philo and Josephus, the Essenes were about 4,000 in number, with settlements between Jericho and Ein Gedi. They maintained communal property. As an ascetic sect, they provided charity for people around the country. They practiced prayer, ritual purity, and cleanliness. Unlike the Sadducees, they believed in the immortality of the soul and absolute predestination through God.[9]

The third formal sect, the already-established Pharisees, studied and followed not only the literal written word of the law, but also the oral teachings—interpretations and under-standings of the law. As challenging new situations and conflicts arose, the Pharisees debated and clarified the law and brought it closer to the people. Earlier, the sages and the priest-scribes had helped the people understand how they could live within their times and circumstances; this same class of sages and scribes, in all likelihood, eventually became the Pharisees.

The Pharisees would come to believe that the Jews had the capacity to determine how to act rightly using a certain amount of free will, but at the same time, fate also cooperated in such actions. The people themselves were not entirely in control of their fate, but some higher divine power intervened to balance free will and fate. The role of the Written Law was to maintain social order and justice, thus creating harmony within the community.

When it came to the soul, the Pharisees believed that the good soul could attain immortality in an afterlife with its just rewards, and the wicked soul would suffer from eternal punishment.[10] The Pharisees' values focused on a humanistic model of interpreting the law—a more integrated and meaningful paradigm for the people to live by. The Sadducees, who held themselves separate from the population and focused on centralized ritual, created greater gaps or disparities among the people.

Alexander Janneus, a violent warrior-king, put many Pharisees to death and exiled the remainder to Alexandria. He then sought to maintain control in his role as both king and high priest through the remaining Sadducees. Into this sectarian situation came Queen Salome, who reversed her husband's decree. She brought the Pharisees back to Jerusalem to teach the people and to lead the Gerousia governance structure in place of the Sadducees.

Where there had once been conflict between the Pharisees and the people, now their influence grew under her rule, making her beloved by everyone and by those Pharisees who had been exiled. The Pharisees instituted social reform through the stabilization of an early Sanhedrin structure.

Queen Salome's leadership brought about the start of a new practice, integral to the value of knowledge and learning by the people. She brought in one of the greatest teachers of the time—Simeon ben Shatach, the Pharisee—to become head of the Great Council.

When asked to head the Council, Simeon ben Shatach tried to waive this responsibility by requesting that Judah ben Tabbai from Alexandria, Egypt, hold this position while Simeon ben Shatach would interpret issues according to the living law. From that point on, the early Sanhedrin would always be headed by dual leaders.[11]

The Sanhedrin and the earlier Gerousia both included a total of seventy-one members. The key role of the Gerousia had been the interpretation and teaching of the living law. Under the Hasmoneans, the Gerousia and later the Sanhedrin developed broader political roles.

Given the above, it made sense to create a leadership structure which functioned in pairs—one person to provide political governance and represent the group, the *Nasi* (Prince), and one known as the *Av Beit-Din* (Head of the Supreme Religious Court) to administer the interpretation of the law.[12]

Among the Gerousia's duties was to oversee implementation of faith-based learning for the people. For the Jews, the Oral Law was the basis of education, to be passed on informally through the family, from father to son. Over time, synagogues evolved, not only to gather people throughout the Greek diaspora to learn the teachings of the first five books of Moses, but also to share in the role of educating sons. Synagogues would eventually provide formal faith-based education and would also add secular subjects, such as reading, writing, and arithmetic similar to the Hellenistic schools. Participation in this schooling at the synagogue level was voluntary and was solely for younger children in these early times.[13]

The family's role in education might have influenced Simeon ben Shatach in 75 BCE to grant an exception to voluntary participation in education. Given a special class of orphaned boys sixteen years or older, he mandated that this group attend faith-based schooling.[14] Lacking fathers who could teach them, orphans still had the obligation to learn and to carry out the laws. This mandatory faith-based education originated in Israel and became the first seed of required schooling.

The value of learning would take a new direction toward formalized education for Jews in the wake of Queen Salome's reign. Had she not selected the Pharisees to be the dominant group to head the Gerousia, this might never have occurred. The Hellenist vision of education was centered on the individual, with the gymnasium becoming the primary source of training in pursuit of physical and intellectual education. This was a philosophy steeped in the egocentric pursuit of culture for the highest pleasure and good of the individual—not for the sake of God. For the Jews, the highest good was living in the light of God and faith—filtering knowledge and culture through the matrix of moral values and wisdom attained from an understanding of the Written and Oral Law.

It appears that the Jews adapted principles from the Hellenists to create a vision based on their own heritage, needs, and aspirations. Rather than allowing the Hellenists' gymnasia to attract wealthier Jews, was it not better to establish their own schools of learning? The creation of the gymnasium and its related secular programs possibly became not only a source of conflict, but also a competitive force pulling people away from the faith toward Hellenism. It was therefore logical for the Jews to create their own model of learning and education in order to teach and strengthen the essentials of the faith.

While the Sadducees might attend the gymnasia for the wealthy, the remainder of the Jewish population would have the same opportunity to attain education by choice through the synagogues. Eventually, academies developed beyond the model of the synagogue schools, functioning at a more advanced level. Academies would remain open to those who could afford them and had the time to continue their education. Here again, we see the early seeds of evolving educational institutions, reminiscent of higher schooling for the more serious and capable disciples.

Academies and synagogue schools of learning were available to all boys, rich or poor. This was an innovation for the time. While girls were not yet attending these voluntary faith-based schools, they were able to attend synagogue, thus shaping the values of all children through learning.

Although it might have been difficult for the poor to attend the more scholarly academies, some, in fact, did so. Was this not the first step to social and class mobility? Here was a mechanism whereby someone poor could become learned, be accepted by the aristocracy and, in that way, achieve a level of authority.

Education as an institution would remain voluntary in the synagogues and academies until 64 CE, when Joshua ben Gamala, a Second Temple High Priest, established the first ordinance that all boys beginning at age six or seven must attend mandatory educational programs in their synagogues. This requirement was established universally throughout Israel and the diaspora lands.[15]

Indeed, over the coming centuries, Jews would become literate, gaining new skills and experiencing social mobility, as distinct from other groups of people. Scholarship would become the fertile ground for the final canonization and preservation of the Hebrew Scriptures, thereby assuring the survival of the faith.

Chapter 16:
Shining the Light on the Golden Rule

E arlier ideological differences within the faith created extreme disunity among the people. The Jews, in their desire to preserve the faith, overthrew the Seleucids who had worked to destroy their belief system. They created their own independent nation under the Hasmonean rulers, who then merged the king and high priest positions into one. They saw the evolution of the two groups within the Sanhedrin—the Sadducees and Pharisees—who represented different classes and ideologies.

Queen Salome finally brought peace and unity to the land by working with the Pharisees and focusing on the people, but her reign ended in 67 BCE. After several of her sons took control and then lost the throne due to their own weaknesses, the Romans took control of Israel in 63 BCE. Eventually, Roman rule led to the destruction of the Second Temple in 70 CE and the subsequent dispersion of the Jews from Jerusalem.

The Jewish faith would only survive this onslaught because of a unifying set of values and institutions. When there is great internal divisiveness amongst a people based on ideology, a new set of cohesive values must emerge to fill the void. A learned Pharisee by the name of Hillel put forth the first of these enduring values. He would establish a new path for the Jews by interpreting the living law of God with compassion. He would lead with a new awareness of justice and mercy. He emphasized an institutionalization of faith and education in the synagogues that would be taught to the young and old alike. Academies would be available for older boys who wished to become scholars.

Hillel was the bridge for unifying the values of the Israelites, just as King Josiah had been earlier. Hillel was a humble man with a message that became pervasive throughout the teachings of the Jewish faith for almost two millennia. Yitzhak Buxbaum created a profile of the sage in *The Life and Teachings of Hillel,* one of the few books written about this man, referencing the leadership that Hillel brought to the Jews.

In the period leading up to Hillel's rise after the Romans conquered Israel, the Hasmonean ethnarchs would continue to rule the land until 37 BCE. Herod I became the first vassal Israelite king under Roman rule, from 37 BCE to 4 CE. He was not a true Israelite, nor from David's line. Herod was an Edomite from a conquered and converted area in the Idumean desert south of Jerusalem. He attempted to legitimize his Israelite lineage through his marriage to Miriam, a Hasmonean daughter of the monarchal line.[1]

Herod I, sometimes called Herod the Great, was a tyrannical king. At the onset of his reign, he killed many of the seventy-one members of the Sanhedrin, most of whom were Sadducees who had risen to power and were aligned with the former Hasmonean rulers following Queen Salome's death. Herod I allowed many of the Pharisees to live, however, including the great dual Nasi of the time—Shamaya and Avtalyon.[2]

Later, Herod I became fearful of the Pharisee sages and teachers and had many of them executed because he thought they were working to incite violent rebellion. Legend has it that Baba ben Buta, a reputed Pharisee elder during the time of Shamaya and Avtalyon, convinced Herod that his fellow Pharisees were not a threat, as the practice of religious freedom and teaching kept the population politically stable and would actually promote peace.[3]

In light of this prescient argument, Herod I realized his mistake. Baba ben Buta was able to convince him to restore the Temple to its former glory and to reinstate the Pharisee sages and teachers as religious leaders. Herod I began enlarging the Temple around 20 BCE and completed its restoration over the course of ten years. He also built one of the largest ports in the land of Israel at Caesarea on the Mediterranean and the great palace fortress of Masada on the southwest shore of the Dead Sea.

Today, the Wailing Wall in Jerusalem is one of the remaining retaining walls of the Temple Mount. The site represents the location of the original Second Temple. The al-Aqsa Mosque now stands on the southern end of the Mount. The Dome of the Rock, also located on the Mount, sits on the site where Abraham would have sacrificed his son Isaac but for God staying his hand. (Genesis 22:1–19)

Herod I also reinstated the Sanhedrin, giving it authority over religious activities but no inherent political power. He brought in two members of a prominent family, the sons of Bathrya, to head the Sanhedrin, thinking they would not be a threat to his position as they came from a region outside of Jerusalem. The sons of Bathrya were not great teachers, and during this time, the people lost touch with much of their knowledge of the living law.

After the sons of Bathrya, Herod I installed a scholar of the Hebrew Scriptures as the Nasi of the Sanhedrin. This was the sage Hillel. Herod perceived that Hillel, coming from outside

Jerusalem, would not pose a direct threat to his rule. Herod was again correct in this regard.

During the time that Hillel was Nasi, the Jews experienced great learning. Hillel set up his famous academy in Jerusalem which produced outstanding scholars and disciples. Hillel the Elder, as he was known, was active between 30 BCE and 10 CE. His teachings and reputation were so esteemed that four hundred years of Hillel's descendants continued as Nasi—Sanhedrin leaders.

Hillel originally came from Babylonia. He was a descendant of the Jews who had remained and grown in number after the exile. He had learned the living law but wanted to study a great deal more. Hillel traveled to Jerusalem so that he might enter the academy taught by Shamaya and Avtalyon, the revered sages and scholars.

Hillel, too poor to pay the daily entrance fee to the academy, demonstrated his passion for learning one cold winter evening. He climbed onto the roof of the academy to sit and listen to the teachers through the skylight and fell asleep. In the morning, the teachers noted that sunlight was not entering the study area as it should. When they looked up, they found a poor student sleeping on the roof, covered with snow. They determined that his thirst for knowledge of God and scriptures was so great that he should enter the academy.

What was so unique and beloved about Hillel? He was a patient, caring, and compassionate teacher, a scholar of the Torah, as well as the Hebrew Scriptures. His faith in the Lord and his vast love of learning had the greatest impact not only on the Jews, whether wealthy, common, or poor, but also on the non-Jewish community, many of whom were interested in learning the living law. He taught in parables, and his teaching framework was always to start from the perspective of the person asking when answering a question. No query was inappropriate or unimportant. His goal was for all people to learn to love God, love the Torah, and love the living law.

Even more important than Hillel's gift for teaching was his ability to create a unifying spiritual message for the people, which he expanded and solidified under Roman rule. This would ultimately help to transform the faith. The Jews had lived under foreign rule for hundreds of years; and even when they had run their nation-state independently under Hasmonean rule, factions still created conflict.

It took a master like Hillel to show everyone a way to reduce discord within the faith, with education being the vehicle for consistently conveying this message. Hillel carried Queen Salome's earlier work forward, and his humane and compassionate approach to the interpretation of the living law and its application became the enduring key to uniting the people.

Hillel was expert at cultivating the Oral Law, which helped adapt the Written Law to changing times. This adaptation and integration of the law into people's daily lives not only allowed them to live in accordance with their faith but ensured that the law remained flexible and relevant, keeping it alive and real for everyone. Laws and interpretations which do not adapt to the times become rigid, dogmatic, overly conservative, and meaningless over time.

For example, Hillel adapted the lighting of the candles over eight days in observance of the rededication of the Temple by Judah Maccabee, this to bring greater joy and relevance to the people. We still follow this tradition today during Hanukkah:

The Sages taught ... the basic mitzva of Hanukkah is each day to have a light kindled by a person, the head of the household, for themselves and their household ...

The [House of] Hillel says: On the first day one kindles one light, and from there on gradually increases the number of lights until, on the last day, they kindle eight lights.

Reason for the [House of Hillel] opinion: "one elevates to a higher level in matters of sanctity, and one does not downgrade."[4]

The more literal interpretation of the day was to light all eight candles on the first day, subtracting one each day until, on day eight, only one candle was left burning. Hillel decided that one light should be lit and added each day until all eight candles burned brightly on the last day. This would represent the greatest joy and hope to the people while under Roman oppression, by aspiring toward a higher level of sanctity each day.

Hillel expertly taught the Oral Law, but there was so much more to this beloved teacher and scholar. He would emphasize a God of righteousness and justice, as well as one that was loving, merciful, and forgiving. These attributes would, at times, seem to be paradoxical. If one came down too hard on the side of justice, all people who turned out to be sinful would suffer. Too much leniency and compassion, and there would be too little justice, which could undermine social order.

Hillel created a body of law and interpretation that balanced the paradox between justice and mercy—he could weigh all sides of an issue within the parameters of justice, then tip the scales in favor of mercy. His love of mankind, his ability to demonstrate patience, and his lovingkindness were foundational. He always erred on the side of compassion and peace.

Hillel emphasized the Golden Rule, which was at the heart of his teachings and decisions. This message is inherent throughout the Torah (Pentateuch) and Hebrew Scriptures as part of God's message. Hillel educated scholarly Jews, the common people, and non-Jews alike. He taught about "loving people" through the commandment "you shall love your neighbor as yourself" (Leviticus 19:18). A famous story about Hillel illustrates his approach.

A certain gentile once came to Hillel and said, "I'm ready to become a Jew, but only if you can teach me the whole Torah while I stand here on one foot." Hillel answered him, "what is hateful to you, don't do to your fellowman; that is the whole Torah, and the rest … is just a commentary. Go then and learn it!"[5]

When teaching the Golden Rule, Hillel first educated in the negative—how *not* to act upon others to avoid harm. With time, Jesus taught the Golden Rule in its positive form, "do unto others as one would have them do unto yourself"— treating others with the same respect and kindness that one would treat oneself and one's loved ones.

Hillel taught the Golden Rule to all, including those outside the faith, at a time of great conflict under Herod I's Roman rule. Hillel recognized the importance of living quietly and practicing kindness to minimize the chance of rebellion or violence, thereby ensuring that the people remained safe from harm. It was important to avoid clashes that could escalate into uprisings. Teaching the concept of the Golden Rule was an excellent way of emphasizing the principle of good relations in such an environment.

While Hillel's faith in God was at the core of all his teachings, it was his love of humanity that reigned. As Nasi, he would be responsible for the High Court of the Sanhedrin that interpreted the law, since Herod I had abolished the political role of this body. The intent of the living law of God was to protect the sanctity of life and to create social order through civil law principles. Hillel based his rulings and teachings on compassion and understanding for the people's needs, even as justice was rendered.

The following story illustrates Hillel's wisdom in avoiding longstanding harm and stigma to the children of certain types of marriages in ancient Alexandria.

> Jewish men in Alexandria, Egypt, would betroth women, but [sometimes] before they took the women to the bridal canopy to wed them, others came and snatched them away [to marry them]. The sages wanted to declare the children of such marriages illegitimate. But Hillel the Elder said to the Alexandrians: "Bring me your mother's marriage contract." When they brought it, he found written therein: "When thou shalt enter under the bridal canopy, be thou my wife, according to the law of Moses and Israel." And they did not declare their children illegitimate. (Bava Metzia 104a)[6]

Jewish marriage in that time had a waiting period of up to a year between the signing of the contract of betrothal and the actual ceremony that took place under the bridal canopy. The first stage was similar to today's engagement period, drafted up as a letter of intent. If another man spirited the bride away (which was not unusual) and later married under the bridal canopy, the children of that marriage might be considered illegitimate.

Unless a correct alternative decision was made, the resulting stigma to these innocent children in Alexandria would be onerous and unjust. Understanding the permanent injustice and humiliation which the children would feel, Hillel remedied this situation by rephrasing the marriage contract, the *ketubah,* that the Jews of Alexandria had devised in an earlier period.

Hillel's philosophy was in conflict with that of his fellow Pharisee, Shammai, who led his own academy and was the second dual Nasi for the Sanhedrin. Both Hillel and Shammai were proponents of the people, unlike the Sadducees who had focused on centralized ritual and interpretation based solely on the Written Law. But Shammai followed a stricter interpretation of the law than Hillel, and without the critical thinking or compassion required to integrate and adapt it to the needs of the people. Shammai's teaching was to interpret the law as stated, even in the face of changing times, an approach which demanded justice at all costs. In contrast, Hillel gave people meaningfulness in the law to help guide their daily lives.

Both academies taught the Hebrew Scriptures and secular subjects such as reading, writing, and mathematics, but espoused competing versions of the Written Law, with Hillel's approach being more humanistic, Shammai's more legalistic. Discussing points of the law is a form of debate, but within the matrix of values that the Jewish way of life taught, both interpretations come into play, taking both sides into account before reaching a final conclusion. Future rabbis, who were the descendants of Pharisee teachers, determined that Hillel's approach was the correct one and that his teachings would become the foundation for the faith. The rabbis would later write that Shammai's rigid teachings would become a notation of the past—a set of interpretations and decisions which had become outmoded.

Hillel's interpretation of the law for both scholars and common people provided an understanding and example of right living during conflict and violence under Roman rule. Because of Hillel's leadership, the Golden Rule became a way of life—a means of faith-driven living even in the face of Roman oppression.

In the tradition of the Pharisees, Hillel taught the immortality of the soul and that reward for living a good life would come after death. Therefore, during the cruel and violent times of the Romans, the people should not expect reward in this life, but their sufferings indeed were meaningful. Man did not go to a netherworld or underworld if he learned to live a good and caring life—if one followed the Golden Rule and studied Torah. In times of conflict with the Romans, there could be hope in this world. Hillel infused this spirit of hope in the people. According to him, the way for Judaism was to follow the teachings of the Lord and to create one's own pathway on earth, knowing that the reward was in the hereafter.

Over four centuries, Hillel's descendants would retain the leadership role of Nasi in the Sanhedrin, which endured beyond the destruction of the Temple. The most significant group included Hillel the Elder, his son, Shimon ben Hillel, and his grandson Gamaliel I as the last Nasi before 70 CE. Rabban Johanan ben Zakkai, who was Hillel's youngest disciple, became the first Nasi following the destruction, and Rabban Gamaliel II, Hillel's great-grandson, held the position following Johanan ben Zakkai.[7]

Joshua ben Gamala was not a direct descendent of Hillel but was High Priest in 64 CE, just prior to the Temple's destruction. He is noted for establishing the ordinance expanding universal education by requiring a synagogue school in each community for all boys from the age of six and older. Mandatory attendance ensured schooling in the faith, the living law, and secular subjects such as reading, writing, and arithmetic for those in Israel, as well as those living in the Greek-Roman and Babylonian diaspora.[8]

It was now required that children be taught the living law as well as literacy and skills for a secular world. Such education would insure a growing institution for the survival of Judaism after the destruction of the Temple. It recognized that children were critical for transferring values involving the living law from one generation to the next.

Families provided education for girls in the home and the synagogue exposed them to Torah readings. Rich, poor, men, women, and children were able to attend synagogue. These proceedings exposed all the people to learning, helping to advance the value of knowledge and education in women over time, and creating the connection that would strengthen the bonds of faith in the home. At a time when women were generally not included in any educational systems, this participation in learning would eventually lead to the emergence of their equality in society.

Ultimately, Hillel taught a critical value. Love of God centered in the heart informs the first five Commandments. Hillel's teachings were heart-centered, emphasizing mercy and lovingkindness. The mind is focused on learning, knowledge, and understanding. The living law was meant to guide us in balancing justice with wisdom, while leading with the heart through the spirit of compassion.

It seems that mind and heart, knowledge and faith cannot be isolated but must be integrated and unified. The Hebrew Scriptures combine mind-centered justice with heart-centered mercy. When given the choice, Hillel would always lead from the heart.

Today, the value of finding the locus of our humanity is all important. We must practice it in our daily actions in a world full of conflict. In searching for our humanity, we must lead with those values which are life-affirming as still taught today in the Torah and Hebrew scriptures.[9]

Hillel's teachings through his disciples would eventually allow the faith of the Jews to formally evolve into Judaism and survive the diaspora after the destruction of the Second Temple in 70 CE. Between the first and second centuries, the Torah and Hebrew Scriptures would be codified, stabilized, and ultimately closed to change for future generations.[10] The youngest disciple of Hillel, Johanan ben Zakkai, began organizing an understanding of the Oral Law, after the destruction of the Temple. The Babylonian rabbis would further advance the codification of the Oral Law through their creation of the Talmud.

Hillel's teachings also preceded those of Jesus, who taught lovingkindness, the Golden Rule, mercy, forgiveness, and free will. Jesus taught others to help the poor and the oppressed, to heal the sick, and to create God's kingdom on earth. Hillel's greatest years of teaching and leadership in Jerusalem took place between 30 BCE and 10 CE. Jesus died in 30 CE. Their paths crossed at least in time; and one might think that it was possible for Hillel's teachings, if not through him, then through his disciples, to have influenced Jesus.

According to the Gospels, Jesus taught in the synagogues of the Galilee for years before arriving in Jerusalem. Jesus's messages led from the heart through his faith in the Lord. His message of the Golden Rule was to strive toward peace for humanity during times of intense conflict, similar to Hillel's values. Jesus's ideas would allow for the universal spread of monotheism.

In deference to the messages of Hillel and Jesus, who taught humanity to both lead from the heart and seek out peace, is it possible that mankind could aspire toward a common set of values? Is there a way for us to begin dissolving our differences between faiths by focusing more on our similarities? Can we overcome our disparities through a shared set of life-affirming values? Disunity from within leads to decline unless humanity can find a way to transcend these divisions while embracing a unified vision.

Chapter 17:
The Value of War

U nder the leadership of Hillel, values began to develop that helped people cope with life under violent rule. We will digress in this chapter to explore the consequences of war as an opposing value and then return to the historical progression of the value of peace.

When rulers hold absolute political and religious power, they often concentrate that power and misuse it, which leads to tyranny and violence. Sectarian ideologies begin to emerge, generating conditions for conflict or rebellion. Social cohesion weakens and produces conditions for new and emergent sets of unifying and transcending values. Such values can either focus on goodness or emphasize the opposite—greater oppression.

Political systems of today, including Western-style democracy, are open to endless conflicts arising from differing underlying ideologies. These can prevent effective decision making and bring about strategic gridlock. Greater diversity—economic, ethnic, and religious—generates new problems requiring innovative solutions. These tensions and their resulting inertia can create a void. What is needed is a new vision to help society enlarge its outlook and come together to solve and move past these issues. If we, or any society, constructively push forward toward greater freedom of the human spirit, we can successfully progress toward a growing global community. If the wrong values fill this void, society can tip the scale backward toward rigidity, abuse, and oppression.

Before we can reach a paradigm shift, we come to a crossroads. People within a nation decide which path to follow. Our values should guide us in the right direction. We can choose the open, courageous path toward goodness, or the closed, violent path of fear and hatred. But once chosen, political, economic, and religious structures begin to lock in, or institutionalize our values, making them more permanent.

In societies espousing violence, fear, and hatred, these structures can constrict people so tightly that it becomes difficult to break out, even for those who desire peace and economic well-being. People have created unity at the expense of others for millennia. It is easier to deflect anger by projecting hatred against specific groups than it is to create unity through acts of harmonious goodness and cooperative achievement. Such is the case with fundamentalist Islam today.

The political Islam of the Arab Middle East is extremely complicated and nuanced. We try to understand it through the eyes of the Western world and its developed democracies. Our world is one that is open, with freedoms we take for granted, and is based on regard for individual rights and the dignity of the human spirit. It is a world in which the rule of law protects the rights of individuals and promotes social order. When we look at the world from this vantage point, we come to the belief that our way of living is the right way for all people.

There is a risk that oppressive systems of governance will develop when central rulership manages society using rigid religious philosophies instead of secular rule of law. Such monarchs, dictators, and leaders use their own rules of law to control their nations and resources.

People who live in such systems may not feel oppressed. Instead, these societies can appear functional, even when closed to long-term human development, economic gains, and security for their people. Muslim fundamentalism is one such system in which some children become suicide bombers, women are hidden and uneducated, and entire populations live hopeless, impoverished lives. Yet, in their hearts and minds, they passionately believe in the righteousness of their chosen path, because they are following God's will as they understand it.

There is no better example of how oppression and the value of war become acceptable than to look at it through the lens of the Ottoman Empire, whose leaders were responsible for a genocide which took the lives of over 1.5 million Christian Armenians in this Muslim society. A point of reference is the deeply moving history which Peter Balakian tells in *The Burning Tigris—The Armenian Genocide and America's Response.*

The Turks were originally a nomadic ethnic group from the steppes of Central Asia who converted to Islam and became the second largest Muslim group in history. By 1453, these Turkish forces, referred to as the Ottomans, had invaded Asia Minor up to the borders of Persia and captured Constantinople, then the seat of the Byzantine Empire, renaming it Istanbul. They then crossed the Bosporus and conquered the Balkans and southeastern Europe. They successfully invaded Europe until they were stopped at Vienna. After defeating the Mamluks in 1516, they continued to conquer most of North Africa, extending their reach to what is today northern Algeria.[1]

From the time of that conquest, the Turks controlled the area known today as the European Balkan states, Greece and Macedonia, Hungary, Turkey, Armenia, Lebanon, Syria, Israel, Iraq, Iran, Egypt, and much of North Africa. By 1877, the Russo-Turkish War inspired many of the Balkan peoples, who were primarily Christian, to fight for their rights and autonomy while under Muslim rule.

Serbia, Montenegro, Bosnia, Herzegovina, and Bulgaria all sought independence from the Ottomans. Serbia, Montenegro, Bulgaria, and Romania became either autonomous, independent, or operated under autonomous administration within the Ottoman Empire. Ottoman leaders then transplanted Muslim refugees from the Balkan areas that had won independence or autonomy, through mass migration, to the eastern Anatolian (Turkish) regions where the Armenian population was mainly located.

While independence and autonomy had been won, many of the Christian Balkan lands were eventually returned to the Caliph, Sultan Abdul Hamid II. His forces then retaliated against targeted Christian populations within the Empire. This war against Balkan independence was referred to as *jihad*.[2]

Coming close on the heels of the Balkan rebellions, the caliph considered all Christians, including the Christian Armenian population, potential enemies within the empire. They already had the status of *dhimmi*: tolerated but second class.[3] As Muslim refugees entered the Armenian provinces, the government sanctioned violent Muslim uprisings targeting the Christian Armenian population.

Most Armenians lived in the central, western, and northwestern regions of Anatolia and the provinces of Armenia and Van in western Turkey. When we think of Mount Ararat, we think of the Armenians who lived in this region for centuries: farmers, tradesmen, artisans, financiers, travelers, scholars, physicians, and pharmacists. They were Christians with a Protestant-style work ethic.

Following the settlement of the Balkan Muslim population into these regions, the Armenians, using political activism, requested human rights improvements from the caliph under Muslim law. In 1890, they protested heavy taxation. In response, the sultan authorized the Muslim population to massacre Armenian men, women, and children. This was the first step in the elimination of the Armenian population.[4]

In 1895, Sultan Abdul Hamid II was again responsible for the slaying of Armenians, over 200,000 throughout the Empire.[5] The Armenians had circulated another petition and rallied on behalf of their human rights in the capital of the Ottoman Empire, Istanbul. In response, Muslims massacred Armenians throughout the city. This then set off a new wave of violence and carnage in the Armenian regions, from Istanbul to the easternmost province of Van.[6]

It is important to understand how such anti-Christian hostility has evolved over the ages. Our societies surround us with values that have been shaped through religious beliefs, political structures, and economics, which then converge in ways to create historical events. Jihad, emphasizing the value of war, creates a different history from one based on the value of peace. Walid Phares, a professor and expert on Middle Eastern studies and ethnic and religious conflict, explains this history in his book *Future Jihad.*

Phares begins with a review of Muslim history. In the year 610 CE, the Prophet Muhammad first received the word of God, Allah, through the Archangel Gabriel. He continued to receive revelations from God for twenty-three years.[7] The Arabs had for centuries been mostly nomadic, tribal people, wandering the desert lands of the Arabian Peninsula. The desert's harsh conditions frequently prompted internecine conflict among the various tribes. Muhammad's prophecies and revelations united these tribes for the first time in history.

Muhammad defined the foundations of Islam with five central pillars of faith: *shahada* (witness, testimony of faith); *salat* (prayer); *zakat* (charity, almsgiving); *swam* (fasting); and *hajj* (pilgrimage to Mecca). Each pillar incorporates elements of Judaism and Christianity that developed in a unique fashion under this new and later monotheistic faith, and Muslims are expected to observe each of these in the conduct of their daily lives.

Some have accused Muslims of elevating jihad to a so-called "sixth pillar" of the faith, the observation of which would come into force if Muslim authorities issued a *fatwa* (edict) calling the faithful to war.

To promote unity amongst nomadic and warring tribes, who at the time lived in and around Mecca, Muhammad formulated the concept of a Muslim nation-state, the *umma*, to bring the tribes together. In 622 CE, the tribes left Mecca and traveled north to Medina in the Arabian Peninsula, then organized themselves to return and successfully conquer Mecca between the years 628 to 630 CE.[8] These settlements in the Arabian Peninsula comprised the core of the Muslim state.

According to Phares, the act of jihad was an "effort at the service of the *umma*, the state, and Allah. Jihad is a call to mobilize the resources, energies, and capabilities of individuals in the service of a higher cause triggered by an order [fatwa] given by a legitimate authority. It is a theological force that cannot be canceled except by a legitimate authority."[9]

Over time, Muslims would control the entire Arabian Peninsula. Eastern orthodox Christians and Jews unwilling to convert to Islam were killed. Four years after Muhammad's death, all existing non-Muslim groups had essentially been wiped out.

After Muhammad, four *Rashidun* Caliphs (Righteous Caliphs), also known as the Patriarchs of Islam—Abu Bakr, Umar, Uthman, and Ali, took control between the years of 632 and 661 CE. When Caliph Umar became head of the Muslim nation, he declared jihad on the surrounding empires. He first brought all of the Arabian Peninsula under the control of the Muslims. In one of the greatest battles in Muslim history, he conquered and took over the territory between what is today Syria and Jordan from the Byzantine Empire.[10]

The men who fought in this region did so in the name of God for the *umma*. A smaller number of men with a fanatical passion for their faith had defeated the Roman Empire. The will to fight and win was seared into their souls. As a result, the empire of Islam, now known as the caliphate, expanded and thrived.

Following this conquest of Syrian lands, the caliph declared jihad on the lands of Palestine and Egypt. He rationalized this as a defensive move. However, in conquering these lands, the Muslims were strategically becoming aggressors in order to expand their empire beyond the Arabian Peninsula. Eventually, the Rashidun Caliphs extended the caliphate to include what is today northern Libya, Egypt, Israel, Syria, Iraq, and western Iran.

In the midst of this expansion, a conflict ensued as to whether the caliph who ran the state should be someone who ably followed the law of Muhammad (*Sunna*) or a direct descendant of Muhammad (*Shia*). Sunni caliphs ruled according to the law through Abu Bakr, Umar, and Uthman. The nation-state became the caliphate, headed by a caliph. Ali, the last of the first four Rashidun Caliphs, was the son-in-law of the Messenger of Allah, and the first Shia to rule through the direct-descent line. He died in a bloody battle between Sunnis and Shias.

The Islamic schism stemmed from two divergent concepts of who would wield authority. Sunnis maintained that rulership depended upon the ability of the ruler. Shia demanded that it reside in a descendant of Muhammad. This division, which continues today, became the principal basis for internal civil strife among the Arab Muslims. Historically, most Muslims have been Sunni, which is the case even today, while Shia were and remain in the minority.[11]

Those advocating for choosing the ruler by ability, the Sunni, gained the leadership of the empire. The Shia, over time, developed a divergent theology and settled in areas that we are familiar with today: Iran, Azerbaijan, and eastern Arabia. Variants of the Shia faith have developed over the centuries, including that of the Druze, whose belief system incorporates elements of Gnosticism, Christianity, Zoroastrianism, Buddhism, Hinduism, and other beliefs, and who have an esoteric interpretation of scripture.

Eventually, regional efforts to enlarge the caliphate expanded into a global jihad. Personal efforts in support of jihad are part of a communal effort which serves to enlarge the Islamic umma. Personal jihad is at the service of, and in preparation for, a wider, ultimate jihad.

Islam divides the world into two territories: *dar al-Islam* (House of Peace) and *dar al-Harb* (House of War). When lands were conquered in the name of Allah for the umma, these fell under *dar al-Islam*. Once a territory was conquered, the next step was to assimilate the people. So-called "People of the Book," Jews and Christians, were subordinated into second-class status; others were either converted to Islam or eliminated. This forced assimilation ensured the successful administration of the empire. People were required to follow Shari'a, the body of Islamic law. All other systems of laws were eliminated. Muslim rulers could collect taxes and ensure domination over conquered nations. Once an individual has converted to Islam, practicing any other religion marks that individual as an apostate—*murtad*, subject to execution.

The historical development of the Muslim nation carried an extremely powerful and passionate message for its people. It was an integrated theocracy of faith institutionalized through its political systems and the economics of conquest. Once a region had become part of the caliphate, it was considered to be under Islamic rule in perpetuity, even if that land was conquered by another group at a later date. The passion for fighting on behalf of God was a powerful calling for many, creating one of the strongest and most resourceful armies.

Islam recognized conquered Jews and Christians as "People of the Book," since both the Hebrew Scriptures and the Bible preceded the Qur'an, and Moses and Jesus preceded the Prophet Muhammad. As the newest religion to have received the divine word, Islam considered itself to have superseded all other faiths. Therefore, conquered Jews and Christians, as people of the Book, could keep their faiths, but only as second-class citizens—*dhimmis*. If they refused to accept this status, they were subject to ethnic genocide.

Until the time of the Crusades in 1099 CE, dhimmi groups were very much in a minority in lands conquered by the Muslims. Dhimmis, as second-class citizens, had to pay a higher tax, the *jizya*, because of their lower status. This tax was often meant to be oppressive. Dhimmis could not hold government positions, had to wear different clothes, and were not permitted to serve in the armed forces. They had to walk on the left side of the street and live in segregated areas. The goal was to pressure these minorities into converting to Islam through submission and humiliation.

Attitudes toward and treatment of the dhimmi came under the authority of the caliph and could change at any time. If, in his determination, it was expedient for them to continue to live under this status, it was permitted. If in his view it did not serve the caliphate, Christians and Jews lost their rights and were left at the mercy of the Muslim population. Muslims would quickly incite violence against the dhimmis, inflicting destruction, theft of property, mass murders, and even genocide.

In 661 CE, the Sunni Caliphate of the Umayyad dynasty arose. Its Muslim capital moved to Damascus and its army enlarged the empire to include Persia, northwest India, and central Asia as well as Algeria, Morocco, and Spain. In 750 CE, the Sunni Abbasid caliph and his armies conquered the Umayyads and moved the capital city to Baghdad in order to attain greater alignment with Persian culture. Under both dynasties, the caliph was both the political and religious head of the caliphate.

Moving forward in time, the Catholic Church under the direction of Pope Urban II initiated the First Crusade against the Muslim world in 1095, eventually conquering Jerusalem and taking back the holiest city of the Christian world. For the first time, Muslims were on the defensive rather than the offensive. The Christian world was also on a "holy crusade" in the name of One God. Its goal was to free the land of Palestine, Christianity's spiritual capital, not to eliminate the entire caliphate.

Genghis Khan, the leader of the Mongols, ultimately conquered the lands of Mesopotamia in the thirteenth century and decimated the Arab empire. He burned Baghdad to the ground. According to Walid Phares, this was the nadir of the Arab-centered caliphate. When the Egyptian dynasty of the Mamluks conquered the Mongols and the Christians and gained control of Palestine and Jerusalem, the Muslim world once again saw that jihad was the savior of Islam from both the Christian crusaders and the pagan Mongols.

After the Ottoman Turks conquered the Byzantine Empire and the Mamluks, they became the new "custodians of the faith and the umma."[12] The head of the Ottoman Empire, the Sunni Sultan, acquired the title of Caliph, ruler of the Caliphate, along with the authority to call for jihad to expand, yet again, the empire through ongoing conquest and occupation.

The Ottomans inherited a caliphate composed of approximately fifty percent Muslims and fifty percent members of other religious faiths, most of whom were Christians and Jews living in Palestine and Arab countries. It included those lands throughout the diaspora, referred to in modern times as Turkey, Greece, and the Balkans. Dhimmitude changed under this new empire. It was impractical to continue forcing everyone to convert to Islam as in the earlier caliphate.

A new version of dhimmitude took hold in non-Muslim communities, headed by a leader who became a direct agent of the regional Ottoman governors. These non-Muslim leaders were expected to follow the rules and orders of the caliph or sultan. These regions were split into administrative areas called *millets*.[13]

Phares notes that many Middle Eastern experts say that Islam under the Ottoman Caliphate liberalized Christians and Jews as People of the Book. Liberal Muslims say it was a system of collaboration that better organized control of the empire. However, the reality was that dhimmitude by any other name was still dhimmitude. Non-Muslims remained second-class citizens under Islamic rule and their safety, involvement in society, and protections were subject to the whims of the caliph.

This background provides context for the actions by the Ottoman caliphs against Christians within their land in modern times. In 1909, most of the Christian population of Bosnia, Herzegovina, and Bulgaria, considered dhimmis or infidels by the ruling Muslims, once again rose up against the Ottomans in the First Balkan War, and declared their independence from the Islamic caliphate. These nation-states became annexed to Christian Austria.

Around this time, a highly nationalistic group called the Young Turks came into power. Sultan Abdul Hamid II was caliph, but the Young Turks felt he was weak and that the empire was disintegrating, triggered by the rebellions of the Balkan states. They placed the Sultan in solitary confinement and in his place, installed his son, Mohammed V, as sultan and caliph—but in name only. The Young Turks then set up an immense bureaucracy to rule the empire, eventually supported by the institution of Shari'a.[14]

The immediate result of this First Balkan War was that the Young Turks scapegoated the Christian Armenian population in the region of Adana, in south central Anatolia near the Mediterranean Sea. The Adana Massacres resulted in the murder of 15,000 to 20,000 Armenians. Turkish Muslims raped and killed women and children and plundered the Armenians' wealth. The amount of destruction, poverty, and disease created by this massacre was directly related to the dhimmi status of those persecuted.[15]

The Second Balkan War occurred between 1912 and 1913. The Turks lost 70 percent of the Balkans to Austria. In 1914, the Armenians once again initiated requests for reforms, this time supported by European allies. This action would trigger the final genocide of the Armenian Christians.[16]

In 1914, the Ottoman Empire entered World War I on the side of the Germans. The Young Turks further established a bureaucratic political machine to exterminate the Armenians. War provided the cover. By the end of the year, the Young Turks had created a so-called "Ten Commandments" document, a secretly developed blueprint for the Armenian genocide.[17] Eyewitness accounts place one of that century's first genocides at the feet of the Ottoman Empire.

In May 1915, the Young Turks established the Temporary Law of Deportation. In conjunction with military and quasi-military leaders, the Young Turks recruited and organized bands of criminals to orchestrate the deportation of the Armenians. They ordered this massacre as a "holy war," with the caliph declaring a fatwa against the Armenians.[18]

While the Temporary Law of Deportation did not specifically mention Armenians, it targeted any group suspected of espionage, treason, or sedition. The Armenians became the scapegoats under this new law, which legitimized massacres of a minority people of faith. In time, the Temporary Law of Deportation turned into the Temporary Law of Deportation and Confiscation. This allowed for the plundering of all wealth and personal belongings of the Armenians.[19]

Muslim Turks massacred Armenians in their homes— men, women, and children. Hundreds of thousands who survived were shipped by train in cattle cars to towns in western Turkey and Syria, key waystations. Others were forced to march in the searing sun to their deaths. Those who made it to Syrian destinations were sent into slave labor, concentration or refugee camps, sold into slavery, or ordered on death marches. Starvation, rape, disease, plunder, and violence were rampant. Muslims opened mass graves for the Armenian dead.

This horror and scourge to humanity ultimately led to the deaths of 1.5 million Christian Armenians. To this day, the Turks will not formally recognize or admit this genocide for which they were directly responsible under Ottoman rule. Henry Morgenthau, Sr., the American ambassador to the Ottoman empire, chronicled these events in *Ambassador Morgenthau's Story—A Personal Account of the Armenian Genocide.*[20]

Much of the genocide was concentrated in the city of Van, in eastern Turkey near the Russian border. There, according to eyewitness accounts from two American nurses, Muslim Turks massacred over 55,000 people.[21] In May 1914, Leslie Davis, US Consul to the ancient city of Harput, in the central plains of Anatolia, witnessed attacks and deportations of the Armenian population and tried to save what lives he could by allowing Armenians to take shelter within the walls of the protected consulate.[22]

With several witnesses, Davis also toured the region of Lake Göeljük, located at the head of the Euphrates River, in 1915. There he found at least 10,000 slaughtered and mutilated Armenians. Bodies and skeletons were strewn individually and in masses in the lake, in the hills and the valleys surrounding the lake. Bodies were tossed facedown onto beaches and buried in the sand. Davis forwarded this eyewitness account of the local area genocide, sanctioned by the Ottoman Empire and its Turkish government, through diplomatic channels to the US Ambassador to the Ottoman Empire, Henry Morgenthau, and other government officials.[23]

The Ottomans' methods of genocide would presage the slave labor and concentration camps that the Nazis used to exterminate over six million Jews in the Holocaust during World War II. The destruction of the Jews officially started with the 1935 Nuremberg Laws, which legitimized discrimination against Jews "for the protection of German blood and German honor." In 1942, top German officials at the Wannsee Conference developed a confidential blueprint for eliminating the Jews.[24] How did one set of values based on war help shape a second society's values within the same generation?

In the early 1880s, Kaiser Wilhelm II, Emperor of Germany and King of Prussia, began sending German officers to rebuild the Ottoman Empire's corrupt and ill-equipped army, providing needed support and military equipment. Over time, Prussian officers ran entire Turkish divisions.[25]

The Kaiser's true aim was to partner with the Ottoman Empire to gain access to its oil reserves.

By 1888, Deutsche Bank had established a subsidiary in Turkey, the Anatolia Railway Company, and constructed a railroad terminating in Ankara. The Ottoman sultan recognized that the eastern Mesopotamian provinces of the empire held enormous oil reserves, and that the Ottoman Empire was not in a position to develop its own oil infrastructure. Through an alliance with Germany, the Sultan would benefit from such explorations.

Consequently, the Sultan partnered with the Germans to build a railway from Ankara to the Mesopotamian provinces, first ending in Baghdad and later continuing on to Basra in the Persian Gulf. This became the Baghdad Railway, which also fell under the auspices of the Anatolia Railway Company. The railway's point of origin was Berlin. This concession granted Germany the oil and mineral rights within twenty kilometers of either side of the railroad, allowing Germany to gain control over unexploited oil reserves. Oil became the economic driver to fuel new technology development in the Industrial Age.[26]

By March 1914, high-ranking German officers commanded key positions in the Ottoman army.[27] These German leaders, in partnership with the Young Turks and the caliph, were responsible for approving and utilizing their resources and railway technology to transport hundreds of thousands of Armenians to their deaths in eastern concentration or refugee camps. The Germans, who owned the Baghdad Railway Company, orchestrated these expulsions. German workers employed by the railway company witnessed the attacks and deportations.[28]

Laws that legitimized the killing of Armenians, secret plans to exterminate the Christian population, massacres, plundering, mass killings, and deportations all originated with the Ottoman Empire. The Young Turks' plans concerning the Armenian population—trains for deportation, concentration camps, death marches, and slave labor camps—all were coordinated with the Germans, who were complicit in the Ottoman Empire's intentions to exterminate the Armenian people. This was one of the first genocides of the twentieth century.

Jihad embodies the value of war. It is embedded within a matrix of theocracy and cultural mores. None of the five pillars speaks of war, conquest, or hatred. But those who seek justification for territorial expansion or subjugation of others can find it in this distorted definition of jihad.

It may be tempting to write off Ottoman empire-building and the associated genocide of the Armenian population as ancient history. But in fact, the Ottoman Caliphate was one of the most powerful modern empires. It existed until 1923, five years after the end of World War I, when the Allies finally dismantled it. Only then did the United Kingdom and the other Entente Powers officially cease their state of war against the Ottoman Empire.

Worse yet, in less than one generation, jihad returned to the Arab Middle East. Evil in the name of jihad has become pervasive once again, finding its expression in terrorism, civil war, genocide, chemical warfare, torture, rape, sexual slavery, and extreme poverty, all for the sake of oil and power.

In Arab lands, wealth from oil resources went to the small percentage of family and friends linked to dictators, monarchs, or leaders. If there was risk of rebellion, leaders dispensed money to people as entitlements to stave off uprisings, but most individuals were left without real jobs or any hope of supporting a family. The people of the poorest nations were left completely impoverished. Rulers and dictators partnered with imams and paid them to oversee the teaching of the faith, which helped keep the population in line. Greed and a quest for power created allies in maintaining brutal autocrats in positions of authority.

Eight or more different jihadist groups with sectarian ideologies were developed based on beliefs within Arab Middle Eastern nations. War and evil emerged as a way of life, catalyzing the creation of the Islamic State of Iraq and Syria (ISIS), whose leaders believe themselves destined to establish a new version of the caliphate. Extremist groups and Arab leaders within many Middle Eastern countries continue to target the remnants of their Jewish and Christian populations.

Once the value of war is embedded in religious doctrine through Shari'a, it is hard to reverse. Times may change and the topographical map for jihad may shift, based on what the West perceives as terrorism, but this value has been perpetuated for centuries.

Islamist extremists see their fight as "good and righteous" within their understanding of the faith. This is why it is so hard to understand their actions from a Western point of view. What we see as senseless terrorism is for zealots a passionately embraced calling underlain by an entrenched and rigid religious doctrine.

Some fear for their lives should they try to break out of the system. Others have no desire to break out, even if they are free to do so. Many who have become initiated to the fight see this as an honorable and passionate cause in the name of God, with their rewards not to be had in this life, but in a glorious afterlife.

Western democracy must come to grips with the significance of this worldview. These values, which date back to the seventh century, have been carried forth into recent history, and are now being played out in today's battlegrounds of war, nuclear threats, and acts of terrorism. We must recognize that if there is to be peace, not only must the killing stop, but the values must change. New values must support and protect human life, compel people to act compassionately toward their fellow man, create an environment which advances the rights of women, and inspire a willingness of leaders to accept all peaceful religious faiths.

Chapter 18:
The Value of Peace

Sometimes war is necessary, as is the case when defending one's land or upholding certain ideals. Such events have occurred throughout history. War turns evil when autocratic rulers use their power to destroy entire groups of people for their individual purposes. This was the case when the Ottomans slaughtered the Christian Armenian population. But ruthless leaders seeking control are not the only causes of war. Sectarianism can also cause devastation, leaving the field open for stronger forces to bring down weaker (or weakened) entities and nation-states. The Romans and Jews fought in the land of Israel under just such circumstances. In spite of this, Jews, who value peace, once again found a way to create unity.

Herod I died in 4 BCE, soon after he rebuilt the Second Temple. Within a decade, Roman procurators oversaw the land of Israel, which they called the province of Judaea. But a succession of descendants of King Herod I actually ruled the land. Growing rebellions and violence between factions eventually led to the First Jewish War against the Romans beginning in 66 CE. This further divided the Jews.

Contrary to prevailing attitudes of the day, Hillel's teachings continued to resonate with his disciples. Synagogues grew and schools for children developed. The values of compassion, hope, and peace would become the wellspring of resilience that the Jews needed to recover from yet another disaster.

Hillel's youngest disciple, Johanan ben Zakkai, was responsible for saving and rebuilding the faith after the destruction of the Second Temple. Where others sowed only extreme division and conflict, he represented the contrary— the value of peace. To understand his role as a leader, we must first comprehend the internecine conflicts taking place in Israel at the time.

The First Jewish War occurred between 66 and 73 CE. This was a period of great disunity among religious and social groups.[1] Significant differences already existed between the Pharisees, Sadducees, Essenes, and early Christians. Then, starting in the Galilee region north of Judaea, additional splinter groups of Jews rose up in a series of revolts against Rome's violent oppression and taxation.

The groups behind these uprisings were the Zealots, the freedom fighters, and the young rebels. The Zealots were for war; the Pharisees were for peace. Eventually, the grip of Roman oppression would become so grave that more and more people favored war. Due to Roman strength, the outcome would clearly be disastrous. The young rebels initiated uprisings in the region of the Galilee, but eventually their focus shifted to Jerusalem, where they combined efforts with the Zealots and a group of freedom fighters from Idumaea. Ultimately, Rome destroyed Jerusalem and the Temple. The center of faith was lost.

Even after the destruction of the Temple, a group of rebels continued to resist in the outpost fortress of Masada. The Romans fought these rebels for years. In 73 CE, when it was inevitable that they would lose this fight, the rebels committed suicide rather than be captured and enslaved.[2]

The Second Jewish War occurred between the years 115 and 117 CE throughout the Roman Empire, notably in Egypt as well as areas of North Africa. Ethnic differences among Jews, Romans, and Hellenists brought on these conflicts. The Alexandrian Jews were essentially decimated by the Romans during this period.[3]

The Third War, better known as the Bar Kochba revolt, was fought between 132 and 135 CE. Hadrian, the Roman emperor, attempted to rebuild Jerusalem, renaming it Aelia Capitolina, with plans for a new temple to honor Jupiter, head of the Roman pantheon. Bar Kochba led a religious war against such idolatry. After the Romans defeated the Jews again, Hadrian banished them from Judaea and officially changed the name of the province to Syria Palaestina, referring to the ancient enemies of the Jews, the Philistines, in an attempt to obliterate the connection between the land and the Jewish nation.[4] After almost 2,000 years of history, but for a small remnant of Jews, the land of Israel no longer existed for its people.

During the First Jewish War in 68 CE, it became clear to Hillel's youngest disciple, Johanan ben Zakkai, that the Jews would lose to the Romans. The Roman armies were too strong. His compassion was for those suffering amidst death and destruction. If Jerusalem and the Temple were destroyed, which was inevitable, how would the Jews sustain their faith?[5] Johanan ben Zakkai became obsessed with the notion that he needed to do something to assure the future survival of the faith. His would be the pathway of peace.

Johanan ben Zakkai was the youngest of all the learned disciples in the academy of Hillel. He would become the father of the faith for future generations after the destruction of the Temple, such was his level of great learnedness compared to Hillel's other students. Herein follows a story about Hillel's eighty disciples, the greatest of whom was [J]onatan ben Uzziel, and the least or youngest, [J]ohanan ben Zakkai.[6]

> *At the hour of Hillel's passing all his disciples gathered in the room where he lay on his bed, but Yohanan ben Zakkai, who also came, did not go in. Noticing his absence, Hillel asked them, "Where is Yohanan?"*
>
> *"He's just outside," they told him, "standing at the doorway."*
>
> *"Let him come in," said Hillel, "he's worthy."*
>
> *When Yohanan came in, Hillel said to them, "The least among you is a father of wisdom and will be a father of generations; as to the greatest among you all, how much more so!" And he said to them further, "About you is it said in the Torah [by Divine Wisdom], 'I will cause those who love me to inherit richly, and I will fill their treasuries.'"*
> (Proverbs 8:21)

Johanan ben Zakkai would play a crucial role after the First Jewish War. To fully comprehend the events surrounding this war, one must first understand its causal elements, all of which demonstrate how sectarianism among the Jews contributed to the Roman destruction of Israel. Josephus, the Roman–Jewish historian, provides the originating source document for most historical summaries of this period in his book *The War of the Jews*.[7]

For many years prior to the start of the First Jewish War in 66 CE, Roman procurators perpetuated oppressive violence and barbarism against the Jewish people, along with extreme taxation. The people could not meet their payments to the

Romans. These rulers greedily plundered entire cities, torturing and murdering the Jewish people.

The most barbaric of them was Gessius Florus, the Roman procurator for Judaea under Cestius Gallus, president of the province of Syria. Gallus was under the direct authority of King Agrippa II, a descendant of King Herod, aligned with the Roman Emperor Nero. As a means of covering up his atrocities and preventing Jewish retaliation, Florus provoked the Jews so that he could blame them for the revolts. Over time, rebellions arose throughout the land, led mainly by young people who had become hardened against such atrocities.[8]

These idealistic Zealots and freedom fighters were young and unsophisticated, battling stronger political forces. They coalesced in Jerusalem and the provinces of the Galilee. They fought their first campaign against the army of Cestius Gallus in Jerusalem, on Mount Scopus, where they prevailed in battle. Inspired, they further organized themselves into groups both in Judaea and the region of the Galilee.[9]

The Romans, under the leadership of Vespasian, mobilized large armies to fight these forces in Galilee. Although the battles were long, the Jews eventually lost as they were outmatched in strength, organization, and discipline. While the Roman forces destroyed most cities, at least one, Giscala, whose people had surrendered to the Romans, survived. Vespasian then began his march on Jerusalem. Who could blame the young rebels for fighting back? It was clear that the Romans were cruelly barbaric and were working to incite hatred and riots. It is unsurprising that the Romans' plundering, torturing, and killing incited rebellion—any people subject to this brutality would done the same.

One rebel leader who survived this ordeal in the Galilee, John of Giscala, moved his men, who were opportunistic robbers and bandits, to Jerusalem to join up with the Zealots of that city. Giscala's men then began plundering the city. The Zealots in Jerusalem had invited Jewish freedom fighters from Idumea to join them in the hope of stopping this criminal activity. But the Idumean fighters, also possessed of a criminal nature, only worsened the situation. These two groups took refuge in the Temple and pillaged the city of Jerusalem, killing their fellow Jews, including women and children.

This was no longer a fight for freedom but one that had somehow devolved into a civil war among factions of Jewish groups within the walls of the city. An elder High Priest at the time, Ananus, along with other wealthy men of Jerusalem, sought to work out an arrangement with the Romans before Vespasian could march on the city and destroy it, but the Zealots and robbers would not allow this to occur. They killed the High Priest and many of the wealthy and continued to plunder the city.[10]

Instead of building unity among the people, the rebels, bandits, and Zealots focused on their own greed. They provoked violent conflicts with the priests and wealthy men of Jerusalem who, had they had their way, would have surrendered to the Romans for the sake of the people. The priests who desired safety and peace were pushed to destruction by their own people.

Roman rulers would never allow the Zealots within the province of Judaea to achieve independence from the empire. The Romans could not let them set an example of revolt for any other region under their control. But had the priests and the people been able to create a unifying, peaceful political offense, this might have enabled the city of Jerusalem to survive. Clearly this became a contest of values—those who stood for war and destruction in opposition to those who stood for peace, even if that peace meant living under the brutal conditions of Roman rule.[11]

The rebels, rather than putting the needs of the people first, were now fighting from a self-destructive stance. Idealism, which had been unifying in the past, had shifted to reckless conflict and warfare. Sadly, the efforts of the zealots and rebels led to a mass slaughter of the people.

Vespasian would become Emperor by the time he reached Jerusalem, handing over command of the war to his son, Titus. Titus and his Roman armies surrounded the city of Jerusalem, causing the worst famine and war the people had ever experienced. The zealots and radical fighters would not allow anyone out of the city, even those who wanted to leave voluntarily. Instead, the rebels further plundered and murdered their own people. At first, Titus allowed the rebels to continue in the direction of their own demise. But the war raged on until the Jewish warriors finally succumbed to the Roman armies in 70 CE. The legions then completed the plunder and destruction of Jerusalem and the Second Temple.

Prior to the First Jewish War, the Sadducees, composed of priests and wealthy Hellenists, made up the majority within the Great Sanhedrin, with the Pharisees being in the minority. After the destruction of the Temple, the Sadducees disappeared completely. In fact, the Zealots may well have killed them all even before the Romans entered Jerusalem.

Titus's soldiers stripped the Temple sanctuary of all its treasures and shipped them to Rome from the great ancient seaport of Caesarea. Vespasian created a display of his success over the Jews as a warning to other groups who might contemplate revolt against Rome. He used the spoils of war, the wealth from the Second Temple, to build the Colosseum in Rome.[12] He constructed a second building near the Colosseum where he stored the remaining gold and silver. This structure, paradoxically named the "Temple of Peace" in its self-aggrandizing glory, would become the repository for all the treasures Vespasian plundered from conquered lands, which he displayed before the people. Last, the Arch of Titus was constructed near the Colosseum to commemorate the victory. These structures were built between the years 72 and 80 CE.[13]

Inside the Arch of Titus, one can see stone carvings depicting Roman soldiers carrying off the gold menorah, the Light of Israel, which had stood in the Holy of Holies of the Second Temple—ironically, the same menorah created under the leadership of Judah Maccabee in 164 BCE to commemorate religious freedom from the Seleucids and the rededication of the Temple. The carving depicts an image of Roman soldiers carrying off the Temple's gold Table of the Divine Presence and a pair of silver trumpets. This carving represented the attempted destruction of the Jewish faith through the destruction of the Temple by the Romans.[14]

Following such a period of intense conflict and sorrow, it was crucial to find a unifying path of peace based on practicing goodness toward others. After the destruction of the Temple, prayer, dialogue, and learning would replace sacrificial offerings. As the youngest disciple of Hillel, Johanan ben Zakkai would become responsible for carrying on the traditions of the great Nasi.

During the earlier onslaught, when Vespasian was still general, Johanan ben Zakkai found a way out of Jerusalem, although at the time of destruction in 68 CE, the Zealots allowed no one to leave the besieged city. Ben Zakkai faked his death, and his disciples placed him in a sealed coffin to be carried past the guards and beyond the gates of Jerusalem. He was taken to General Vespasian, where his reputation for pursuing peace preceded him. Legend has it that Johanan predicted that Vespasian would become the emperor of the Roman world. Vespasian was so impressed and flattered when the prediction came true in 69 CE, he granted Johanan ben Zakkai permission to leave for Yavneh, near the Mediterranean coast, where he established his great academy for the study of the Hebrew Scriptures.[15]

Johanan ben Zakkai's quest for a unified faith would be based on the Jews learning to live peacefully among the Romans, not on conflict, destruction, or sectarianism. As stated earlier, most Jews of the time would have preferred peace under the Romans. Yavneh would become the new central place of scholarship and study.

After the destruction of the Temple, Johanan ben Zakkai realized that the scrolls of the Written Law would be lost. The Oral Law had also never been written down. A more unifying value, based on the Written Law, was needed to fill the void.[16] The value of war was clearly not a sustainable one. Only the values of compassion and peace would last over time and ensure the survival of the people.

The Sanhedrin relocated to the city of Yavneh. Johanan ben Zakkai took on the role of Nasi during this period. He was followed by an additional three descendants of Hillel, all of whom were significant in stabilizing the faith until circa 220 CE.[17] The Sanhedrin, in its later years, met in the capital of the Galilee region, Sepphoris.[18]

Johanan ben Zakkai and his disciples, along with his colleagues and scholars, took on the enormous task of recalling and debating each characteristic of the Oral Law. This was based on the matrix of values embedded in the Pentateuch—kindness, love of humanity, peace, justice with mercy, compassion, charity, forgiveness, and faith in One God. During times of suffering and sorrow, the path forward was paved with hope and understanding. Ben Zakkai and his disciples posited redemption through immortality of the soul in the afterlife, a concept originating with the Jews during the Hellenistic and Roman periods.[19]

Johanan ben Zakkai brought together all the remaining scholars at Yavneh. He and his colleagues were responsible for saving the Oral Law interpretations of the Great Sages, concluding with the teachings of Hillel. The great scholars of the academies in Yavneh associated with the Pharisees would become the forerunners of the rabbis. These rabbis became the scholarly teachers of the Written and Oral Law. In this way, the practice of learning and scholarship was strengthened, bringing resilience and vibrance to the faith.

Until this time, the Oral Law did not exist in any preserved form. Teachers passed it on verbally to their students, from generation to generation. The act of debating it with one another as well as reaching verbal conclusions helped students learn the Oral Law and integrate it into their lives. The Oral Law helped strengthen the values of the Jews. It created an ultimate code of conduct for people to follow; it emphasized peace in an empire filled with conflict. However, the Oral Law only existed in the minds of the great scholars, which meant it could be forgotten and lost.

Over time, the Oral Law became so complex that it required a more methodical form of study. Rabbi Akiba ben

Joseph of Yavneh was best known for being the first to collate this enormous amount of information into general classifications which allowed disciples to learn the teachings more easily. With this organization, the Oral Law could be written in its final form.[20]

The last task of organizing, documenting, and editing the Oral Law so it could be preserved fell to Rabbi Jehudah ben Nasi, the great Nasi of the Sanhedrin and son of Rabbi Gamaliel II. He was the sixth descendant of Hillel to hold the Nasi position. By this time, Gamaliel II had relocated the academies of Yavneh and the Sanhedrin court to the town of Sepphoris in the Galilee. The Oral Law, once written and codified, formally became known as the *Mishnah*.[21]

The Mishnah was based on the learned positions of the sages, giving recognition to all these scholarly people. But only one final viewpoint would become the ultimate guide for living. This understanding through the Oral Law, and its concluding viewpoint, helped preserve the values of the Written Law. The final decisions in the Oral Law, guided by the rabbis, focused on a path of peace, practiced through justice with mercy, and acted upon with compassion for others. In this way, the living law would be a source of discovery for how God wanted humanity to live in society, even as society changed.[22]

Also, beginning with the time of Johanan ben Zakkai and the emergence of the Mishnah, the final books of the Hebrew Scriptures were chosen and completed. Recall that the Torah and Nevi'im (Prophets) had been written during earlier times. The books of Daniel and Esther were now added, as well as the books of Ezra, Nehemiah, and Chronicles. The Hebrew Scriptures were canonized during this period, meaning that all the books of the scriptures had come together and been recorded in their final form. The canon closed these books permanently. They were no longer subject to change.

What was so significant about the closing of these texts? Prior to canonization, evidence of additional scrolls which had been written based on alternative interpretations was found. As a result, the writings changed slightly over time. For example, the Dead Sea Scrolls reflected minor, "fluid" interpretative revisions in the text of Torah and Nevi'im.[23]

Once canonized, the scrolls could be copied by scribes and distributed to synagogues throughout the diaspora lands without the risk of altering the Hebrew text. Such canonized scrolls were read by the people, teachers, and scholars living in the lands of Babylonia, Alexandria, Rome, and areas of the Roman Empire including Asia Minor (present-day Turkey), where Jews had settled. The teachings of the Torah and Tanakh had now become standardized. People could gather in synagogues and learn from precisely the same writings.

The uniformity of text also allowed for standardized education to flourish in synagogues and academies through-out the diaspora. Sermons were given on portions of the teachings, sharing and elucidating meaning according to the Oral Law. All of this encouraged further and deeper scholarship.

When the books were closed to changes, scholars and teachers could stop focusing on how the Hebrew Scriptures should be written, and instead develop a new path of critical thinking based on the understanding of the Oral Law through the Mishnah.[24] In fact, such focused learning would generate an expansion of thought through the creativity of newly generated ideas. This allowed for the eventual adaptation of the faith to the needs and requirements of the people now exiled from Jerusalem and spreading into a larger diaspora—growing geographically with new cultures to contend with throughout Babylonia and the Roman Empire. This ultimately led to the development of the Talmud, which became the cornerstone of learning, intellectual stimulation, and the focusing of the mind on matters practical and religious.[25]

Earlier, the Roman Emperor Hadrian had quelled most of the Jewish uprisings and banished all Jews from Jerusalem. He had changed the name of Judaea to emphasize the severing of the Jews' connection to the region. As a result, by 200 CE, the land of Palaestina experienced a decline. With the exception of a small contingent of Jews, Jerusalem was no longer physically accessible to the people.

Yavneh, as the new center of Judaism, had served its purpose as the center for the canonizing of the final texts of the Hebrew Scriptures and the organizing of the Oral Law, the Mishnah. This continued to set Judaism on its course toward survival. Because of ongoing political instability in northern Palestine, scholarship moved away from this region, shifting toward Babylonian lands.[26]

Chapter 19:
Expansion of Thought

M any religions or faiths are too rigid—too literally interpreted, causing beliefs to become dogmatic and outmoded. These faiths seek to hold on to people tightly, thereby creating division within their ranks and generating internal strife. Such division, pushed to the extreme, can cause conflict and rebellion. In contrast, Judaism, whether by intentionally or by accident, and as a function of the forced exile of the people after the destruction of the Temple, would become adaptable and resilient in meeting the needs of the Jews. Scholarship, learning, and questioning facilitated Judaism's survival.

As Yavneh and Sepphoris lost their authority as key centers of scholarship, the academies of the Babylonian Jews, which existed outside the Roman Empire, grew in scholarly stature. This portion of the Babylonian empire came under control of the Parthians in 247 BCE, and then the Sassanids in 224 CE, avoiding the destabilizing rule of the Roman Empire.[1] The original Babylonian Jews who had remained after the first exile had grown in number within the Persian and Greek empires.

One such Babylonian Jew who trained in Jerusalem was Hillel, who returned to his homeland, and later became head of his own academy and the Sanhedrin in Jerusalem. Consequently, Babylonian scholars would travel back and forth to Yavneh and later Sepphoris to augment their learning. They would return with their new knowledge to the towns along the Euphrates, where the academies were concentrated, in Nehardea, Pumbedita, and Sura.[2]

The Babylonian academies grew in number, just as they had in Yavneh, and the scholars flourished in this much more stable setting; they could apply their entire focus to study. The rabbis developed additional lines of critical thought about the Written and Oral Law. New teachings and scholarly thought beyond the Mishnah became known as *Gemara*. Whereas the Mishnah focused solely on an understanding of the Oral Law, Gemara provided further discussion of and commentary on the Mishnah. It not only developed an additional understanding of the laws from both the Torah and the Mishnah (known as *halakah*) but also included stories, parables, and legends which illustrated the morals meant to be conveyed by these laws (known as the *aggadah*).

By 425 CE, Babylonian scholars and rabbis had arranged the major categories and topics of the law, building on the work of the earlier scholars and rabbis from both Yavneh and Babylonia.[3] The Mishnah and the Gemara collectively composed the Babylonian Talmud, which was completed by 500 CE.[4] It was the greatest work yet to be developed by the Jewish world. It set the foundation for the development of Judaism as we know it today.

Based on overall themes, the Talmud was organized into six Orders and sixty-three Tractates. The core of a page of the Talmud first presented a section from the Mishnah, which referred to the Oral Law. Subsequent rabbis then commented in the Gemara, additional commentary on issues raised in the Mishnah. Each page of the Talmud was hand-written within this organized structure until the invention of the Gutenberg printing press (circa 1450 CE), which standardized the text, enabling it to be distributed more widely.

Abraham Cohen's *Everyman's Talmud* describes the general organizational breakout of major themes in the Talmud. These groupings encourage people to study how their values and actions carry over into all areas of life. They include:

- the doctrine of God (omniscience and omnipresence),
- God and the universe (transcendence, creation, and cosmology),
- the doctrine of man (free will, faith and prayer, sin, repentance and atonement, reward and punishment),
- revelation through the Torah (prophecy, Torah, study of Torah, Written and Oral Torah, Practice of Torah),
- domestic life (family, children, and education),
- social life (work and community, peace and justice),
- the moral life (brotherly love, humility, charity, forgiveness, and temperance),
- physical life (health and disease),
- folklore,
- jurisprudence (civil and criminal law), and
- the hereafter.

As the Jewish population in the diaspora grew, synagogues expanded their teachings of the Torah. They sent questions by letter to the major religious centers, Yavneh and later, Babylonia, about how to adapt the Law to their new circumstances. The rabbis' replies, called *Responsa*, were based on their knowledge and critical analysis of the Written and Oral Law. These were disseminated via sermons and shared with the people in other ways in all major synagogue communities.[5]

The synagogues continued their established faith-based education, combining it with secular subjects for children. Over time, these literary rulings (Responsa) became part of the curricula along with the Torah and the Talmud. By such means, the authority of the faith reached people in different lands, lending them support, intellectual insights, and direction.

Rabbis became the new authority in a fluid diaspora. The codified commentaries of key erudite Rabbis appear in the Talmud today. Eventually, the greatest of the future medieval rabbis, Rashi (Rabbi Shlomo ben Yitzchaki, Hebrew for Solomon ben Isaac), established a center for academic learning in Troyes, France, in 1077. He developed commentaries that explained and elucidated the Babylonian Talmud and Hebrew Scriptures.

Often, in the face of suffering or conflict with evil, the question arises: how could God have allowed such events to take place? What is the purpose of this suffering? Such conditions can inspire a people to get back up and find new direction. The Romans destroyed the Second Temple; without this calamity, the expansion of critical thought that sustained and informed the Judaism of the diaspora would never have occurred. Without a unifying matrix of values based on peace and compassion, a more relevant and adaptable faith would not have emerged. These instruments of faith allowed Judaism to become transportable.

The Hebrew Scriptures would establish the foundation of the Christian Bible, and synagogues would establish a model for early churches. Prayer would solidify faith in God throughout the Christian world. Mandatory synagogue-based education would become the precursor for public education for all, and the academies would be early versions of faith-based, and later, secular university settings.

Learning and scholarship would remain a driving force for the Jewish people no matter where they traveled, what circumstances they encountered, or what travails they experienced. Such institutional values enabled them to recognize that there was a better and different future, which served to provide greater resiliency to the people throughout the diaspora.

Learning within the framework of the living law collected in the Torah, Tanakh, and Talmud would stimulate the intellect of the people, encouraging hard work and ethical living. This focus on scholarship would promote a new type of social mobility for all Jews, rich or poor alike, while it encouraged a directedness toward actions based on achieving the greater good. A religion which strives to hold the light of goodness in its hands will create unity within its people. A faith which grows in its love for humanity and pursues the path of peace will inspire adherents to a higher purpose.

To conclude, the following Jewish prayer illustrates the path first chosen by Hillel, then by Johanan ben Zakkai, and finally by the Rabbis who edited the Babylonian Talmud. This is the path which would survive the ages. When times and circumstances constantly change because of conflict and war, how will the right values be known or become evident?

These Endure in Every Age[6]

These endure in every age
The transforming power of love
The redeeming power of compassion,
The healing power of forgiveness,
These endure in every age.

The joy which comes from sharing.
The strength which comes from striving
The nourishment which comes from beauty,
These endure in every age.

The sanctity of life,
The value of truth,
The primacy of justice,
These endure in every age.

The abiding worth of prayer,
The purifying promise of repentance,
The striving to know God's will,
These endure in every age.

Grant us, O God, amidst relentless change,
The wisdom to know and to cherish,
These teachings which endure for all time.

Chapter 20:
The Path to Universal Monotheism

Jesus, who grew up in Nazareth in the Galilee and became a carpenter, was born toward the end of Herod I's reign. He lived a span of thirty years or so and died at the hands of Pontius Pilate. Given his humble beginnings, he could easily understand the plight of the poor under the Romans. Born into the House of David, Jesus was raised a Jew among the common people, and preached as a Jew during his lifetime. He lived and taught prior to the period of the First Jewish War against the Romans. The Temple was the central foundation of the Jewish faith during his time.

But who was this Jesus, and what gave rise to his group of disciples? James Carroll, in his book *Christ Actually*, highlights the need to understand the context in which Jesus lived.[1] Jesus preached at a time of Roman oppression and exploitation. Carroll makes clear that Jesus taught the people of Galilee as a Jew about the Jewish law.

Following Herod I's death, the Romans made Israel a province, revoking its independently-ruled status and re-naming it Judaea. A series of Roman prefects, who became progressively more oppressive and barbaric toward the Jews, ruled over Judaea and Samaria. The people of the Galilee and Israel were in need of guidance, direction, and encouragement. Educated as a Pharisee, Jesus taught them the living law.

During this period, the Sadducees were the dominant political force in Jerusalem. A social rift had developed between the priests and the common people, possibly because the priests had aligned so closely with the Roman rulers. No doubt the High Priest and elite Jews were concerned about political power and authority; but people were concerned with how to live their faith from day to day in an atmosphere of persecution.

The priests may not have met the needs of the Jews, but that in no way made the role of the Temple any less significant. In fact, Herod I had completed its reconstruction toward the end of his life, and it had become recognizable as the majestic structure we see in pictures today. Nevertheless, this did not help the people deal with their extreme circumstances.

As conditions grew yet harsher, some people turned toward a new hope, the imminent arrival of a Messiah. Most Jews believed he would be a warrior hero similar to King David, one who would free them from their oppressors and return to them control of the land of Israel.[2] Most of these were poor, common people seeking relief from the direness of their circumstances.

Emphasizing the needs of the people under the Romans, the Pharisees maintained Hillel's school of thought, which promulgated a compassionate and humane view of the law. Jesus's message, within the context of Pharisaic teachings, emphasized values inherent in the teachings of the Torah and the Hebrew Scriptures—that all Jews should follow the Golden Rule (Leviticus 19:18), act with forgiveness, and care for the sick and poor. Jesus gave people hope by creating a pathway to compassion and living in peace.

Most Jews were in need of an empowering message, one based on a vision of hope and reward for righteous behavior. Some believed that Jesus was the foretold Messiah. His message sustained hope for the future. He taught the values inherent in God's law. Jesus taught that the way to live on Earth was to avoid fighting one's ruler, to know God and to remain humble and confident in the grace of the Lord. Alignment with such a life meant people could seek God on Earth through their daily thoughts and actions.

Most people in Israel at the time were poor; they farmed the land in the area of the Galilee and fished the sea.[3] And so as a true Pharisaic teacher, Jesus spoke to the people and their humanity. In the face of cruelty, he preached redemption, resurrection, and just rewards for living a good and peaceful life.

Jesus gave these people another message: the sanctity of life. The living law reveres life through the commandment "You shall not murder." It declares that life is precious. Jesus would help people preserve their lives during turbulent times when the Romans were oppressing poor Jews through violence and taxation. The goal was to learn to live quietly and peacefully.

Following the First Jewish War, two groups survived. The first followed the path of peace as taught in the Torah and the Hebrew Scriptures. The second group was the "Jesus people," who also followed a path of peace.[4] It is possible that most of the Jesus people did not fight in the First Jewish War since, for them, the only way to reconcile Jesus's message with their beliefs was to abstain from rebellious conflict. At the time of the Temple's destruction, forty years after his death, the Jesus people were Jews who believed in Jesus.

The Church of the Beatitudes now stands where Jesus gave his famous Sermon on the Mount. On the eastern shore of the Sea of Galilee, he preached to the Jews that "the meek shall inherit the earth," emphasizing that the people could live in peace, even under Roman rule. In times of suffering, through their belief in the immortality of the soul, they would be sustained, knowing that just rewards awaited them in the hereafter. Is it any wonder that Roman leaders including Pontius Pilate, upon hearing about this messianic figure, suspected that Jesus was encouraging the people to overthrow them? This was a constant worry for Rome, but especially for the rulers of Judaea. So, when Jesus traveled to Jerusalem, according to the Gospels, he knew he would meet his fate there.

Once in Jerusalem, Jesus confronted the money changers at the Temple, who collected fees in exchange for ritual offerings. They were linked to the Sadducees in charge of the Sanhedrin. Understanding the role of the Sanhedrin is crucial to the events which occurred next in Jerusalem.

Recall that under Herod I, the Sanhedrin had lost all political power, though their religious authority remained intact through Hillel as the Prince or Nasi. The Great Sanhedrin, by 30 CE, had regained political power while still retaining its religious authority through the *Beit-Din* (the House of Judgement). Hillel's grandson, Gamaliel I (the Elder), then Nasi and a Pharisee, headed the Sanhedrin at this time. But Roman rulers forbade the Sanhedrin from addressing criminal law issues, including those related to capital punishment.

Seventy elders went up to Mount Sinai with Moses to receive the Word of God; the Great Sanhedrin maintained seventy members, with Moses as the seventy-first. Criminal issues required all seventy-one to preside, but interpretations of civil law only required a minimum of twenty-three members. The Great Sanhedrin met at the Temple in the Hall of Hewn Stone. It is also thought that there were two Sanhedrins at the time, with the second focusing on religious law interpretation and instruction.[5]

The Sadducee majority of this period focused on those aspects of the living law that dealt with ritual offerings, including sacrifices, tithes, food and dietary laws, ritual ceremony, and the role of the Temple priests. People would make pilgrimage to the Temple from all over Judaea and the diaspora lands. If they were able to bring their own animals for sacrifice, they would meet their obligations. For those unable to bring their own animals, they could exchange coins with the money changers for sacrificial animals. This money exchange would occur at or by the Temple court.

At some point during Jesus's time, the sacrificial ritual must have become more focused on money and the ritual acts than on the connection between God, the priests, and the people. As most people were poor, this ritual act ought to have been more intimate, significant, and meaningful. The medium of money exchange may have diminished the value of the act of sacrifice in those difficult times, which led to corruption.

The people who could least afford to put forth funds for such offerings were the ones most in need of solace, comfort, and hope. The priests could have intervened to create greater meaning for the people, thus strengthening the bond between the priests, the Temple, their ritual acts, and the living law.

There was no question that the Jewish people of that time still valued the ritual practices of the Temple because, forty years later, their greatest sadness would be its ultimate destruction. But their daily lives necessitated additional hope and an intensified spiritual connection. No wonder Jesus's message to the money changers was inherent in his overturning the tables of those who were avaricious and had ignored the needs of the people. However, Jesus would not have condoned the elimination of the Temple or eliminating ritual offerings. Jesus was a Jew; his point in upsetting the tables was that the priests and money changers had become too uncaring and corrupt.

The Pharisees, on the other hand, saw their role as being interpreters of the living law, teaching people how it could bring greater meaning and direction to their lives. They would have been knowledgeable in both the Written and Oral Law. Just as Hillel, a Pharisee, had taught people the meaning of the Golden Rule in a time of violence under Herod I, so too Jesus spread the Word of God based on the Golden Rule as a means of coping with the brutality of Roman rule. Both taught others how to live peacefully, focused on their humanity, in accordance with the law.

Other Pharisees, of the school of Hillel's contemporary Shammai, interpreted the law more harshly. Jesus, aware of this, preached to this group that a too strict or literal interpretation of the law would burden people rather than bringing them comfort or solace. A rigid and narrow implementation of justice would not meet their challenging needs during times of conflict. Rather than aiding them, it would impede them.

Jesus preached Jewish values to all Jews, but now emphasized a more enhanced and adaptable message—the values of peace, love, and forgiveness—all of which were based on the teachings of the Torah. People had the free will to choose to live according to the Golden Rule. By weaving peace and the living law into their daily lives, Jews following Jesus could preserve their own lives and the lives of their families. They could adapt to living under Roman rule by turning spiritually inward to find God.

Many Jews saw Jesus as the Messiah whose coming had been prophesied—he was the embodiment of hope during times of intense struggle; he allowed them to find meaning and purpose in their suffering. If the people bore the difficulties of this life by choosing to live in peace, they would be rewarded in the afterlife. The key was to live by the same values as taught in God's living law.

Hence, Jesus also had a message directed at those Pharisees following Shammai's literal teachings of the law. It was to interpret the Word of God with compassion and focus on meeting the needs of the people. Jesus's message was aligned with Hillel's teachings, both of which were timeless and eternal.

Did Jesus predict the destruction of the Temple and the elimination of ritual offerings? For many believers, this is the case. But James Carroll, in his book *Christ Actually*, again demonstrates the importance of understanding the Gospels in light of the times. Just as the Hebrew Scriptures reflected their historical circumstances, there is every reason to believe that the Gospels did the same.

According to Carroll, the Gospel of Mark was written around 70 CE, during or shortly after the destruction of the Temple. The Gospels of Matthew, Luke, and John were all written well after the destruction of the Second Temple. None of the Gospels were written during the years Jesus was alive and preaching, around 28 or 29 CE, or written by any of the disciples of Jesus.[6] These writings were not so much a prophecy or prediction of destruction, but a statement of events that had already taken place during the First Jewish War. Jesus's ultimate message through the Gospels' authors was meant to help surviving Jews realize there was another way to live with God now that the Temple was gone and brutal Roman rule remained.

The Jesus people, Jews who looked to Jesus's memory and who followed his teachings of peace, would not have fought in the civil wars in Jerusalem that finally led to the destruction of the Temple by the army of Titus. This means that, like the disciples of Johanan ben Zakkai and the Jews who did survive Jerusalem's destruction, many people who believed in Jesus's message also survived.

In this context, the Gospel of Mark, whose true author remains unknown, would have reinforced Jesus's teachings, encompassing the need to remain separate from ongoing conflict. This writing would keep Jesus's memory alive as the people sought a way to maintain their faith without the Temple. It brought God closer to the people through the image of a loving Father. The Gospel would become the necessary literature for consolation of a people who survived the horrors of the First Jewish War and Roman occupation.

The Gospel of Mark exemplifies the values Jesus taught based on the Torah and Hebrew Scriptures. Speaking to one expert on the law, Jesus quotes the *Shema*: "Hear, O Israel: the Lord is our God, the Lord is One," and continues with the instruction that the people should love their neighbors as themselves.

Then one of the lawyers, who had been listening to these discussions and had noted how well he answered, came forward and asked him, "Which commandment is first of all?"

Jesus answered, "The first is, 'Hear, O Israel: the LORD our God is the only Lord; love the Lord your God with all your heart, with all your soul, with all your mind, and with all your strength.' The second is this: 'Love your neighbour as yourself.'"

The lawyer said to him, "Well said, Master. You are right in saying that God is one and beside him there is no other. And to love him with all your heart, all your understanding, and all your strength, and to love your neighbour as yourself— that is far more than any burnt offerings or sacrifices." When Jesus saw how sensibly he answered, he said to him, "You are not far from the kingdom of God." And from then on no one dared ask him any more questions. (Mark 12:28– 34)

It is this message that was carried into the Gospels: to have faith in one God and to follow the Golden Rule in order to survive Roman destruction.

The Gospel of Matthew, written in 80 CE, ten years after the destruction of the Temple, spoke about Jesus and his crucifixion. It presented the values he professed in his lifetime, the story of the miracles he performed, and the representation of his death as a means of cleansing man of all sin through redemption and resurrection. Jesus's life, and ultimately his death, signified that his message and values could be passed on even without the existence of the Temple. Jesus's crucifixion at the hands of the Romans came to symbolize the world of suffering under this violent empire. Resurrection represented the reward for continuing to live by righteous values under foreign domination to preserve one's immortal soul. Jesus, as Christ, became the symbol of hope for the people when, without the Temple, they did not yet know how to survive and adapt their faith.

The Gospels of Matthew and Mark preserved the memory of Jesus's message for the benefit of those who survived the First Jewish War, both in Judaea and in the diaspora lands. To these people, God the Father cared enough about their suffering to reach down and touch them through Jesus, the Son of God.

The Gospel of Luke was written near Rome around 80 CE. His Gospel, according to James Carroll, would speak to the possibility that Luke was a traveling companion of Paul while Paul was speaking to the people in Asia Minor and Greece. Paul became a believer after experiencing a life-changing vision of Jesus on the road to Damascus almost twenty years after Jesus's death.

Luke wrote his Gospel during trying times in Rome, when the monuments of conquest were on clear display. Vespasian constructed the Colosseum between 72 and 80 CE. The Arch of Titus was constructed circa 80 CE. Early Christians, then still the Jesus people, were being persecuted in Rome and in Asia Minor, along with Jews in the diaspora who had been imprisoned by the Romans. Many of these captives would become slaves or fodder for games held in the Roman Colosseum.

Luke, a physician known for his healing skills, created a Gospel to help heal the wounds of persecuted Jews and Jesus people alike in Rome. While all the Gospels emphasize the values held and preached by Jesus, Luke's Gospel compassionately seeks to reach and to heal those who had lost their hope and their spirit. Yet the Gospel of Luke also recognized Jesus as a Jew for the sake of the Jesus followers who had been taken to Rome.

Luke also spoke of the destruction of the Temple; but since this Gospel was written after the Temple's destruction, it may have described actual history. This portion of the Gospel of Luke reads like a chronicle of events during the First Jewish War in Jerusalem and describes how those who believed in

Jesus as the Messiah might have saved their lives from Roman destruction.

> But when you see Jerusalem encircled by armies, then you may be sure that her destruction is near. Then those who are in Judaea must take to the hills; those who are in the city itself must leave it, and those who are out in the country must not enter; because this is the time of retribution, when all that stands written is to be fulfilled. Alas for women who are with child in those days or have children at the breast! For there will be great distress in the land and a terrible judgment upon this people. They will fall at the sword's point; they will be carried captive into all countries; and Jerusalem will be trampled down by foreigners until their day has run its course. (Luke 21:20–24)

Here was a message to the followers of Jesus: save yourselves; do not fight the Roman army surrounding the city during the destruction of Jerusalem.

It is believed that the gospel according to John was written around the year 100 CE. While it is not clear who wrote this gospel, this version of Jesus's life, more than any other, emphasizes the distinction in beliefs between the Jews and the followers of Jesus. It might have been written within a diaspora Jewish community of Jesus followers, with the dynamics between the two Jewish sects reflecting their intense disparities. But it would have been written as representing the differences from within the Jewish community—before the transition to early Christianity.

John's Gospel brings Jesus closer to divinity as the Son of God more than any other. It was written much later, close to a decade before the diaspora Jewish rebellions against the Romans and at a time of rising tensions between Jews and Romans in these outlying lands. This Gospel may have represented a more urgent message for the Jesus followers to remain steadfast in maintaining peace, while emphasizing the polemic of Jesus's relationship to God. This would further differentiate the Jewish sects during a time of escalating conflict with the Romans.

Christianity as it appears today diverges from Judaism at this point. After the destruction of the Temple, the Jews followed the path of compassion and peace, embodied first in the Hebrew Scriptures and, later, in the Mishnah and the Talmud. These values were strengthened through study, prayer, and scholarship. Universal monotheism, as the basis for the one God of Christianity, previously unknown to the Romans or the Hellenistic world, had its origin in Judaism. It emphasized similar values that later evolved from a Messianic message. This bifurcation occurred during the period of the Roman Empire. The Gospels would guide a new world of non-Jews as they came to believe in the values taught by Jesus.

Romans and Greeks still worshipped their many gods and idols. However, following the First Jewish War and during the first century CE, many Romans and Greeks became interested in the worship of the one God of the Jews, but without having to follow all the obligations commanded in the living law. Jesus's teachings would now offer an easier path for non-Jews of the Greek and Roman world to follow the one God.

It was the gospel teachings which led non-Jews to believe in the one God and understand what Jesus represented in his divine nature as God made manifest on earth. If the people could not personally know Jesus and the message he taught, they could at least come to know him through the Gospels.

The message to those Jews who were Jesus followers was to follow the path of peace. They were not to engage in the ongoing conflict with Rome. They still followed the living law, but without the requirement for ritual offerings.

James Carroll in *Christ Actually* reflects that it was Paul who first reached out to Jews and non-Jews alike about the teachings of Jesus and created the catalyst for achieving universal monotheism. Paul was born Saul of Tarsus, in what is modern-day Turkey. He was a devoted Pharisee taught by a direct descendant of Hillel, Gamaliel I, the Nasi of the Sanhedrin.[7] Therefore, Paul's views had to be based on the teachings of the living law. Early on, Saul sought to persecute and imprison the Jesus followers.

The Letters of Paul—the Epistles—ultimately reshaped the new faith and created the first break from the traditional practices of the Jews. After receiving a vision of Jesus on the road to Damascus, Paul became a believer, living and preaching around the year 50 CE, well before the start of the First Jewish War and the destruction of the Temple. Many of his writings in the Bible, such as his letter to the Romans, predate the destruction of the Temple. However, in none of Paul's letters did he condone the Temple's destruction.

Paul not only reached out to many of the Jews in Jerusalem and the diaspora, but also to non-Jews who were attracted to the principles of the Jewish faith, but not the stringent requirements of following the living law. To the non-Jews who might have been interested in converting, committing to the full law set forth in Hebrew scripture would have been challenging. Paul simplified the message by eliminating the requirement to follow all of the law. Paul's teachings of Jesus instead focused on experiencing the inner faith and belief in the one God, and the exhortation to "love your neighbor as yourself." These simple and compassionate words as taught by Jesus reflected the same teachings that Hillel spoke of to the non-Jews, passed down through his descendant, Gamliel I.

Acts of the Apostles, thought to have been written by the same author as the Gospel of Luke, is a continuation of the teachings of Jesus and a rendering of the circumstances of Paul. Acts highlights statements reflecting Paul's faith as a Jew. The Jews take Paul into custody for his heretical preaching to non-Jews. His first statement is made in the presence of the Roman Governor over Judaea, Porcius Festus, in the Roman tribunal located at Caesarea. Paul is consistently portrayed as supportive of the Temple, even though he has become one of the Jesus people:

> After spending eight or ten days at most in Jerusalem, he
> [Porcius Festus] went down to Caesarea, and next day he
> took his seat in court and ordered Paul to be brought up.
> When he appeared, the Jews who had come down from
> Jerusalem stood round bringing many grave charges, which
> they were unable to prove. Paul's plea was: "I have
> committed no offence, either against the Jewish law, or
> against the temple, or against the Emperor." (Acts 25:6–8)

Then King Agrippa, grandson of Herod I and the Jewish vassal king over Judaea and Samaria under Roman rule, arrived in Caesarea to listen further to the pleadings of Paul.

> "My life from my youth up, the life I led from the beginning,
> among my people and in Jerusalem, is familiar to all Jews.
> Indeed, they have known me long enough and could testify,
> if they only would, that I belonged to the strictest group in
> our religion: I lived as a Pharisee. And it is for a hope
> kindled by God's promise to our forefathers that I stand in
> the dock today. Our twelve tribes hope to see the fulfillment

of that promise, worshipping with intense devotion day and night; and for this very hope I am impeached, and impeached by Jews, Your Majesty. Why is it considered incredible among you that God should raise dead men to life?" (Acts 26:4–8)

Paul's pleadings confirm his faith in the Jewish law, but with the belief that Jesus, as Christ, arose from the dead. Paul was not speaking against the living law but affirming the position of many of the Pharisees regarding immortality and resurrection. Recall that the Sadducees did not believe in resurrection, angels, or spirits.[8]

Emperor Constantine continued the official bifurcation of Judaism and Christianity in 313 CE with the Edict of Milan, which decreed toleration of Christianity throughout the Roman Empire. This reinforced the formal schism which the Jewish king over Judaea and Samaria under Roman rule had clearly originated with Paul's teachings. Constantine brought together two hundred and fifty bishops at Nicaea in 325 CE to create one formal belief system which would act as a unifier of all the diverse people within the Empire.[9] This established Christianity as the fastest-growing religion.

Embedded within Judaism and Christianity are the values of caring for the poor and the sick, acting with kindness and compassion, as well as pursuing a peaceful path. These faiths show us, through a dynamic upward evolution of values, the road to a better life through everyday actions, even in today's modern world.

While living these values today should lead to a world of peace, unfortunately, this is not the case. Living by these values does not mean that suffering and war will end. The scourges of pain and violence will always be present. But such stressors allow people, both individually and collectively, to recognize when they are on the right path or when they are on the wrong one; when they are serving the greater good, or when they must change course. Despite the ebbs and flows of history, compassion and peace are still the way forward.

Only when events reach a crisis point do people recognize the need to make a conscious course change and redefine that which leads to goodness. Humanity experiences freedom of agency to choose right or wrong. People's values, ethically, morally, and socially, determine whether they live destructively or constructively in peace. It is through the experience of these tensions that humanity learns how to achieve a higher purpose.

Most faiths contain within them beliefs promoting goodness, compassion, and redemption. But they must also meet societal needs by adapting to modern times. Instead, doctrine and beliefs so often can harden into narrowed interpretations, falling short of helping people live out these values.

Religion, as an institution, has adapted by strengthening community. But we must also foster a more spiritual, inclusive understanding of God in this changing world, one which fosters an openness to different religions. The focus needs to be on similarities in belief rather than differences.

A more literal, fundamentalist approach to faith spurs even greater conflicts between groups. This is apparent in the radical Islam of Middle Eastern countries, which has aligned to protect socio-political leadership structures, as well as those outlier groups which have carried out violent actions against others. Extremes can lead to intolerance and oppression against others who do not adhere to established beliefs.

Strict interpretations of religion will not permit adaptation or change. All faiths must retain their ability to adjust and incorporate new ways of thinking. The goal is not to renounce those values that faiths teach but to enable modernization of them within the context of the times and to be accepting of new and different needs, especially during periods of significant societal change.

Most religions, however, are also not adapting to the need for a new social consciousness. In response, people turn away from them in hope of finding answers elsewhere. The teaching of values used to be rooted in families, but the traditional family has also changed and often cannot sustain this role. Mobility and society's hectic pace have caused people to lose sight of their values, especially when wealth has become a top priority. Large socio-economic gaps, with increasing disparities and constraints on economic advancement among groups, have lowered the threshold for rebellion, conflict, and violence.

Any religion, once formalized, risks creating divisions between its followers and people of other faiths. Groups come to believe in the superiority of their religion. Faith, which is meant to pass on values of goodness, defeats itself when it creates walls of separation. Foundational values ought to drive toward unifying diverse elements of humanity. For the ultimate meaning of God is unity itself, and ideal actions, both individually and collectively, should strive toward this transcendent goal.

James Carroll in *Christ Actually* suggests it is most important today for people to act in accordance with the teachings of Jesus, which focus on advancing humanity. Emphasis ought to be on those values which permeate the Hebrew Scriptures and the New Testament, for in these ancient texts may be the solutions to help guide nations at a time of significant societal upheaval.

Righteousness today means living and following our ethical beliefs and the secular law while implementing them with grace and mercy, forgiveness and charity, as well as kindness and compassion. Most people will seek out goodness and abundance in their lives when given the chance, unless taught to do otherwise.

The focus on foundational values must turn to unifying mankind while still celebrating its differences. Only then does the betterment of humanity become served. The fork in the road which allowed Judaism and Christianity to evolve, following different paths, also helped to both spread universal monotheism throughout the Western world and embed a new matrix of enhanced values—peace, love, and forgiveness—thereby institutionalizing them in today's religions.

Chapter 21:
Defining the Transformative Cycle of Values

The rise of Christianity spread universal monotheism throughout the Western world, advancing the values of faith, peace, and the Golden Rule. Judaism further developed in the Babylonian academies and spread throughout the diaspora, with the values of faith, justice, peace, and learning supported by themes from the Talmud. Through individual and collective study, the Jewish people sought to discover the will of God and how to apply it in their daily lives. This strengthened their social connections and unified them, thereby creating a milieu based on the living law.

Religious, political, and economic institutions shape values and, in turn, are also shaped by values. But in times of significant change, when people look for answers to guide them in new directions, old solutions may prove insufficient. Modern times require new courses of action, while current models remain somewhat resistant to change. The result places religious dogma in conflict with people's moral expectations, while political clashes create societal cynicism and anger.

People may move away from religion in times of stress to pay attention to more immediate needs. Yet, the world requires a paradigm shift that emphasizes humanity over a primary focus on accumulating wealth. Do history and religion become less relevant or more important during such times? Do sacred texts lose relevance in a changing world? Or can people derive new meaning from texts and traditions to create a transformative set of values that will help shape a better future?

This chapter will seek to define values and how they are necessary in the formation of today's society. First, let us review the evolution of values and patterns that emerged from the tight-knit society of ancient Israel. **Values are "the moral principles and beliefs or accepted standards of a person or social group."**[1] The Torah and Tanakh have values embedded in them that consistently realign and combine at essential points to meet societal needs, or when corruption and evil demand corrective action.

Beginning with the Jews' faith in God, self-determination and free will developed in the guise of individual responsibility and accountability. These early seed or core values emerge as Abraham honors God, and they are under-scored with the trials by which Abraham demonstrates responsibility through his life choices and actions.

When Abraham and Sarah traveled to Egypt, Abraham gave Sarah over to Pharaoh to protect his own life—a dishonorable choice which the Lord reversed. Through this episode, Abraham learned to value the bond between husband and wife. By extension, he learned to value all his relations. So, when King Chedorlaomer attacked Sodom and Gomorrah, Abraham defended and saved his nephew Lot along with Lot's family and possessions.

The core values of taking responsibility and exercising free will evolved over time and eventually became institutionalized. Each generation successively carries this foundational value forward, affecting whole groups of people, tribes, and extended families. A prime example of this is Joseph saving the lives of the entire Egyptian nation, as well as those of his brothers and his father.

Having left bondage in Egypt, the Hebrews, building on the strength of the twelve tribes, fashioned a nation in the land of Israel. The Ten Commandments and accompanying Torah law, emphasizing the core value of justice with mercy, enlightened the people and informed them on how they should live together. In the forty years that two generations of Israelites wandered and lived in the desert, they learned and assimilated the laws that Moses had taught them. They applied these laws and their respective underlying values between the periods of Judges and early Kings. Eventually, under the monarchy of Solomon, the value of justice with mercy was formalized through the development of a political structure.

Once a peak in a core value is achieved, decline can set in. Institutions capture and build upon these values, but they may ultimately become rigid, cumbersome, and abusive based on established power structures, or else become bloated from wealth and corruption. Solomon built a great economic empire based on trade and the value of peace. The system declined after an abundance of wealth allowed corruption to develop. Because of this, the Assyrians were able to conquer northern Israel.

In the Southern Kingdom of Judah, the prophets warned time and time again of the need for a paradigm shift to counteract the decline due to corruption. During King Josiah's rule, a new core value drew upon the newly discovered scroll of the Teachings of Moses. The priests began teaching the Law to the people in order to both initiate an internalized discipline of faith in God and to strengthen prayer in the hearts of the people. The captive people carried these values with them into the Babylonian exile.

As the Second Temple period began, the core values of inner faith, learning, and scholarship took hold, with Ezra and Nehemiah joining forces to teach the people the living law. Throughout the Hellenistic period, the Sages became leaders in interpreting the law, so it became meaningful to all Jews. Furthered through the early teachings of the Pharisee Hillel, the people joined their hearts and their minds in intensifying their faith. A new political structure also took shape in the form of the men of the Great Assembly, which eventually transitioned into the Gerousia, and later to the Sanhedrin. More importantly, the living law sustained the people with the development of synagogues as the central focus of faith-based schools that promoted learning and scholarship.

Decline once again set in as sectarian conflict grew between the Sadducees and the Pharisees, first under the rule of the Hasmonean kings, and then under the Romans during the First Jewish War. Before the First Jewish War occurred, Hillel, and later Jesus, identified new core values based on the Golden Rule, ones centered in kindness, compassion, and peace. After the war, the Jews gained insight into the value of peace as they sought to study and learn from the Hebrew texts and the Talmud. Education continued with the growth of synagogues and academies throughout the diaspora. Originating with the Pharisees, the role of the rabbis evolved as they became teachers and community leaders.

In light of Roman military supremacy, Jesus's teachings about peace, as disseminated through the Gospels, became the core value for the survival of the Jesus people. The Golden Rule may have taught those who survived war how to live in an environment of threat and violence. More importantly, it presented many non-Jews with a path to the ways of God, helping to bring monotheism to the Western world. These values grew as Christianity developed. After the canonization of the Bible, faith became institutionalized as the Church evolved.

We have identified a cyclical pattern in the early evolution of values. A value can become foundational when new needs arise. As societal demands grow, broad values must emerge to help address them. Eventually, once integral to a culture, these values become beliefs. But there is a difference between beliefs and values.

Beliefs are based on established worldviews. Beliefs are generated from within people, rather than being imposed by an external source. They are derived from mindsets or perceptions about how people see themselves in relationship to the world. If they are secure, having experienced trustworthy people, trusting others becomes a primary mindset. If they believe in free will, having experienced this themselves, they are more likely to emphasize an individualistic approach to our world.

Beliefs based on perceptions frequently generate emotional reactions. For example, stereotyping immigrants as criminals causes others to fear them. Negative emotional reactions of fear and anger can easily go viral in today's digital world. Groups adopt them on a large-scale basis. Beliefs can be used to unify a group by setting one group against another, thereby emphasizing differences while creating and worsening divisiveness.

Beliefs that are chaotic and destructive spread more easily in society as the world becomes more digitally connected. To illustrate, the media tends to focus attention on negative or self-serving human-interest stories rather than emphasizing positive events. Night and day, murders, fires, wars, and pandemic outbreaks dominate the news. This information spreads digitally almost instantaneously.

Beliefs that are life-affirming and unifying take greater effort and energy to convey and embed into society's thought system. But in the end, these are necessary for building positive and progressive cultures. Energizing, positive beliefs can be transformational and can endure over time, while viral beliefs born of fear-based emotions tend to erode society.

Beliefs are slow to change. Take, for example, the issue of slavery. Congress voted in 1865 to add the Thirteenth Amendment to the US Constitution, abolishing slavery and involuntary servitude. President Abraham Lincoln had declined the opportunity to negotiate a settlement ending the Civil War before dealing with the issue of abolishing slavery. Lincoln chose to seek passage of the amendment first, thereby delaying the end of the Civil War.

When the law went into effect, the belief that all men are created equal was translated into a codified, aspirational value for our country. This belief was a value that first had to permeate society to result in the ending of slavery. However, just because a law changes does not mean that people's fundamental beliefs change. In this case, many citizens of the United States at the time were not ready to give up the perceived socio-economic advantages of slavery, especially in the South. Yes, a law had to be put in place before change could occur. But since the belief system in a large portion of the population had not yet altered, those emotions congruent with resisting such a belief in real-world equality simply went underground.

Groups such as the Ku Klux Klan went on murderous rampages against Black men, women, children, and sometimes entire towns. The doctrine of "separate but equal" accommodation was entrenched into the law of the land by the infamous 1896 Plessy v. Ferguson decision. Civil rights progressed in the 1950s with court decisions such as Brown v. Board of Education and actions like those of Rosa Parks. Her protest of segregated seating on Montgomery, Alabama city buses and the subsequent boycott eventually led to a decision requiring equal accommodation on public transportation. Martin Luther King, Jr. brought the civil rights struggle to the nation's capital in 1963 with his famous "I Have a Dream" speech, in which he pointed out that the founders' words, "all men are created equal," constituted an unpaid promissory note to America's citizens of color. Even given these courageous deeds and speeches, there is need for more progress to ensure equality for all citizens.

Values are broader than beliefs and focus on our orientation to the external world. Values are based on ideals and evolve from beliefs; they are generally congruent with beliefs, but since they are broader and influence the outside world, they begin to drive societal change and interactions. Values are important and motivating to people. As they grow in society, values are transmitted as memes, cultural items and actions which are repetitively shared and experienced among individuals and groups. An online video of a popular subject transmitted between individuals can grow into a meme. Memes are vehicles which can help spread and develop ideas and values.

Values also influence peer-to-peer interactions through societal trends. They are disseminated through families, faith-based communities, work settings, educational systems, cultural centers, and the digital world. These values should flow in the right direction—in a direction toward goodness as we best define it. If they flow in the opposite direction, the wrong values may emerge and expand within the culture.

Values can inspire humanity to intentionally affect the cultural environment. As values grow and become more permanent within a society's institutions, such as the rise in democratic laws, individuals begin to internalize these values, establishing new, personalized belief systems. People learn through actions and experiences which become congruent with established cultural norms over time. Values influence societal trends, and society's values influence an individual's personal belief structure.

Values are further strengthened when they align with existing social structures, such as those of religious institutions or those spelled out in documents supporting human rights and democracy. The basic values of truth, honesty, and integrity of character are built on fundamental beliefs in free will, responsibility, and justice tempered by mercy. Eventually these are instilled into a system—the rule of law—and governance supporting such ideals.

Further core values such as learning, knowledge, and scholarship ultimately translate into wisdom, and hopefully, a more nuanced moral wisdom. These values in turn become more permanent over time, giving rise to the establishment of institutions of public education, universities, and research. As the values of love, compassion, and peace evolved, religious institutions grew, emphasizing congruent action. And while many nations are still at war, most of the world lives in peace.

Over time, fundamental values of truth, integrity, love, and forgiveness become embedded in people's lives and accepted and ingrained in society. Such values are then accepted as personal ethical beliefs grounded in our inherent perceptions, emotions, and actions. We come to expect the world to function in such a manner, even when it does not— and when it does not, some of us are moved to take action.

As in Abraham Maslow's hierarchy of needs, earlier values become foundational and integral to a society's culture while more complex ones begin to emerge. Subsequent values grow out of earlier ones and can transform a society, bringing about a new and hopefully more equitable way of living. All these values, again, appear to be embedded within our religious texts in some form, with certain values becoming more ascendant at certain times than others.

As values arise within society, grow, and become institutionalized, there comes a point when the system may become inflexible. In most cases, this leads to corruption, exploitation, or a decline in effectiveness. Times change, but systems are slower to change. Traditional ways of solving problems are no longer as effective in meeting new challenges. A different set of values is required to push societal progress forward. Crisis points may arise, forcing transformation.

At certain notable points in history, some societies' values have veered completely off track. Such was the case in German culture, which created repeated, deadly crisis points for the Jews. As democracy progressed in most of Western civilization, dark periods in history occurred. Antisemitism was present throughout European history, but never more so than during World War II. By the time the war ended in 1945, the Holocaust had claimed the lives of six million Jews.

Given that Germany, as a nation, was disorganized and on the verge of collapse, the values that the Nazis had imposed gave rise to leaders who sought to create exclusive group protections and cohesion based on racial identity, singling out and scapegoating minority people. Germany spread its ideology and beliefs which were based on fear, race-hatred, and a self-serving nationalism. This levelling of the masses and a totalitarian political system gained traction over democracy and individual human rights.

In 1933, German President Hindenburg appointed Adolf Hitler, the Nationalist Socialist German Workers Party candidate, as Chancellor. He became dictator in 1934. Nazi racist teachings from the eugenics movement engendered violence and murder. But the real appeal to the Germans was the prospect of bringing a better life to the common German who had lost ground in the aftermath of the Great War and the Great Depression.[2]

In their victory over Germany in WWI, the Allied Powers, led by France and Great Britain, had imposed massive reparations on the Germans with the Treaty of Versailles. Most Germans viewed such payments as an imposed humiliation. Beginning in 1923, hyperinflation demolished what little was left of middle-class savings. Then came the Great Depression in 1929. German unemployment reached its highest level. People experienced severe food shortages. Conditions were dire.

The Nazis promised organization and a plan to bring Germany back to power. Publicly addressing both food shortages and unemployment were their first priorities. Behind the scenes, the Party set in motion a plan to conquer land in the eastern territories of Europe, especially Poland, in order to expand agriculture. German citizens would relocate to these lands and grow food for the German population, thus reducing the number of people in German cities. The Nazis would displace, expel, or exterminate the local populations of these conquered nations in the name of *Lebensraum*, their "living space" plan.[3]

Upon becoming chancellor, Hitler began rebuilding the German military, in violation of the Treaty of Versailles. Rearmament was the true objective of nationalist policies. In 1935, Germany stopped all reparations payments so that they could update their industrial infrastructure and rebuild their war machine. They established compulsory military service and printed money to support the effort, accumulating mass debt.[4]

The movement to scapegoat the Jews in Germany was underway. According to Götz Aly in *Hitler's Beneficiaries*, this started with the systematic expropriation of Jewish wealth to help fund the German military effort. The Nazis first passed racial discrimination laws in 1935, defining Jews by parentage, forbidding marriage and extramarital relations between Jews and non-Jewish Germans, and eliminating the rights of Jews as German citizens. This was the first step in socially isolating the Jews.

In 1937, Jews were expelled from employment in government, university, and professional jobs. Jewish doctors, lawyers, and professors lost their livelihoods. As they were removed from their positions, non-Jewish Germans took their places, even if they lacked qualifications.

This became a visible political step to putting Germans back to work.

In 1938, the Jews, many of whom owned businesses, were required to itemize all their real estate, business, and security assets. The German government Aryanized these businesses and property by simply turning them over to non-Jewish German owners or by selling the assets to Germans, which provided additional funds to the Reich. Five German banks became accessories to the Reich in the transfer of Jewish currency and securities. This was often done in the guise of forcing Jews to purchase German government war bonds with no guarantee of future payment.

On November 9 and 10, 1938, the devastating pogrom Kristallnacht took place. With a silent nod from the Nazis, the German people attacked and violated the Jews. They burned buildings, stole possessions, and killed people throughout Germany. Hitler next authorized an "atonement tax" payment in the amount of 1 billion Reichsmarks to the government, to be paid by the Jews over one year in four installments, to clean up after the authorized plunder and property destruction that followed the pogrom. Fiscal policy combined with violence forced a sell-off of Jewish assets and increased state revenues by 6 percent.[5]

Germany now had an explicit plan for seizing Jewish assets to fund Germany's military on an ongoing basis. The Nazis transferred homes and apartments to non-Jewish Germans. They stole property, money, securities, gold, silver, jewelry, and art objects, and sold these on the open market to raise cash for the Reich. They took food, goods, and furnishings from the Jews and gave these to German families. This became another immediate and visible sign of the government meeting the needs of the German people.

Each time Germany conquered another nation, such as Austria, Poland, Czechoslovakia, Hungary, Belgium, Holland, Denmark, Norway, France, and Greece, upon setting up the occupational government, the first step put into place was to identify the Jewish population and itemize their money and possessions. The occupational government then eliminated their jobs, Aryanized their businesses and properties, and stole their wealth. They plundered food, goods, and furnishings for German citizens back home and for German military members and their families. The Nazis then deported the Jewish people to ghettos or to concentration camps. Each country may have set up the plundering differently, but the outcome was the same.

Poland, however, was at the heart of the Lebensraum expansion. The country had over 3.5 million Jews. The Nazis relocated poor and unemployed citizens from the Reich to Poland and gave them their own farms to grow crops. Both Jews and Poles lost their land, businesses, and wealth. The Jews were then relocated to become slave laborers, living in established ghettos or in concentration camps, while the regime exterminated others. The Nazis had a plan to deport Jews from Germany, Austria, Poland, and other conquered nations to camps in Poland and Germany, where they were killed or starved to death. They did this while their captives performed hard labor.

When we think of the Holocaust, we think of ghettos, cattle cars, and mass graves, as well as work and death camps—the German government's systematic devaluation and destruction of human lives. We think less about the impact of an organized plan to plunder Jewish wealth to help finance the Third Reich and transfer assets to the German people. Exploitation became an acceptable method for solving the economic problems and satisfying the immediate needs of the German people.

Through the dynamic alignment of the political structure, economics, and the churches, Hitler advanced the devaluing of human life. He made the German people, as well as people from other lands, complicit in the sacrifice of their human values by engaging their self-interest and greed. Once the people got used to the practice, they grew comfortable with receiving stolen goods and living in expropriated apartments.

When people ask why, or how the Holocaust could have occurred, most will answer that the Germans made Jews the scapegoats. Scapegoating does not even begin to describe the profound depth of sorrow that comes with the emergence and growth of such destructive actions as organized theft, mass murder, and the violation of human lives. It was not just about the violence and destruction of life, which could possibly be explained away as a lack of meaningful values. By first stealing from, and then destroying the Jewish people, a nation willfully and calculatingly raised funds to build a war machine and publicly satiated the needs of the German people, taking the cycle of destructive values to a whole new level.

Greed and hatred can never extinguish the flame of the human spirit. Even if suppressed in life, the spirit continues through the Jews who survived and emigrated from Europe to America and into British-controlled Mandatory Jewish Palestine, which became Israel. Their first goal was to re-enter society, raise families, and have children. This would grow their numbers once again, focusing not only on the present, but on future generations. Their second goal was to seek out new opportunities under the protection of democratic laws which guaranteed their freedom. The third was to create a better life for their children by emphasizing education. Drawing on their historical values and finding themselves to be resilient, they grew as a population once again.

Let us now return to addressing the dynamic cycle of values. Today's democratic and free-market societies are based on a complex set of values, usually pushing humanity toward a raised social consciousness. But values can move us in either direction—positive, with good outcomes, or negative, with destructive ones. New values must arise to both shape and drive our forward momentum.

Traditional solutions expected from democratic and free-market systems are being used to solve challenges with methods which worked well at one time but are no longer successful. Such values do not appear to catalyze societal progress and may, in fact, move society into decline. Influences, such as an overvalued focus on money and wealth as driving forces, embed themselves in the process, thereby corrupting existing values and calling for the wrong kind of change.

Moving toward a higher and more unifying hierarchy of values, the former do not disappear but are assimilated and evolve, giving rise to a new, more resonant model benefitting society. Therefore, values must first transform by being *forward progressing*, guiding society on a future path toward a higher evolutionary state. They must resonate with goodness (i.e., be life–affirming) as opposed to perpetuating oppressive or rigid conditions; they must empower people so that the collective society can progress together. If, for example, a society fails to recognize a particular group's rights, then equality for all cannot arise. Values must push society in the right direction to encourage individuals to alter their underlying belief structure and engage in congruent actions.

Second, these values must actively drive us to achieve a higher purpose, an aspirational purpose. If, for example, serving God represents a higher purpose, and God is good by definition, we are seeking a higher ideal for all of humanity to create in the direction of goodness—that which empowers people to create in a positive and constructive manner. We are in need of raising our social consciousness. Our society is presently characterized by being regressive, reactionary, and focused on economic wealth. We must identify the correct path for our forward progression to stage a paradigm shift.

Even as the global society aspires toward peace, it also has evolved values predicated on money, spurred by the growth of consumerism in society. Money has become a living value which seems to dictate the direction of our lives instead of being the tool it was meant to be—supporting our efforts to achieve the greater good in society.

We have institutionalized the value of money through corporations, high finance, and economic policy. The corporate focus on the concentration of profits and wealth drives our political system. This translates into the demand for more consumer goods and short-term profit taking, making everything a commodity purchasable for a price.

If we use economics and political systems alone to drive society forward, there is as much chance that poor outcomes will result from the system as good ones. If there are no meaningful ideals and values that shape, strengthen, or unify society toward a higher purpose, that society ultimately begins to decline. Instead, if we establish positive ideals and aspirational values, then it is more likely that our values will shape economic and political systems. While not every organization will necessarily shift toward this new direction, there is a possibility that these very values will shape more outcomes than not, thereby creating a new, directional tipping point.

Recall, earlier in the chapter on Solomon's kingdom, a discussion related to Michael Sandel's insightful comments on the moral limits of markets.[6] Traditional economic growth is based on supply and demand models, which work well in less complex societies and are more predictable in constrained and limited economies. This has been the case since the Industrial Revolution. New scientific discoveries helped Western society become wealthier and more efficient, allowing people to do more with fewer resources. Simple models of supply and demand were understood even as increasing quantities of goods were produced and purchased. Economic predictions could accurately suggest wise courses of action.

But over time, economics has become global and more complex. We can no longer predict which models work best. Unintended consequences arise, requiring interventions from our financial, political, and legal systems. Even as economic interventions are put into place, adaptive behaviors develop, and unexpected emergent phenomena arise. A complex global economy with new and sometimes unexpected exponential technologies acts unpredictably. Such complicated international economies behave differently from individual or local economies.

According to Sandel, because of a greater emphasis on profits and wealth, almost everything has become a commodity. All things are measured by their monetary worth, and everything can be bought and sold for a price.

Actions which were freely given in the past have become commoditized. The public is consistently bombarded by advertisements for goods that the manufacturers think they should want. Rampant consumerism is not good for society; nonetheless, it has become a way of life.

More importantly, Sandel emphasizes that such wealth and a focus on purchasing goods creates greater wealth inequality in society. A small percentage of people possess the majority of wealth, while the masses have less and less. And even when opportunities for more people to own businesses exist, larger companies with more concentrated wealth and power often buy out smaller ones—sometimes to acquire their capabilities, sometimes to just get rid of competition. This serves to move the economy away from multiple competitors to oligopolies which can then inflate prices over the long run—further concentrating wealth, risking abuse of economic power, and fostering corruption.

While economic self-interest will always be a strong temptation, competition will not and should not disappear. Instead, we should identify those values which best align future actions and activities with the greatest common good to society. How best to tame this beast?

The world has been shaken by the spread of the coronavirus in 2020. Some countries stood by their people, focusing on solutions which reduced the spread of the virus as early as possible. They controlled the price of necessary medical supplies and food. Other nations' governance systems failed. Iran was one of those failures. Governance did not put humanity first, and its institutions were not adequately focused on the wellbeing of its people.

The United States was one of the last nations to address the issue. The confusion between treating the disease, containing it, and creating an adequate supply chain versus the need to open the economy led to failed communications and planning, which should have prioritized the essential value of life over economics and politics. However, people also made a rare attempt to come together, based on a unified approach to adversity, to learn from each another—quickly, through the instant spread of necessary information. Some countries acted more swiftly than others.

This event may become the catalyst for initiating a global paradigm shift. Technological change may also provide opportunities to transform the world. It is humanity's responsibility to identify those values appropriate to shaping the future. And this must happen quickly, because technology and economics have a way of moving beyond our present understanding, let alone control. If technology can be prioritized to focus toward solving humanity's problems, then wealth can be aligned to successfully support this goal. However, if money continues to be the primary driver of the process, then poor outcomes as well as good ones may emerge.

In Germany, in the 1930s and 1940s, the underlying justifications for Nazism were economic hardship, scarcity, conquest, and domination, which led to racism, claims of supremacy, and the ostracization of certain groups of people, primarily German Jews. The Nazis used technology to support these destructive values. They employed military industrialization and early forms of computer technology to appropriate other nations' wealth and resources while enslaving and destroying their people. Fear and a need for domination, supercharged by the use of technology, allowed the Holocaust to occur.[7]

It is much harder for society to shape its ideals, values, and goals based on an aspiring faith in the ultimate good or for a higher purpose, one which honors the human spirit. It takes more energy and a stronger value system to generate positive transformation. A society must willingly choose to live out possible ideals and embed them in daily actions in order to make them meaningful.

Therefore, what will our next set of values be for the future? Before addressing this question in the last chapter, let us first revise our model of growth in values. Earlier in the chapter, we hypothesized that values evolved from core values to a growth phase, and then to a plateau through institutionalization, making such values more permanent. Ultimately, decline sets in with old mindsets becoming narrow and inflexible.

Dr. Donald Beck, the protégé of Dr. Clare Graves, who was the founder of the concept "Spiral Dynamics," developed a model of progressively upward, evolving trajectories of societal development in the shape of a spiral which drives sociological and economic development.[8] The concept of the spiral also explains the upward, cyclical progression of evolving values. This model demonstrates that higher levels of accepted values integrate the former levels in order to become more transformative, and societies move through these evolutionary spirals one cycle at a time.

Each level of the spiral represents a period of upward movement of growth from the basic, core value on the evolutionary cycle. This is strengthened as institutionalization of the value sets in until, finally, the structure begins to weaken, and the downward turn of the spiral begins. However, if society develops a more advanced set of core values—especially during periods of decline, the turn of the spiral allows for paradigm shifts and transformations to take place.

Today there is a need for a paradigm shift. We need more than a narrow focus on accumulating money and wealth. Better answers require a balance of what is good or right for the world's people, individually and collectively as well as nationally and globally. The need for this shift is no different from the need answered by the messages of the prophets and the words of Jesus recorded in the Gospels. These messages helped Western civilization put forth a new way of living through grace.

What might a different model of values look like for a changing world? Can such a different model be used to guide the development of new technology for good? What should be the role of older institutions? Can people be empowered to create more with less and with greater access to innovations? If technology can assist in accomplishing such goals, then systems and institutions need to emerge to strengthen these values so that there will be less misuse and abuse of technology. Transcendent core values will arise even as people maintain their traditional values, but we must also allow tradition and innovation to stand together, side by side, so a positive paradigm shift can successfully take place.

Chapter 22:
Values That Shape the Future— Co-Creativity Driven by Compassion

Technology is expanding globally, creating more opportunities than one could ever imagine. We are on the cusp of combining new research, artificial intelligence, and biotechnology in ways which will give us incredible power to innovate. We must use this power wisely. How do we shape the fabric of our culture while still allowing for the freedom of the human spirit? What will be the new set of transformative values that will guide us to solve today's problems, help people thrive, and sustain the earth's resources?

New core values are beginning to emerge, much like there was a critical transformation of values which took place in the life cycles of Israel and the Jews. This shift is similar to former times, as when King Josiah brought about reform and unity of inner faith before the Israelites' exile to Babylon, and when Johanan ben Zakkai guided the people to live peacefully by bringing study and knowledge to bear in a dangerous world.

I will name this new set of values *Co-Creativity Driven by Compassion*. We are creators exploring a path of newly discovered knowledge. We humans have always been innovators, but the pace of innovation throughout the course of history has been slow, only beginning to speed up with the advent of the Industrial Revolution. Today it is accelerating exponentially, and we must act responsibly with some urgency.

Compassion

Our first priority emphasizes the value of *compassion*. This value focuses on the needs of humanity. We must learn to solve challenging problems to support society's progress. People must come first. We must be accountable for reforming public policy, which includes improving social conditions, strengthening education, supporting health care, reducing poverty and wealth inequality, and stimulating economic mobility.

Not only must we focus on solving societal problems, but we must also strengthen human relationships in an ever-more complex world. We must build livable spaces in which families and communities can thrive, because when the younger generation can no longer afford to buy homes and raise families, we surely have a problem. The requirements of providing for home and family should also leave us room and time to connect with the natural world around us.

We must ensure that corporations and governments advance solutions, not only to meet business challenges, but also to support a sustainable environment. Along with the spread of an uncontrollable virus, we are dealing with a crisis associated with climate change. We see Earth's temperature changing, adverse weather patterns, and other related disasters. Do we need a major event to force us to change, or are we willing to face up to our problems and begin coping with them now?

Creativity

The second priority emphasizes the value of *creativity*. By combining new and existing technologies in novel ways, we have more opportunities to channel our efforts into finding solutions to the major challenges of today. Dr. Brian Arthur, father of Complexity Theory in Economics, states that while there is ongoing research and development in the United States, it appears to be diminishing. Instead, combining existing technology in new ways is on the rise.[1] But how can we attempt to shape our efforts for better future outcomes?

Creativity must be used to responsibly tackle social issues. For example, smartphones connect billions of people around the world. At a fraction of the cost of traditional business models, cell phones in poorer African countries are now being used for banking and selling crops or exports in the market.

Farmers in these countries historically did not have the capital to establish complex legal entities, major banking arrangements, and agricultural distribution systems which help bring food to market. Neither can some of these countries afford to establish the necessary infrastructure. They have been able to leapfrog these challenges because of advancements in cell phone technology, which is being used to help people in ways that can lead to higher levels of self-sufficiency and wellbeing. For example, between 2008 and 2014, Kenya's mobile banking system, M-PESA, helped to lift two percent of Kenya's population out of poverty.[2] This illustrates the value of creativity and innovation in helping people solve long-standing problems.

Using new scientific knowledge and technology wisely can create greater abundance for everyone. Such is the case with agricultural innovation leading to increased food production. Growing food in solutions rich in nutrients, as is being done with advances in hydroponics, increases crop yields and nutritional content significantly, and is up to seventy percent more efficient than traditional agriculture. This demonstrates the value of creativity in solving food shortages and promoting health.

Push-pull farming, or agroecology, is a form of intercropping where one type of plant is grown, then different plants are interspersed between rows. It is a method that naturally attracts protective insects and repels others, thereby reducing reliance on pesticides. It has been used in at least 57 countries, with 80 to 116 percent enhanced crop yields. And while there may be legitimate concerns about genetically modified organisms (GMOs), these crops are more weather-tolerant, more resistant to pests and disease, and produce more output per acre than traditional seed crops.[3]

Nanotechnology, genomics, immunology, and pharmacology are aligning in new combinations to bring about desirable solutions in medicine. One example is the effort to heal cancers through targeted cell destruction. A second example involves collecting a patient's own cells as the foundation for generating small organs such as bone or cartilage using biomaterials, along with structural scaffolding technologies composed of artificial or natural materials to support the shape of new tissue growth. A third example involves the extraction of stem cells from our own bodies, combined with digital imaging and 3D printing technology, to produce viable organs for transplant that involve little or no risk of rejection and eliminate the need of waiting for a donor. Wellness and health emanating from creativity are admirable examples of compassionate solutions derived from new technology.[4]

Creativity must help people thrive. As current challenges are met, our freedom to determine how best to improve the quality of our lives expands. A focus on humanity means finding ways to enhance our human relationships, both at home and in our communities, as well as encouraging people to connect more meaningfully with others. This should counterbalance the increasing emphasis on advanced technology, which causes electronic addictions, shifts and reductions in jobs, as well as superficial social connections.

Cell phones and computers in our work settings easily promote longer work weeks and make us feel as though we are on the job 24/7. The goal of today's corporations is to make money and increase productivity—often at the expense of our health. People struggle to be passionate about their work, to be able to learn based on personal interests, and to promote for themselves a work-life balance.

Corporations need to return to good corporate citizenship and raise their social consciousness by being willing to invest in their employees through ongoing education, flexibility, and stable benefits, while still helping to address the needs of society. Starbucks has developed an approach to retain its workers by helping to fund their college educations. Amazon has recognized the future impact of using automation and robotics in their warehouses and the disruption to jobs that such automation creates. In 2019, they developed a strategic plan to retrain lower-wage workers for more complex jobs by teaching them software coding and computer expertise. This boosts employee retention and job opportunities for lower-wage workers.

Lifelong learning is critical for maintaining skills, reinventing ourselves in a changing job market, and engaging in lifelong pursuits to help people *thrive*. It has become the new norm. Online platforms and apps, together with books, seminars, and flexible university courses on topics of interest, have allowed more people to gain access to such learning.

Online discussions and interviews, YouTube videos, TED Talks, and online courses facilitate new avenues of personal growth for everyone—anywhere in the world. However, technology alone cannot provide a quality education. Maintaining the human connection while participating in skill development is also necessary, whether on campus, via distance learning, or through seminars. Building relationships through experiential learning is and has been the norm but can now be supplemented with technology.

People in urban settings must form communities that include networks of individuals who are willing to become friends and help each other, sharing childcare services, computer and educational resources, and promoting recreation. The future demands livable cities. It is our responsibility to develop new ways of promoting an enhanced quality of life for the younger generation, and for the elderly who are experiencing greater isolation. During the COVID-19 pandemic, we found that most children need face-to-face classroom time along with their digital learning, not just for academic subjects but for learning to interact with each other.

People thrive best when they can connect to the outdoor environment. Each of us needs to periodically reconnect with nature, to experience quiet time for ourselves, to feel the rhythm of life, and to center ourselves in an exceedingly fast-paced world. Nature can help us unplug from our high-tech world. Just as people can become addicted to drugs, so people can become addicted to technology. When we live on a constant diet of electronics such as video games, e-mails, social media, and texting, we often close ourselves off from necessary, deeper conversations and relationships.

Creativity is the key to finding ways to ecologically sustain our world as new technologies and science develop. The Earth and its resources are finite. When we waste them, we endanger future generations as well as ourselves. We have a responsibility to create mechanisms for sustainability in our world through such methods as recycling waste, using renewable energy, reclaiming wastewater, and diminishing our carbon footprint. We must also find ways to reduce air and water pollution, both of which are health hazards. Climate change becomes real as rising global levels of carbon dioxide and other greenhouse gases trap heat and melt ice in the polar regions, impacting water tables and altering weather patterns around the world.

Solutions exist for generating clean water in drought-stricken areas where climate change is worsening. Within a nation that has a large percentage of desert land, Israel has used emerging technologies in water development and application to ensure a supply of this limited resource. Since the 1950s, Israel has become self-sufficient, providing enough clean water to its citizens at all times. The country can grow its own food and still have enough water to share with poorer countries such as Jordan. It exports its technology to other nations or regions that are experiencing shortages such as India, Africa, China, and California.

Combining wind and solar energy with the development and use of powerful lithium batteries may help bring affordable energy solutions to a world that is drowning in carbon-based fossil fuel emissions, which cause pollution and illness. Technology used in electric cars should eventually allow further reductions in greenhouse gas emissions. Alternative energy sources will help to reduce the cost of utilities in new smart homes, making them both more affordable and more efficient. Ironically, as energy experts know, green revolution solutions can still produce carbon emissions and chemical pollutants unless industries take appropriate measures.

The "Co" in Co-Creativity

The third priority underscores the value of *"co"* in *co-creativity*. Co-creativity means we must work collaboratively to create and innovate. We must also balance the collective good with the needs of the individual rather than emphasizing the individual at the expense of the collective good. Communication and problem-solving can lead to greater responsibility and accountability to one another and to ourselves, thereby strengthening personal, peer, and group interactions.

Power in the hands of the few inevitably leads to power abused. This results in wealth inequality in the world and concentrated, monopolistic markets. In an unregulated free-market economy, the owners of the means of production and distribution accumulate wealth, thereby creating a phenomenon in which a very small percentage of the population benefits from the majority of the wealth. In the past, jobs shifted away from certain areas of production because of globalization; now, jobs are shifting because of the rise of technology and automation. Both scenarios are facilitating further concentrations of wealth. We see the middle class in

America shrinking and barriers to increased social mobility rising for adults and our younger generation.

We must create the means to share power and wealth among a larger number of people to achieve greater overall abundance. This means working together on participative forms of capitalism, economics, and political structures that support democracy. I am not suggesting a redistribution of wealth or a new form of socialism but rather creating greater avenues of access for mainstream individuals to increase their income.

One proposal is to reduce regulations that create barriers for small businesses to access capital and promote entrepreneurship. Another is for government to mandate the strengthening of benefits for lower-wage workers. Technology can also facilitate collaboration between governments by improving the efficiency of administrative systems for better access. If issues such as these are not addressed, our country's current anger and resentment may lead to even greater emotional turmoil, divisiveness, and violence.

There will always be competition in the world. But competition, which creates healthy and balanced tensions, can become a catalyst for collaboration, and a tool to overcome the constraints of corporate inertia. Societies that have evolved successfully have done so by working together to build a civilization or a nation.

Competition can inspire collaboration as new ecosystems develop within industries. For example, NASA, which was previously the sole provider of American space launch capability, has developed cooperative arrangements with other countries as well as with private companies. To date, SpaceX, working with NASA, has demonstrated numerous successful launches of the Crew Dragon module. The public-private partnership with SpaceX allows both organizations to innovate more quickly than either could have alone while maintaining safety and reliability standards.

Technology used in space travel is being developed synergistically to promote growth in alternative energy sources. Research into space travel has always generated new materials and technologies which have produced spinoff products. Tesla develops electric cars and lithium batteries. The battery design, enlarged for solar energy use, can support electric grids that service large urban areas. These cities can purchase unused electricity generated from smart homes that produce excess solar energy and send it to power grids.

Competition sees the world through the eyes of scarcity and a win-lose mentality. Cooperation sees the world as one of opportunities and solutions. The combined power of people striving to achieve unifying goals will eventually, and inevitably, move us closer to solving today's challenging problems and may help us make new discoveries which benefit humanity.

Co-creativity means we work together to create shared outcomes that help people, not harm them. While financial success and economic growth is certainly important, they must not be a means to an end themselves. Financial success should not be the primary goal, but must be *aligned* as a secondary goal, one which supports our efforts at achieving greater purpose.

Co-creativity also means that we not only have the freedom to create and innovate but that we must do so responsibly. Once money, consumerism, and economic growth become primary motivations, we lose sight of our true purpose, which is to improve people's lives. Remember, value is conferred on money and consumer goods by people who desire position and power.

It is the *quality* of what we create with money and goods that brings meaning and purpose to our lives. A sole primary focus on wealth emerges from the darker emotions of greed, envy, hatred, and anger, easily leading to negative outcomes rather than the positive ones of aiding people in improving themselves, their families, and society as a whole.

We must find a way to lead with this value of co-creativity driven by compassion. How do we accomplish this when change moves at a rapid and unstoppable pace? How do we regain purpose and passion in our lives? Even if we agree to seek these desirable values, to ensure that we move on a path toward goodness, how do we achieve consensus and embed these values into our lives?

If the rate of change of technology is outstripping society's pace, then we must somehow find a way to address this issue. Developing and strengthening this new value of *co-creativity driven by compassion* will take time, and we must capture that time. We must confer together on these issues, day after day, one-on-one and in groups, to develop common values, directions, and solutions that clearly demonstrate that we *can* lead as *co-creators* for the betterment of society— before technology completely outpaces us and gains control over our lives.

Alternatively, many of us can find new ways to reconnect with nature, to enjoy quiet time and to become more centered, so we can think through issues of great importance to ourselves. This allows us to become rejuvenated. We can find new sources of ideas that will become integrated into our psyches and focus us on positive goals toward encouraging a better humanity.

The path will be different for each individual. For some it will be about holding down a job to live better, but hopefully in ways that strengthen family and community ties. For others, it will be about developing new solutions at the corporate, state, or national level, by improving systems and services which help meet societal needs.

Today, more people are trying to create these deeper connections with family, friends, and co-workers—to responsibly innovate and co-create together. We will find that the traditional model of top-down hierarchies will not disappear, but it will become outmoded. Instead, we need to develop new leadership styles which provide guidance, resources, and frameworks for people to innovate, to achieve shared solutions, and to help people thrive. Otherwise, traditional hierarchy, over time, will cause bottlenecks that stifle creativity and growth.

The Hebrew Scriptures have taught us that our past traditions remain relevant to our current challenges. But the future asks how we will take those values that are important to us and use them to discover new ones to guide our present and future decision-making processes. The rabbis helped us interpret the living laws in order to coexist in earlier times, within a social order that encouraged us to care for one another. Their lesson is that once we stop caring, and instead start thinking too much about wealth and power, society becomes corrupt.

Finding the right shared path for our values of peace, kindness, empathy, and compassion was the key in former times—and is still the key in all major faiths today. The rabbis drew these values from the Hebrew Scriptures and the Talmud and introduced them in synagogues. Christian thinkers canonized them in the New Testament and introduced them in churches to guide people's lives throughout the world. But the values of the past are no longer sufficient to shape the world of tomorrow. We must dig deeper into our ancient texts for new insights and draw out values that will work for the future. These require us to both co-exist and co-create a better world.

Israel's Future Values Success Story

Israel already embodies this value of the future—*co-creativity driven by compassion.* Israel has become a beacon of "light unto other nations." Having a common heritage of three religions—Judaism, Christianity, and Islam, it is a nation that values peace. Furthermore, it is the only democracy in its part of the world.

Israel is surrounded by Arab nations adhering to religious fundamentalism. This has promoted war and terrorism. The tensions of the region consistently threaten the safety and wellbeing of Israel and its people. Such dynamics have led to the need for Israel to rapidly innovate technologically, in collaborative ways, for both short- and long-term gains, which will maintain a qualitative advantage and allow for survival. Finding its way toward unity through regional adversity requires constant vigilance and, therefore, resilient, adaptive thinking.

Israel has created one of the strongest and most moral defense forces in the world. Its military system has become the basis for strong networks, lifelong friendships, and most important, innovative technology. During their military service, young Israelis have the opportunity to develop critical thinking, problem-solving, and leadership skills prior to entering university because the military operates more as a horizontal organization rather than as a traditional hierarchy. Military service becomes the seed bed for developing advanced technology and out-of-the box thinking, with incentives to support a high level of entrepreneurship among Israeli youth.

Israel maintains one of the best systems of higher education in the world. The country has achieved the highest level of spending in research and development on a global per capita basis. Major international corporations are constantly acquiring Israeli companies to boost their research and product development and have also established their own core research divisions in Israel. One of Israel's goals is to generate technological leadership with an emphasis on solving many of humanity's problems.

Creativity and innovation in Israel are already operating to enhance the common good—to support security, health, agriculture, sustainability of nature, and infrastructure development. The baseline value of learning and knowledge is the country's greatest strength. Such efforts have developed because the impact of these values on its people encourages them to work, explore, create, and learn together in a cohesive manner.

Israel has emerged as a world leader in research in such areas as agriculture, water purification, medicine, pharmacology, and genomics. It is on the forefront of digital technology, cybersecurity, and newly engineered materials, along with artificial intelligence, robotics, drones, military technology, and nanotechnology.

Israel's water technology, as described earlier in this section, is already one of the best in the world. For example, its reclamation of wastewater ranks the highest of any nation. Innovative irrigation methods and renewable water sources allow for targeted water use on crops, thereby reducing waste and yielding a higher output per acre. Cheaper and more advanced Israeli desalination methods have brought fresh water to many arid countries.

Futurists predict that water shortages will cause much conflict. Many parts of the world are already experiencing such shortages. Egypt has been in conflict with Ethiopia over the damming of the Blue Nile near the Sudanese border because of concerns over Nile water levels flowing into Egypt, and the impact it may have on Egyptian agriculture.[5] Other countries, like Morocco, are battling desertification as sands claim more and more of their arable land. Israel is able and willing to help lead the way with global solutions to water problems.

As the country progresses in all these areas, Israeli companies license and share their technologies to help other nations overcome food shortages and solve major social problems, as well as promote sustainability in natural resources. Israel is one of the first nations to arrive on the scene when catastrophes, such as earthquakes, hurricanes and tsunamis, strike. Israel knows where its priorities lie. It aspires to be a model in facilitating the changes that make a difference in people's lives throughout the world.

Such a model is becoming a reality as Israel and the United Arab Emirates begin to implement the Abraham Accords. This treaty promotes peace and economic opportunities between the two countries. While other Middle Eastern fundamentalist states and groups may continue actively opposing Israel, this alliance signals that future openings for cooperation and innovative partnerships are possible.

As the coronavirus pandemic has impacted the world, scientists the world over have rapidly employed technology to search for solutions. This includes discoveries in diagnostic and post-illness antibody testing, medication, treatments, and vaccine development. Over fifty countries have come together on various open-source, cross-disciplinary electronic platforms to share information, reducing the learning curve for breakthrough solutions. This kind of effort is unprecedented in human history and can set an example for similar future collaborative efforts.

At the same time, the United States lacked coordination in establishing well-thought-out clinical trials and making decisions based on scientific fact. The pandemic has exposed weaknesses in supply chains, which crashed. Our most valuable front-line workers and first responders had to fight for protective masks and gowns. Money was allocated to companies that had discovered potential solutions, many of which did not pan out. These early efforts were often leaderless and uncoordinated.

Stimulus money was budgeted to prevent economic collapse. The bulk of the initial round of funding went to large companies to support their employees, yet those companies were the among the first to announce layoffs. Many smaller companies did not receive adequate funds to remain viable. Over forty million people went on unemployment. Stimulus checks to the poor were slow in arriving. Both processes were slowed because the systems available to handle distribution to such large numbers of people were inadequate. As a result, economic hardship will have markedly worsened in our country by the time the pandemic is over.

If there were ever a time for a crisis to bring out the core values needed for the future—*co-creativity driven by compassion*—it is now. While technology has and will provide many of the answers in our future, those future solutions also require leadership, good governance, and aligned business practices—all of which must put people's lives first.

The pandemic also makes us think hard about implementing programs which, in the long run, may be problematic. For example, stockpiling medications whose effectiveness is unproven, using smartphones to track the spread of the virus, and engaging drones to monitor temperature clusters all involve definite and dangerous downsides. After the crisis is over, will we be able to step back and assess whether we have given up too much of our individual freedoms to enable the use of potentially invasive technology?

We must be wise enough to know that once a specific technology is unleashed, it becomes difficult to step back and be more judicious in our use of it. Once privacy has been invaded, it may be difficult to change course. New technology leads to unintended consequences, which requires recognition of those consequences as well as thoughtful resolutions. We must be willing to explore this challenging terrain and what it means to us in the context of human rights as well as democratic and economic principles.

The fundamental understanding of how we want our future values to guide us will set the stage for making such ethical choices. We must lead with moral wisdom in our collaborative decisions in order to uphold society and improve the world. We must educate ourselves, our children, and our neighbors in new methods of problem-solving so we can optimistically and responsibly approach solutions.

Schools must teach these values and institutions must integrate them into their practices. Institutions that cannot change will give rise to new ones. We must address these issues over time in a multidimensional manner, one which involves education, economics, politics, and culture. Alignment in all areas is the only way to ensure success.

Co-creativity driven by compassion must be our new unifying value which guides the spirit of society based on the congruent integration of the shared principles of faith, science, and governance. Only then will we find new direction and purpose that will inform our decisions justly, wisely, and compassionately as co-creators in an ever-evolving world.

These values are embedded within the Torah, Tanakh, and our ancient Judeo-Christian texts, ready for us to adapt them for today's times and our future. We can see how the originating values have evolved throughout the millennia, in different cultures, among all faiths. We must study our history and understand how they emerged, developed, and resonated during certain times, and how they might elevate society's values while still assimilating prior ones. We can see how some values guide people down the wrong fork in the road, leading to their destruction. It is always our choice and our responsibility to determine which path we will travel and choose what values will guide our future.

Afterword

Major Sources

Appendix

Notes

Index

Afterword:
Values and Essential Scholarship

Since the 1960s, there has been a concerted and, sadly, very successful effort by some to literally destroy more than three thousand years of Judaic ethical, moral, and social teachings. This has ignited an all-out assault on the Judeo-Christian value system of the Western world with the goal of replacing it with a human-centered set of so-called "ethics" and a morality designed to rationalize and normalize every vice that a person could possibly imagine. The pursuit of unbridled pleasure as well as an implementation of horribly unjust, unfair, immoral, corrupt legal and ethical codes are now the canon taught in educational institutes from kindergarten through the end of graduate school in most of the Western world. For those of us who grew up and were educated before this inversion of morality and decency was implemented, it feels like we have been transported into a bizarre world where, on one the hand, there is very advanced technology; yet, on the other hand, many act as though they have never heard of justice or morality.

In *Values That Shape the World*, Faye Lincoln has written a desperately-needed book that reminds those of us who were educated before our world was redefined, and calls out to those being educated today in the "new" version of this historic period, what a God-centered and value-centered existence the world believed in and was striving to achieve. *Values That Shape the World* reminds us that there exists a brilliant and insightful handbook on how humans should behave when it comes to our interactions with each other and the world around us. It defines in detail what morality and ethics are when given by the Creator. This book is, of course, what is called the Tanach/Bible by the Jewish world, the Old Testament by the Christian world, and the First Revelation by the Islamic world. Lincoln takes us on a whirlwind tour of the Tanach/Bible and shows us how many incredible, significant eternal truths were laid out by our Creator for humans to live by. It is a wake-up call to all of us—a reminder that to successfully move forward as a civilized society, we need to return to the ideals and values of the Tanach/Bible. Furthermore, when one reads through this book, it is easy to contrast the powerful and restraining ideals and values of the Tanach/Bible with the intellectually flimsy and lazy approach of the last sixty years that has left most of the Western world with no hope, with broken and collapsing families, increased depression, the birth of a new brand of dangerous nihilism, and the destruction of communities and entire cultures.

God bless Faye Lincoln for showing us that being a Biblical scholar means that one can be a true expert on morality and ethics. Being such an expert means that one can offer many solutions to what ails society in this twenty-first century.

Rabbi Yotav Eliach
Lawrence, NY
June 23, 2021 / 13 Tammuz 5781

Rabbi Yotav Eliach is the principal of the prestigious Rambam Mesivta in Long Island and the author of Judaism, Zionism, and the Land of Israel.

Major Sources

A wide variety of sources, primary, secondary, and online, were consulted during the writing of this book. Dates in parentheses after online sources, e.g., (05/01/2021) (US format), indicate the date that the source was most recently accessed.

Sacred Texts

Tanakh: The Holy Scriptures: The New JPS Translation According to the Traditional Hebrew Text. Philadelphia: Jewish Publication Society, 1985.

The Chumash: The Stone Edition (English and Hebrew Edition): The Torah: Haftaros and Five Megillos with a Commentary Anthologized from the Rabbinic Writings. Edited by Nosson Scherman. New York: Mesorah Publications, 1993.

The Essential Talmud 30th ed. Edited by Adin Steinsaltz. New York: Basic Books, 2006.

Everyman's Talmud: The Major Teachings of the Rabbinic Sages. Edited by Abraham Cohen. New York: Schocken Books, 1995.

The William Davidson Talmud at the Sefaria Library. Jerusalem, Koren Publishers. www.sefaria.org/texts/Talmud.

The Jerusalem Bible. Edited by Alexander Jones. Garden City, NY: Doubleday & Company, 1996.

The Jewish Study Bible 2nd ed. Edited by Adele Berlin and Marc Zvi Brettler. Oxford: Oxford University Press, 2014.

The New English Bible, with the Apocrypha. Edited by Samuel Sandmel, Jack Suggs, and Arnold J. Tkacik. New York: Oxford University Press, 1976.

The New International Version Study Bible. Edited by Kenneth L. Barker. Grand Rapids, MI: Zondervan, 2011

The Holy Qur'an: Text, Translation, and Commentary. Edited and translated by Abdullah Yusuf Ali. Brentwood, MD: Amana Corporation, 1983.

Articles

Moskowitz, Nathan. "The Book of Daniel: Part I: A Theological-Political Tractate Addressed to Judean Hasidim Under Seleucid-Greek Rule," *Jewish Bible Quarterly* 38, no. 2 (2010), 98–105, archived at valuesthatshapetheworld.com/docs/Book-of-Daniel-Part-I-Moskowitz-JBQ-38-2.pdf.

"Continental Disconnect: Mobile phones are transforming Africa." *The Economist*, Dec 10, 2016. Archived at valuesthatshapetheworld.com/docs/continental-disconnect-mobile-phones-transforming-africa-economist-2016-12-10.

"Templum Pacis, the Temple of Peace." In *Encyclopaedia Romana*, edited by Aelus Stylo. penelope.uchicago.edu/~grout/encyclopaedia_romana/imperialfora/vespasian/templumpacis.html (04/26/2021).

Reference Works

Encyclopaedia Britannica, Encyclopaedia Britannica, Inc., continuously updated at www.britannica.com.

The Interpreter's Dictionary of the Bible, edited by George Arthur Buttrick (Nashville: Abingdon Press, 1962).

The Jewish Encyclopedia: The Unedited Text of the 1906 Jewish Encyclopedia, The Kopelman Foundation. www.jewishencyclopedia.com.

The Jewish Virtual Library (JVL), The American-Israeli Cooperative Enterprise. www.jewishvirtuallibrary.org.

Oxford's English and Spanish Dictionary, Dictionary.com LLC, continuously updated at www.dictionary.com.

Webster's Third New International Dictionary of the English Language. Springfield, MA: Merriam-Webster, 1993. Continually updated, as *The Merriam-Webster Dictionary*, at merriam-webster.com.

Lectures

Arthur, Brian W. "Complexity Theory in Economics," lecture in *Short Course—Complexity in Social and Economic Systems*, Santa Fe Institute for Complexity Theory, Santa Fe NM, Jan 2016.

Atala, Anthony. "Printing a Human Kidney." Filmed March 2011. TEDed Video, 16:54. www.youtube.com/watch?v=bX3C201O4MA. (04/29/2021).

Sandel, Michael. "Why We Shouldn't Trust Markets with our Civic Life." Filmed August 26, 2016, Edinburgh. TED video, 14:37. www.youtube.com/watch?v=3nsoN-LS8RQ (04/30/2021).

Films

Indiana Jones and the Last Crusade. Directed by Steven Spielberg. Screenplay by Jeffery Boam. Performances by Harrison Ford, Denholm Elliott, Alison Doody, John Rhys-Davies, Julian Glover, Sean Connery. Lucasfilm, Paramount, 1989.

Lincoln. Directed by Stephen Spielberg. Screenplay by Tony Kushner. Performances by Daniel Day-Lewis, Sally Field, Joseph Gordon-Levitt, Hal Holbrook, Tommy Lee Jones. Dreamworks, 20th Century Fox, 2012.

Books

Ali, Ayaan Hirsi. *Heretic—Why Islam Needs a Reformation Now.* New York: Harper Collins Publishers, 2015.

Atkinson, Kenneth. *Queen Salome: Jerusalem's Warrior Monarch of the First Century BCE.* London, NC: McFarland & Company, Inc., 1960, 2012.

Bader, Gershom. *The Encyclopedia of Talmudic Sages.* Translated by Solomon Katz. London, Northvale, NJ: Jason Aronson Inc., 1988.

Balakian, Peter. *The Burning Tigris.* New York: HarperCollins Publishing, 2003.

Barnavi, Eli, ed. *A Historical Atlas of the Jewish People, from the Time of the Patriarchs to the Present* 2nd ed. Paris: Hachette Littératures; New York: Schocken Books, 2002.

Beck, Donald E. and Christopher Cowan. *Spiral Dynamics: Mastering Values, Leadership and Change.* Malden, MA: Blackwell Publishing, 1996, 2006.

Berman, Ilan. *Iran's Deadly Ambition.* New York: Encounter Books, 2015.

Black, Edwin. *IBM and the Holocaust: The Strategic Alliance between Nazi Germany and America's Most Powerful Corporation.* Washington, DC: Dialog Press, 2001, 2009.

Black, Edwin. *The Farhud: Roots of the Arab-Nazi Alliance in the Holocaust.* Washington, DC: Dialog Press, 2010.

Buxbaum, Yitzhak. *The Life and Teachings of Hillel.* Lanham, MD: Rowman & Littlefield Publishers, Inc., 1994.

Carroll, James. *Christ Actually: The Son of God for the Secular Age.* New York: Viking, Penguin Group, 2014.

Carroll, James. *Constantine's Sword—The Church and the Jews: A History.* Boston, New York: Houghton Mifflin, 2001.

Cohen, Shaye J. D. *From the Maccabees to the Mishnah* 2nd ed. Louisville, KY: Westminster John Knox Press, 2006.

Dawlabani, Said Elias. *MEMEnomics—The Next Generation Economic System.* New York: Select Books, 2013.

De Vaux, Roland. *Ancient Israel: Its Life and Institutions.* Translated by John McHugh. New York: McGraw-Hill, 1961.

Dershowitz, Alan M. *The Genesis of Justice.* New York: Warner Books, 2000.

Deutsch, David. *The Beginning of Infinity: Explanations That Transform the World.* New York: Penguin Books, 2011.

Diamandis, Peter H. and Steven Kotler. *Abundance: The Future is Better Than You Think.* New York: Free Press (Simon & Schuster), 2012.

Dimont, Max I. *Jews God and History* 2nd ed. Edited and revised by Ethel Dimont. New York: Signet Classics, 1994.

Durant, Will. *The Story of Civilization: The Life of Greece.* New York: Simon & Schuster, 1939, 1966.

Feiler, Bruce. *Walking the Bible.* New York: HarperCollins, 2001.

Flavius, Josephus. *Josephus: The Complete Works of Josephus by Josephus Flavius.* Translated by William A. M. Whiston. Nashville: Thomas Nielsen Publishers, 1737, 1998.

Friedman, Thomas L. *Thank You for Being Late.* New York: Farrar, Straus, and Giroux, 2016.

Gilbert, Martin. *The Atlas of Jewish History* 7th ed. New York: Routledge, 2009.

Götz, Aly. *Hitler's Beneficiaries.* New York: Henry Holt & Company, 2005, 2006.

Grant, Michael. *The Jews in the Roman World.* New York: Charles Scribner's Sons, 1973.

Heschel, Abraham. *The Prophets.* New York: Harper Perennial Modern Classics, 1995.

Holtz, Barry W., ed., *Back to the Sources*. New York: Simon & Schuster Paperbacks, 1984.

House, Karen Elliott. *On Saudi Arabia*. New York: Alfred A. Knopf, 2012.

Kingsley, Sean. *Gold's Gold*. New York: HarperCollins, 2007.

Kramer, Samuel Noah. *The Sumerians: Their History, Culture, and Character*. Chicago: The University of Chicago Press, 1963.

Lau, Binyamin. *The Sages: Character, Context & Creativity*. Translated by Ilana Kur-shan and Joshua Prawer. New Milford, CT: Koren Publishers, 2010.

Morgenthau Sr., Henry. *Ambassador Morgenthau's Story: A Personal Account of the Armenian Genocide*. New York: Cosimo, 1918, 2008.

Myss, Caroline. *Defy Gravity: Healing Beyond the Bounds of Reason*. New York: Hay House, 2009.

Phares, Walid. *Future Jihad: Terrorist Strategies Against America*. New York: Palgrave Macmillan, 2005.

Philo of Alexandria. *De Vita Mosis*. Translated by F. H. Colson. Edited by G. P. Goold. In *Philo* Vol. VI. Cambridge: Harvard University Press; London: William Heineman: 1935, 1984.

Pollack, Kenneth. *A Path Out of the Desert: A Grand Strategy for America in the Middle East*. New York: Random House, 2008.

Pollard, Justin and Howard Reid. *The Rise and Fall of Alexandria: Birthplace of the Modern World*. New York: Penguin Group, 2006.

Prager, Dennis and Joseph Telushkin. *Why the Jews? The Reason for Antisemitism*. New York: Touchstone, 1983, 2003.

Greenberg, Sidney and Jonathan D. Levine. *Siddur Hadash for All Sabbath & Festival Services*. Bridgeport (CT), New York: The Prayer Book Press of Media Judaica, 2000.

Rainey, Anson F. and Steven R. Notley. *The Sacred Bridge: Carta's Atlas of the Biblical World*. Jerusalem: Carta Jerusalem, 2006.

Saldarini, Anthony J. *Pharisees, Scribes and Sadducees in Palestinian Society*. Wilmington, DE: Michael Glazier, Inc., 1988; Grand Rapids, MI: Wm. B. Eerdmans Publishing, 2001.

Schiffman, Lawrence H. *From Text to Tradition—A History of the Second Temple & Rabbinic Judaism*. Hoboken: Ktav Publishing House, Inc., 1991.

Schwartz, Leo W., ed. *Great Ages and Ideas of the Jewish People.* New York: Random House, Inc., 1956.

Schwartz, Stephan A. *The 8 Laws of Change: How to be an Agent of Personal and Social Transformation.* Rochester, VT: Park Street Press, 2015.

Senor, Dan and Saul Singer. *Start-Up Nation—The Story of Israel's Economic Miracle.* New York: Hachette Book Group, 2009.

Siegal, Seth M. *Let There Be Water: Israel's Solution for a Water-Starved World.* New York: Thomas Dunne Books, St. Martin's Press, 2015.

Smith, Huston. *The World's Religions: Our Great Wisdom Traditions.* New York: HarperCollins Publishers, 1958, 1991.

Swift, Fletcher Harper. *Education in Ancient Israel—From Earliest Times to 70 A.D.* Chicago: Open Court Publishing, 1919.

Tooze, Adam. *The Wages of Destruction: The Making and Breaking of the Nazi Economy.* London, New York: Penguin Books, 2007, 2008.

Wasserstein, Abraham and David J. Wasserstein. *The Legend of the Septuagint— From Classical Antiquity to Today.* New York: Cambridge University Press, 2006, 2009.

Appendix:
The Twelve Tribes of Israel

Abraham fathered Isaac, whose second son Jacob (later named Israel) fathered twelve sons: Reuben, Simeon, Levi, Judah, Dan, Naphtali, Gad, Asher, Issachar, Zebulun, Joseph, and Benjamin. These twelve sons became the founders of the Twelve Tribes.

When Joshua led the people to the Promised Land after their desert post-Exodus wandering, each Tribe settled in its own territory except Levi. The Levites did not establish their own region; they served in the Temple and lived among the people throughout the land.

The Tribes of Judah and Benjamin established the Kingdom of Judah in the south; the remaining ten joined together in the north to create the Kingdom of Israel. It is these ten northern Tribes that were lost subsequent to the Assyrian invasion and the victory of Sennacherib in approximately 722 BCE.

The text of *Values That Shape the World* refers to clans and tribes interchangeably.

The term "House" is synonymous with family and dynasty. At its broadest, there is the House of Israel, i.e., Jacob's descendants, i.e., the Twelve Tribes. Other Israelite Houses of significance include the House of Saul, the House of Omri, and the House of David.

Notes

Chapter 1: Beliefs That Change Our Worldview

[1] Huston Smith, *The World's Religions: Our Great Wisdom Traditions* (New York: HarperCollins, 1991), 274–275.

[2] Samuel Noah Kramer, *The Sumerians: Their History, Culture, and Character* (Chicago: The University of Chicago Press, 1963), 126.

[3] Kramer, *The Sumerians,* 81–84, 123. Adele Berlin and Mark Zvi Brettler, eds., The Jewish Study Bible 2nd ed. (New York: Oxford University Press, 2014), 2222–2223. Between the period of 2400 and 2000 BCE, the Third Dynasty of Ur, Sumerian kings and their people cherished goodness, truth, law, order, justice and freedom, righteousness, mercy and compassion. Ur-Nammu wrote the first law code in 2050 BCE, probably on a stele. Kings were responsible for law and justice. Governors, *ensi,* were responsible for administering their local areas of oversight. We are most familiar with the later written code of Hammurabi (1792–1750 BCE), formalized after he had conquered and united Upper and Lower Mesopotamia. The Sumerians had been known for their law in earlier times.

[4] Kramer, *The Sumerians,* 79–81.

[5] Kramer, *The Sumerians,* 123.

[6] Kramer, *The Sumerians,* 117.

[7] Tanakh—The Hebrew Scriptures. Throughout this text, Lord and God will be used separately, together, and interchangeably. Adonai may also be used to refer to the Lord.

[8] In ancient times, in some cultures, it was common practice to share wives. But as common as this practice was, it was often not conducive to developing a strong sense of family.

[9] The binding of Isaac is central to Genesis and to the story of Abraham's relationship with God. While not discussed here, it is recognized that Abraham must have suffered extreme inner turmoil before finally trusting God that his son would live to continue the patriarchal line of the Hebrews through the twelve tribes of Jacob. From this Scripture, children become most precious in carrying on the generativity of free will and self-determination from the time of Abraham.

Chapter 2: The Exodus—Faith in God

[1] Nosson Scherman, ed., *The Chumash: The Stone Edition* (English and Hebrew Edition): *The Torah: Haftaros and Five Megillos With a Commentary Anthologized from the Rabbinic Writings* (Brooklyn: Mesorah Publications, 1993), 359–360. Commentary 40 discusses the duration of the Egyptian exile. (Exodus 12:40–41). This section indicates that the Hebrews were in Egypt for 430 years. The Rabbinic tradition references this timeframe from Genesis 15:13, beginning with the birth of Isaac to the Exodus from Egypt, a period of 400 years. Rashi's commentary on Exodus places the duration at 210 years: "Rashi on Exodus 12:40," in The William Davidson Talmud, www.sefaria.org/Rashi_on_Exodus.12.40?lang=bi (05/01/2021)

[2] Exodus and Leviticus not only identify the traditional Ten Commandments, but also additional laws and commandments referred to in Judaism as the 613 Mitzvot and the "ethical law."

[3] The JPS version of the Tanakh places "You shall have no other gods besides Me" in the first commandment. Many editions of the Bible include this as part of the second. We will continue to be guided by the JPS translation.

Chapter 3: The Exodus—Unity through Adversity

[1] Exodus 40:1–14. Exodus 26:1–33.
[2] Exodus 29:10–41.
[3] Exodus 28:1–30.
[4] Exodus 23:10–11. Exodus 21:12–35. Exodus 22:1–14.

Chapter 4: The Books of Judges and Kings—The Law Treats Everyone Equally

[1] Eli Barnavi, general ed., *A Historical Atlas of the Jewish People, From the Time of the Patriarchs to the Present* (New York: Schocken Books, 2002), 14.

[2] In battle today, it is the custom to spare women and children. In ancient times, men who conquered other lands and groups would rape women and take men, women, and children as slaves. It was considered more compassionate at the time to forbid rape and enslavement, and instead take everyone's life.

[3] Barnavi, *Historical Atlas of the Jewish People*, 14.
[4] Barnavi, *Historical Atlas of the Jewish People*, 15.

Chapter 5: Embedding the Law in the Economic and Political Systems

[1] Barnavi, *Historical Atlas of the Jewish People*, 16–17.

[2] "Cubit," in *The Interpreter's Dictionary of the Bible—An Illustrated Encyclopedia*, George Arthur Buttrick, ed. (New York: Abington Press, 1962), 748. A cubit is defined as a unit of measurement based on the length of a man's arm from elbow to tip of the middle finger, equivalent to about eighteen inches.

[3] "Polygamy," in *Dictionary of the Bible*. Polygamy was widespread in ancient Israel. It assumed the form of polygyny (a man married to more than one woman). Social position and economic status usually determined the ability to support more than one wife. Social change and the breakdown of the seminomadic way of life, as well as the influences of other cultures, reduced the practice of polygyny (polygamy) and encouraged the more general practice of monogyny.

[4] "What is Sharia and how is it applied?," *BBC News*, May 7, 2014. www.bbc.com/news/world-27307249 (05/01/2021).

[5] David Deutsch, *The Beginning of Infinity—Explanations That Transform the World* (New York: Penguin Books, 2011), 381–390.

[6] Michael Sandel, "Why We Shouldn't Trust Markets with Our Civic Life," TEDed Talk, Aug 26, 2014, www.youtube.com/watch?v=3nson-LS8RQ. (04/28/2021).

Chapter 6: The Inevitable Decline of Kings

[1] Roland de Vaux, *Ancient Israel: Its Life and Institutions*, John McHugh, trans. (New York: McGraw-Hill, 1961), 80–85.

[2] De Vaux, *Ancient Israel*, 82–86.

[3] Barnavi, *Historical Atlas of the Jewish People*, 20.

Chapter 7: King Josiah and The Survival of the Israelites

[1] Barnavi, *Historical Atlas of the Jewish People*, 24.

[2] Max I. Dimont, *Jews, God and History* 2nd ed. (New York: Signet Classics, 2004), 54–56.

[3] Barnavi, *Historical Atlas of the Jewish People*, 24.

[4] Dimont, *Jews, God and History*, 53–54.

[5] Before the canonization of Deuteronomy, early versions of this Hebrew Scripture were referred to as the Scroll of the Teaching of Moses. There were several revisions over

time, such as described in the chapter, until the version which appeared during the reign of King Josiah and the priests.

[6] Dimont, *Jews, God and History*, 31.

[7] Genesis sporadically uses "LORD, God" while using LORD and God separately throughout.

[8] Dimont, *Jews, God and History*, 55.

Chapter 8: The Israelites in Exile—Time for a Paradigm Shift

[1] Barnavi, *Historical Atlas of the Jewish People*, 25.

[2] Henceforth, "the law" will be called the "living law" because it will become the province of the people and adapt based on the needs of the Israelites over time.

Chapter 9: The Second Temple Era—Return from Exile

[1] Barnavi, *Historical Atlas of the Jewish People*, 28–29.

[2] The name applied to the Israelites changed to "Jews" during their exile in Babylon.

[3] Binyamin Lau, Joshua Prawer, and Ilana Kurshan. *The Sages: Character, Context & Creativity* (Jerusalem: Maggid Books, 2010), 6.

[4] Barnavi, *Historical Atlas of the Jewish People*, 28–29.

[5] Barnavi, *Historical Atlas of the Jewish People*, 28.

[6] Barnavi, *Historical Atlas of the Jewish People*, 33.

[7] Josephus Flavius, "Antiquities of the Jews," in *Josephus: The Complete Works by Josephus Flavius*, William Whiston, trans. (Nashville: Thomas Nelson Publishers, 1998), Book 11:5 (2), 353.

[8] The Jewish Study Bible, 2225.

[9] Barnavi, *Historical Atlas of the Jewish People*, 22. Lawrence Schiffman, *From Text to Tradition: A History of Second Temple and Rabbinic Judaism* (Hoboken, NJ: Ktav Publishing House, 1991), 31.

[10] Lau, *The Sages*, 14.

[11] Lau, *The Sages*, 12, 14–15.

[12] Lau, *The Sages*, 14–15.

Chapter 10: The Sages of the Great Assembly

[1] Lau, *The Sages*, 17.

² Canon: The Scrolls of the Torah—also referred to as the First Five Books of Moses and the Pentateuch—were completed prior to the period of Ezra, but changes could still be made. Once a scroll was canonized, however, it could no longer be changed. The canonization of the Torah was most likely completed during the time of The Great Sages.

³ Lau, *The Sages*, 10.

⁴ Lau, *The Sages*, 8.

⁵ Lau, *The Sages*, 9, 17.

⁶ Lau, *The Sages*, 10–11.

⁷ Kenneth M. Pollack, *A Path Out of the Desert* (New York: Random House, 2008), 89–94. Walid Phares, *Future Jihad: Terrorist Strategies Against America* (New York: Palgrave Macmillan, 2005), 72–73, 63. Ayaan Hirsi Ali, *Heretic: Why Islam Needs a Reformation Now* (New York: HarperCollins, 2015), 30–32, 37–39.

⁸ Dennis Prager and Joseph Telushkin, *Why the Jews? The Reason for Antisemitism* (New York: Touchstone, 2003), 190–191.

Chapter 11: The Ptolemaic Empire, Hellenism, and the Jews

¹ Justin Pollard and Howard Reid, *The Rise and Fall of Alexandria* (New York: Penguin Books, 2006), 6–12.

² Pollard and Reid, *Alexandria*, 54.

³ Pollard and Reid, *Alexandria*, 54

⁴ Pollard and Reid, *Alexandria*, 14–19, 33.

⁵ Pollard and Reid, *Alexandria*, 17–34.

⁶ Pollard and Reid, *Alexandria*, 45.

⁷ Pollard and Reid, *Alexandria*, 43.

⁸ Pollard and Reid, *Alexandria*, 35–43.

⁹ "Chronological Table of Rulers," The Jewish Study Bible, 2228.

¹⁰ Pollard and Reid, *Alexandria*, 93.

¹¹ Pollard and Reid, *Alexandria*, 63.

¹² Pollard and Reid, *Alexandria*, 120.

¹³ Pollard and Reid, *Alexandria*, 64–69.

¹⁴ Pollard and Reid, *Alexandria*, 102–105.

¹⁵ Pollard and Reid, *Alexandria*, 108–13, 117.

¹⁶ Pollard and Reid, *Alexandria*, 102–127.

¹⁷ Schiffman, *From Text to Tradition*, 82, 84–85.

¹⁸ Schiffman, *From Text to Tradition*, 64–65.

Chapter 12: The Legend of the Septuagint

[1] "Chronological Table of Rulers," The Jewish Study Bible, 2228.

[2] Pollard and Reid, *Alexandria*, 70–74.

[3] Flavius, "Introduction," in *The Complete Works*. Abraham Wasserstein and David J. Wasserstein, *The Legend of the Septuagint: From Classical Antiquity to Today* (New York: Cambridge University Press, 2006), 20, 45–50 discusses Josephus's writing from the "Letter of Aristeas."

[4] Flavius, "Antiquities of the Jews," 12.2–15, in *The Complete Works*, 371–379.

[5] Wasserstein and Wasserstein, *Legend of the Septuagint*, 20.

[6] Wasserstein and Wasserstein, *Legend of the Septuagint*, 19–26.

[7] Pollard and Reid, *Alexandria*, 192–200.

[8] Wasserstein and Wasserstein, *Legend of the Septuagint*, 35.

[9] Wasserstein and Wasserstein, *Legend of the Septuagint*, 35–37. Philo of Alexandria, *De Vita Mosis* Book II, F. H. Colson, trans., G. P. Goold, ed. in *Philo* Vol. VI (Cambridge: Harvard University Press; London: William Heineman: 1935, 1984), Sections V–VIII.

[10] Schiffman, *From Text to Tradition*, 89–90, 94.

[11] Schiffman, *From Text to Tradition*, 85.

[12] "Synagogue," in www.dictionary.com/browse/synagogue (04/29/2021).

[13] Schiffman, *From Text to Tradition*, 86–87.

[14] Michael Grant, *The Jews in the Roman World* (New York: Charles Scribner's Sons, 1973), 23.

[15] Schiffman, *From Text to Tradition*, 94.

[16] "Chronological Table of Rulers," The Jewish Study Bible, 2229.

Chapter 13: The Struggle for Religious Freedom

[1] The Jewish Study Bible, 2153–2158.

[2] Schiffman, *From Text to Tradition*, 64–74.

[3] Schiffman, *From Text to Tradition*, 65–66, 68–70. Richard Gottheil and Samuel Krauss, "Gerusia," in *The Jewish Encyclopedia*, www.jewishencyclopedia.com/articles/6633-gerusia (04/30/2021). Wilhelm Bacher and Jacob Zallel Lauterbach, "Sanhedrin," in *The Jewish Encyclopedia*, www.jewishencyclopedia.com/articles/13178-sanhedrin (06/05/2020).

[4] Schiffman, *From Text to Tradition*, 64.

[5] Barnavi, *Historical Atlas of Israel*, 40.

[6] Schiffman, *From Text to Tradition*, 63, 65, 72–75.

[7] The Jerusalem Bible, Alexander Jones, ed. (Garden City, NY: Doubleday & Company, 1966), 654–655.

[8] I Maccabees 1:20, footnotes 1(e) and 1(g), The Jerusalem Bible. The year 143 represents the number of years from the beginning of the Seleucid empire in 312 BCE.

[9] Schiffman, *From Text to Tradition*, 74, 76.

[10] Schiffman, *From Text to Tradition*, 76.

[11] Schiffman, *From Text to Tradition*, 76.

[12] Schiffman, *From Text to Tradition*, 74–77.

[13] I Maccabees 2:1–28, The Jerusalem Bible.

[14] Barnavi, *Atlas of Jewish History*, 44.

Chapter 14: The Book of Daniel

[1] Apocrypha: Books of unknown origin or authorship that are included in the Septuagint (the Greek translation of the Tanakh plus various apocrypha and deuterocanonical books) and the Vulgate Bible (the principal Latin version of the Bible, adopted as the official Roman Catholic Church text after its 1592 revision) but excluded from the Jewish and Protestant Bibles. "Apocrypha," in *Merriam-Webster*, www.merriam-webster.com/dictionary/apocrypha (04/28/2021).

[2] Nathan Moskowitz, "The Book of Daniel: Part I—A Theological-Political Tractate Addressed to Judean Hasidim under Seleucic-Greek Rule," *Jewish Bible Quarterly* 38, No. 2 (2010): 98–105, archived at valuesthatshapetheworld.com/docs/Book-of-Daniel-Part-I-Moskowitz-JBQ-38-2.pdf.

[3] The Jewish Study Bible, 1635.

[4] In the commentary to this section, "Kittim" refers to the Romans as a western Mediterranean power.

[5] This section refers to General Appollonius, who spoke to the more aligned Hellenist Jews and encouraged the Hasidim to "stand firm" in their faith.

[6] These sections are also described in I Maccabees in the Jerusalem Bible, lending further weight to the Book of Daniel originating during the period of the Maccabees.

[7] Afterlife and resurrection are not basic tenets of early or current Judaism, even though they were introduced during the period of the Maccabees and continued under Roman conquest. During times of such intense violence, hope had to come in the form of some type of reward in order to sustain the Hasidim. In this case, the Hasidim martyred themselves because of their belief in non-violence. Martyrdom eventually disappears as Judaism focuses on a path of living in peace within violent empires after the destruction of the Second Temple.

[8] Barnavi, *Historical Atlas of the Jewish People*, 42.

Chapter 15: The Birth of Universal Education

[1] Schiffman, *From Text to Tradition*, 78, 98–99.
[2] Schiffman, *From Text to Tradition*, 99–100.
[3] Barnavi, *Historical Atlas of the Jewish People*, 46–47.
[4] Schiffman, *From Text to Tradition*, 100. J. Hyrcanus ruled between 134 BCE and 104 BCE; Aristobulus I between 104 and 103 BCE; and Alexander Janneus between 103 and 76 BCE.
[5] Kenneth Atkinson, *Queen Salome: Jerusalem's Warrior Monarch of the First Century BCE* (London: McFarland & Company, 2012).
[6] Schiffman, *From Text to Tradition*, 102–119.
[7] Saldarini, *Pharisees, Scribes and Sadducees*, 109–114.
[8] Schiffman, *From Text to Tradition*, 110–111, 116–119. This interpretation may have originated with the Dead Sea Sect and may have also been associated with the Essenes because of proximity.
[9] Schiffman, *Text to Tradition*, 113–116.
[10] Schiffman, *Text to Tradition*, 104–107. Saldarini, *Pharisees, Scribes and Sadducees*, 109–114. Both sources reference the ideological differences between the Sadducees, Pharisees, and Essenes.
[11] Fletcher Harper Swift, *Education in Ancient Israel, From Earliest Times to 70 A.D.* (Chicago: Open Court, 1919), 92–93.
[12] Yitzhak Buxbaum, *The Life and Teachings of Hillel* (London, Rowman & Littlefield, 1983), 16.
[13] Swift, *Education in Ancient Israel*, 76–79, 87–93.
[14] Swift, *Education in Ancient Israel*, 94.
[15] Swift, *Education in Ancient Israel*, 94–99.

Chapter 16: Shining the Light on the Golden Rule

[1] Barnavi, *Historical Atlas of the Jewish People*, 48–49.
[2] Buxbaum, *Hillel*, 65–66.
[3] Buxbaum, *Hillel*, 55–56, 66.
[4] "Shabbat 21b:5–6," in The William Davidson Talmud, www.sefaria.org/Shabbat.21b.5-6?lang=bi (05/01/2021). Author's discussion with Rabbi Joel Schwartzman.
[5] Buxbaum, *Hillel*, 95. "Shabbat 31a," Davidson Talmud, www.sefaria.org/Shabbat.31a?lang=bi. (04/30/2021).

[6] Buxbaum, *Hillel*, 37. "Bava Metzia 104a," Davidson Talmud, www.sefaria.org/Bava_Metzia.104a?lang=bi (05/02/2021).

[7] Solomon Schechter and Wilhelm Bacher, "Gamaliel I," in *The Jewish Encyclopedia*, www.jewishencyclopedia.com/articles/6494-gamaliel-i. (08/06/2020). Schechter and Bacher, "Gamaliel II," in *The Jewish Encyclopedia*, www.jewishencyclopedia.com/articles/6495-gamaliel-ii. (08/06/2020)

[8] Swift, *Education in Ancient Israel*, 94–96. Referenced by Emil G. Hirsch, Kaufmann Kohler, et al., in "Education," in *The Jewish Encyclopedia*, jewishencyclopedia.com/articles/5438-education. (04/29/2021).

[9] Stephan A. Schwartz, *The 8 Laws of Change, How to be an Agent of Personal and Social Transformation* (Rochester, VT: Park Street Press, 2015), 181.

[10] The Jewish Study Bible, 2157–2158.

Chapter 17: The Value of War

[1] Peter Balakian, *The Burning Tigris: The Armenian Genocide and America's Response* (New York: HarperCollins, 2003), 160.

[2] Balakian, *Burning Tigris*, 38.

[3] Balakian, *Burning Tigris*, 31.

[4] Balakian, *Burning Tigris*, 43–44.

[5] Henry Morgenthau, *Ambassador Henry Morgenthau's Story: A Personal Account of The Armenian Genocide* (New York: Cosimo Classics, 2008), 199. Balakian, *Burning Tigris*, 233.

[6] Balakian, *Burning Tigris*, 57–59.

[7] William Montgomery Watt, "Muhammad," in *Encyclopaedia Britannica*, www.britannica.com/biography/Muhammad (07/02/2020)

[8] Watt, "Muhammad."

[9] Phares, *Future Jihad*, 23.

[10] Phares, *Future Jihad*, 30. The famous Battle of Yarmuk took place in 636 BCE on the plateau near the Yarmuk River, near what is today called the Golan Heights (between Syria and Jordan). The smaller Muslim armies fought and defeated the Roman army. This allowed the Muslims to further advance and conquer the lands of Palestine, Syria, and later, Asia Minor.

[11] BBC News Staff, "Sunnis and Shia: Islam's Ancient Schism," *BBC News*, Jan 4, 2016, www.bbc.com/news/world-middle-east-16047709 (04/29/2021).

[12] Phares, *Future Jihad*, 43.

[13] Balakian, *Burning Tigris*, 40.

[14] Balakian, *Burning Tigris*, 145–146.

[15] Balakian, *Burning Tigris*, 154.

[16] Balakian, *Burning Tigris*, 161.

[17] Balakian, *Burning Tigris*, 189.

[18] Balakian, *Burning Tigris*, 180–184.

[19] Balakian, *Burning Tigris*, 187.

[20] Mogenthau, *Ambassador Morgenthau's Story*, 202–249.

[21] Balakian, *Burning Tigris*, 197, 204.

[22] Balakian, *Burning Tigris*, 225–240.

[23] Balakian, *Burning Tigris*, 241–249.

[24] Edwin Black, *IBM and the Holocaust: The Strategic Alliance Between Nazi Germany and America's Most Powerful Corporation* (Washington, DC: Dialog Press, 2012), 109–110, 366–367.

[25] Black, *The Farhud: Roots of The Arab-Nazi Alliance in the Holocaust* (Washington, DC: Dialog Press, 2010), 183–184.

[26] Black, *The Farhud*, 47–49.

[27] Balakian, *Burning Tigris*, 167.

[28] Balakian, *Burning Tigris*, 190–193.

Chapter 18: The Value of Peace

[1] Barnavi, *Historical Atlas of the Jewish People*, 52.

[2] Barnavi, *Historical Atlas of the Jewish People*, 52.

[3] Barnavi, *Historical Atlas of the Jewish People*, 52.

[4] Barnavi, *Historical Atlas of the Jewish People*, 49. "Origins of the Name 'Palestine,'" in *JVL*, www.jewishvirtuallibrary.org/origin-of-quot-palestine-quot (07/23/2020).

[5] "Rabban Jochanan ben Zakkai," in *Encyclopedia of Talmudic Sages*, Gershom Bader and Solomon Katz, trans. (Northvale, NJ: Jason Aronson, 1988), 152–154.

[6] Buxbaum, *Hillel*, 265. *Avot D'Rabbi Natan (Fathers of Rabbi Nathan)* ch. 28, in Davidson Talmud, www.sefaria.org/Avot_D'Rabbi_Natan.28?lang=bi. (04/29/2021).

[7] Flavius, *Wars of the Jews* Book 2, in *The Complete Works*, 737–899. Titus Flavius Josephus, born Yosef ben Matityahu, fought on the side of the Jews in the Galilee, was captured by the Romans. He was later freed and became a Roman citizen. His writings on the First Jewish War are important source documents, even if written for a Roman audience. "Flavius Josephus," in *Encyclopaedia Britannica*, www.britannica.com/biography/Flavius-Josephus. (04/29/2021)

[8] Flavius, *Wars of the Jews* Book 2:2 (14.2–15.6), in *The Complete Works*, 738–742.

[9] Flavius, *Wars of the Jews* Book 2:2 (19.7–19.9), in *The Complete Works*, 757–758.

[10] Flavius, *Wars of the Jews* Book 2:4 (3.7–5.2), in *The Complete Works*, 804–815.

[11] Dimont, *Jews, God and History,* 97.

[12] Sean Kingsley, *Gold's Gold* (New York: HarperCollins Publishers, 2007), 15, 101.

[13] Aelus Stylo, ed., "The Temple of Peace," in *Encyclopaedia Romana,* penelope.uchicago.edu/~grout/encyclopaedia_romana/imperialfora/vespasian/templumpacis.html. (08/08/2020). Archeologists have located the remnants of the great marble floor of the Temple of Peace. Roberto Bartoloni, "Rome Jubilee Digs Uncover Artifacts," *Archaeology,* Jan 11, 2000, archive.archaeology.org/online/news/jubilee.html (04/30/2021).

[14] Kingsley, *Gold's Gold,* 117–134.

[15] Bader and Katz, *Encyclopedia of Talmudic Sages,* 152–153.

[16] Leo W. Schwarz, ed., *Great Ages and Ideas of the Jewish People* (New York: Random House, 1956), 162.

[17] Eleven descendants of Hillel held the role of *Nasi* of the Sanhedrin after Johanan ben Zakkai, through 425 CE, but the first three after Johanan ben Zakkai were the most important contributors to stabilizing the faith after the destruction of the Second Temple.

[18] Bader and Katz, *Encyclopedia of Talmudic Sages,* 121, 127, 182, 312, 371.

[19] The concept of immortality of the soul first appears during the period of the Maccabees and is discussed in the earlier chapter on the Book of Daniel. This remains a key concept with the Pharisees after the First Jewish War. During times of extreme suffering and privation, when rewards in this life are difficult to come by, people place their hopes in the concept of an afterlife.

[20] Bader and Katz, *Encyclopedia of Talmudic Sages,* 261.

[21] Bader and Katz, *Encyclopedia of Talmudic Sages,* 371–393.

[22] Bader and Katz, *Encyclopedia of Talmudic Sages,* 155

[23] Schiffman, *Text to Tradition,* 133.

[24] Shane J. D. Cohen, *From the Maccabees to the Mishnah* 3rd ed. (Louisville: Westminster John Knox Press, 2006), 173, 185, 197.

[25] Cohen, *Maccabees to the Mishnah,* 185.

[26] Adin Steinsaltz, ed., The Essential Talmud (New York: Basic Books 2006), 12. Over the years, additional commentary was added to the Mishnah, which later was compiled and written down to become the foundation of the early Jerusalem Talmud. This first Talmud was completed hastily and in a disorganized fashion.

Chapter 19: Expansion of Thought

[1] Barnavi, *Historical Atlas of the Jewish People,* 34–35, 65.

[2] Abraham Cohen, ed., *Everyman's Talmud: The Major Teachings of the Rabbinic Sages* (New York: Schocken Books, 1995), xlix. Barnavi, *Historical Atlas of the Jewish People*, 64. Ancient city location map of Babylonia.

[3] Bader and Katz, *Encyclopedia of Talmudic Sages*, 757–760.

[4] Bader and Katz, *Encyclopedia of Talmudic Sages*, 771–774.

[5] Steinsaltz, Essential Talmud, 87–88. Barry Holtz, ed., *Back to the Sources* (New York: Simon & Schuster, 1984), 186.

[6] Sidney Greenberg and Jonathan D. Levine, *Siddur Hadash for All Sabbath & Festival Services* (Bridgeport, CT: The Prayer Book Press of Media Judaica, 2000), 248.

Chapter 20: The Path to Universal Monotheism

[1] James Carroll, *Christ Actually: The Son of God for the Secular Age* (New York: Penguin Group, 2014), 201.

[2] Schiffman, *Text to Tradition*, 148–150.

[3] Saldarini, *Pharisees, Scribes and Sadducees*, 35–43.

[4] Carroll, *Christ Actually*, 141.

[5] Bacher and Lauterbach, "Sanhedrin," in *The Jewish Encyclopedia*, www.jewishencyclopedia.com/articles/13178-sanhedrin (06/05/2020).

[6] Carroll, *Christ Actually*, 66.

[7] Schechter and Bacher, "Gamaliel I."

[8] Acts of the Apostles 23:8–9, The New English Bible.

[9] James Carroll, *Constantine's Sword—The Church and the Jews: A History* (Boston: Houghton Mifflin, 2001), 189–190.

Chapter 21: Defining the Transformative Cycle of Values

[1] "Values," in *Collins English Dictionary*, www.collinsdictionary.com/dictionary/english/values (05/04/2020).

[2] Götz Aly, *Hitler's Beneficiaries: Plunder, Racial War, and the Nazi Welfare State*, Jefferson Chase, trans. (New York: Henry Holt & Company, 2006), 30.

[3] Adam Tooze, *The Wages of Destruction* (New York: The Penguin Group, 2006), 166–186.

[4] Tooze, *Wages of Destruction*, 37–59. Hitler's early military infrastructure planning, between 1933 and 1934, included building strategic roads, barracks, and waterways. This involved the creation of the Autobahn as the "lifeline" of a reconstructed national defense system (45–46).

[5] Aly, *Hitler's Beneficiaries*, 46–47.

[6] Sandel, "Why We Shouldn't Trust Markets."

[7] Black, *IBM and the Holocaust.*

[8] Don Edward Beck and Christopher C. Cowan, *Spiral Dynamics: Mastering Values, Leadership and Change* (Malden, MA: Blackwell Publishing, 2006).

Chapter 22: Values That Shape The Future

[1] Brian W. Arthur, lecture, "Complexity Theory in Economics," in *Short Course in Social and Economic Systems* (Santa Fe: Santa Fe Institute for Complexity Theory, Summer, 2016).

[2] Peter H. Diamandis and Steven Kotler, *Abundance: The Future Is Better Than You Think* (New York: Free Press, 2012), 145–146. "Mobile Phones are Transforming Africa," *The Economist*, Dec 10, 2016, archived at valuesthatshapetheworld.com/docs/continental-disconnect-mobile-phones-transforming-africa-economist-2016-12-10.pdf.

[3] Diamandis and Kotler, *Abundance*, 102–109, 114.

[4] Dr. Anthony Atala, "Printing a Human Kidney," March 2011, TEDed Video, 16:54, www.youtube.com/watch?v=bX3C20104MA. (04/29/2021).

[5] Declan Walsh and Somini Sengupta, "For Thousands of Years, Egypt Controlled the Nile. A New Dam Threatens That," *NYT*, Feb 9, 2020. www.nytimes.com/interactive/2020/02/09/world/africa/nile-river-dam.html. (04/30/2021).

Index

Made in the USA
Las Vegas, NV
15 August 2021